My utmost to
and reside
kindness ....

MW01595064

ff,
r

Black Dad/White Dad

Part One – The Fathers

By

Bernard F. Blanche

Bernard F. Blanche

Sorry I missed the chance to
speak to you all about my writing.

Love and
Best Wishes,

Bernie

Strategic Book Publishing and Rights Co.

Strategic Book Publishing & Rights Co., LLC
USA | Singapore
www.sbpra.com

For information about special discounts for bulk purchases, please contact Strategic Book Publishing and Rights Co. Special Sales, at bookorder@sbpra.net.

ISBN: 978-1-68181-433-9

Book Design: Dataworks, India
Cover Concept: Noah Miller, Souderton, PA

<u>Dedication</u>

Black Dad/White Dad is dedicated to the Blanche and Bernot families, whose untiring gifts of time, love, patience, and caring have molded the stories and events in the life of Francis J. Blanche, his children, and those he blessed with his heroic personal sacrifices. This represents the success of a dysfunctional family.

Acknowledgments

The author is indebted to Mary C. Mc Monagle whose thorough research into the Arthur Blanchfield family has contributed much to this effort.

The assistance of Patricia Hennessy, Albert Pastino and Francis B. Blanche was invaluable in providing an accurate atmosphere for the events remembered and recorded in this work.

My sincerest gratitude to the members of the Douglas Crane family: Diane Oresto, Janice Coppelt and Colleen Barneman and to Kathy Aaroe Barbieri for assistance in locating family.

The people of Meade, Kansas, have given much background information, especially Janette Friesen and the staffs of the library, museum, and courthouse.

The author offers a special "thank you" to Dorothy A. Blanche and Suzanne Moffitt for their patience and their editing of this manuscript.

Table of Contents - Part One – The Fathers

Chapter One

"The Western Sunset"

The gray wind chased after the departing horse and sleigh toward the town of Meade, Kansas. Martin stood watching its dark form shrink into the distant, icy horizon. With his back drenched in the warm glow of the farmhouse fireplace, the fifteen year old teetered on a thought. One certain finality dawned upon him with the harvest of 1909. Martin abandoned his childhood with the illnesses to his parents. The labor of reaping and the care of his parents prodded him into manhood.

He could step into the frigid winter day or return to the people gathered in the parlor behind him. He became aware of the unusual hum of polite conversation behind him. The farmhouse rarely held visitors as the local tenant farmers generally kept to themselves. The round faced youth pulled down a ruffle of black hair atop his head and entered the home.

The front room had been modified by the guests into a waiting room. Weathered and reddened visages greeted his return. The landowner ceased his soft chatter with a cluster of townspeople, and Martin surveyed the faces of his teacher, the grocer, and the Dutils. Church clothes put their appearance at odds with Martin's familiarity of them. The Dutils were neighboring tenant farmers like Martin's parents. Their heritage in the Northeast of France molded their countenances, and Martin could have passed for one of their children. Two young girls plied at the dress of Mlle. Dutil, and the boy stood vigilant at his father's left side.

The lanky form of the landowner moved to bring Martin closer to the group. The Dutil boy was sent from his father's side to close the door behind Martin.

"The Reverend did a fine service for your parents, Martin," delivered the self-appointed spokesperson. Like many of the area Mennonite people, the landowner held a religious respect for the land and the people who worked it. "We've been discussing some options for you here." Kindness flavored the delivery, and Martin managed a coy smile in return.

"Thank you, but I wasn't considering such particular matters yet," stumbled Martin, caught off his own musings.

"The Dutils are willing to take you in at their place. You can hire out to them." His politeness gave way to concern, and then to the ambivalence of practical business. The transition to cold reality in his last words etched his tone.

"I don't think I could impose on them like that," muttered Martin, a little bewildered by the adult situation of the moment.

"Well, you know I've arranged for new tenants to take up this parcel next month. They'll need the time to prepare for the upcoming spring plowing and planting."

A rustle of shutters and a creaking of rafters drew Martin momentarily to remember the fallen oak, pushed from its roots by the strong wind of last October's storm. Some of its timbers now heated the room. Martin felt uprooted.

Several of those present also worked the land for this man. His soft physical features set him apart from those who plowed and tilled. He was university educated, and it infected his language. The dialect and accents of the farmers were heavy with Austrian and some German undertones. Martin's parents and the Dutils left Alsace-Lorraine in 1891 for Canada. Russian Mennonites joined them; and, soon afterward, both groups immigrated to The United States for the opportunity to farm the rich soil of Kansas.

"I have grown and worked here, but my mother and father have given me stories," the young man paused. A tablet of papers on a table with a kerosene lamp drew his attention. He gently picked them up and placed them in the crook of his left arm. The art was a mixture of rough childish art from his Third and Fourth Grade and the more sophisticated sketches etched with care during his final year of schooling. His Eighth Grade teacher had praised his talent and encouraged his skill. "My sketches and drawings take me far from this place," he mused, almost to himself.

"You may stay with the Dutils," their heads bobbed in agreement to the landowner's invitation. "Then you can make any plans you wish." His words gave no comfort, but rather signaled the end of the formalities.

The cold of the winter settled into the gathering as the mourners began to leave. Martin Bernot finalized plans with the Dutil family and determined to see them for breakfast the next morning.

Shards of bright sunlight forced their glare through the windows of the house. The rays danced and crackled like a white fire, mixing with the windblown snow as it swept over the Kansas farm. Martin managed to gather his entire life into a canvass duffle bag. A sleepless night full of self-awareness prompted his unrest. Pleased that an unexpected excitement pumped through his mundane tasks, Martin Bernot readied for departure.

The weathered and unpainted back door thrust itself open before him, having gained impetus from the driving wind that crossed the property. The youth shouldered the knapsack and bent into the wintery day. A few strong and purposeful strides ushered in his commitment to hold to his decision. The dark of the night had led him to this moment.

Abruptly, he pulled his bowed body erect as he caught sight of the two blackened scars of upturned earth that lay just before the fence-line of the corn field. The driven snow made an effort to shroud them as it had the land, but their rounded forms fought its encroachment. Martin found prayers from his Catholic up-bringing to drive the pain away and ease his farewell. He stood until a sense of peacefulness overtook him: it was longer than he intended. They were gone, John Martin Bernot and Mathilda Louise Struhalsey Bernot, driven away by influenza. He too would be gone – prodded by dreams of an unseen future.

Breakfast with the Dutils happened out of respect to his parents. As friends and fellow ex-patriots of Alsace-Lorraine, Martin could not flee the homestead without their blessing and consent. The morning conversation enriched the Dutil family. Martin shared stories of his parents, his hopes, and his drawings. He joined the morning chores after the meal. The moments felt like family, but they could not entice him to linger. He embarked on his set course.

The first leg put him on the road to Denver, Colorado. He found some work as a laborer and managed to make some extra money selling some new sketches, portraits and some commercial ad signs. His parents' stories continued to pull him like a passenger car behind a huge steam locomotive. People he met teased him with vistas of the big eastern cities and the exotic lands that lay across the vast oceans. The Rocky Mountains could not contain or seduce him, and by 1910 he was again on the road.

The journey cross-country toward the East taught him the ways of the hobo. Railcars and foot travel filled his time, and progress to New York City was agonizingly slow. Odd jobs kept his coffer filled sufficiently to sustain his needs. He sold some sketches of the new places and people that he met and with whom he visited. Eventually, the city rose before him, and the task of completing his plans presented Martin with a serious dilemma.

He located the Merchant Marine headquarters with relative ease, but soon learned that recruits had to have reached eighteen years of age. His five foot, five inch frame was solid and well-worked. His weathered, outer skin aged his countenance; and, standing amid the New Yorkers, he looked the part of a worldly man in his twenties. Born on December 16, 1894, he had just turned sixteen, and Martin took up a pen and managed to doctor some papers to confirm that he was of age to enlist as Merchant Seaman, Martin Aloysius Bernot.

World War I was soon underway, but that news did not daunt the young Kansan from his pursuit of his ambition. The Bernots had spoken often of the world beyond their farm, and he was smitten with an unquenchable thirst to see the vast and remote wonders of Europe, the Far East, and Africa. The sea lanes of the oceans opened grand horizons to Martin, and he spent most of the war trekking from one mysterious place to another inspiring land. He developed a fondness for strong cigarettes in Turkey, and Greece introduced Martin to strong liquor. Like souvenirs, these two vices went with him as companions during his life.

When weariness overtook him after seven years of travel, he returned to The United States on the Carpathia, debarking from London on March 20, 1917, and due in New York on April 2, 1917. Government draft regulations and the war caught him, and the young world-wide traveler was inducted into the Army out of Erie, New York, on June 5, 1917. Records showed him active and on duty on April 15, 1918. By November 15, 1918, the war was ending, and Martin was a veteran. He left the service with the rank of private and headed to New York City. The metropolis had changed: its streets and work places oozed with the offal of the war.

The influx of post war immigrants forced Martin south. The bigger eastern cities became engorged with European refugees. Even the City of Brotherly Love held little employment opportunities for him. Philadelphia, though, became a gateway for western and southern job seekers. Warm memories of a brief stay in the city prompted him to seek employment nearby in Wilmington, Delaware, as a commercial artist.

He had many hours at sea to practice this trade and found a ready market for his skills in the advertising shops in and around town. Working as a craftsman and having a regular routine, he evolved into a normal citizen, no longer the vagabond, lured by distant and mysterious adventures. While rooming at 223 Market Street in Wilmington, he made the acquaintance of locals at bars and drew the interest of a young lady.

Miss Mary McNamara, from an Irish immigrant family in Philadelphia, found him intriguing. The lady spiced his sense of the exotic. Mary was stoic, a quiet, pensive person. Martin enjoyed the solitude with her, for she required little entertainment. The louder and more energetic "Flappers" threatened the polite and demure Kansan. With Mary, however, there was comfort, and their dating evolved into a hurried marriage in 1920 in Philadelphia. Mr. Patrick McNamara and his wife, Annie, hosted the festivities as the proud parents of Mary. Local friends and the nearby family attended the ceremony.

The big city hosted the small town wedding. Martin accompanied his own loneliness amid the clan of well-wishers, for he was the only stranger present at his own wedding.

Back in the environs of Wilmington, the couple soon welcomed their daughter, Camille Marie, on September 4, 1921. Mary brought a forced sophistication to the marriage and a classical love of ballet to Camille. Martin's contribution featured his kind and caring disposition with the child, but alcohol overshadowed his relationship with Mary.

Prodded by Mary, Martin took a more favorable painting position in Montclair, New Jersey. Normal never came, but the family held together on its own, despite the growing frequency of trials and arguments.

Martin fought new demons as the McNamara family remained aloof from him. His seaman upbringing allowed him to blend sufficiently into the blue collar ambiance that surrounded Mary McNamara Bernot. Mary took the young Camille to ballet lessons where she thrived. The child's radiant smile and caring personality were more a gift from Martin than from her mother.

The parents enrolled the six year old Camille in a local school. Classmates soon grew to love her generous, happy spirit, and they cherished her presence. She danced when she spoke to classmates, swaying to some unheard classical rhythm. She pranced before classes, spun in beautiful turns during recess in the school yard, and padded and leapt on her way to and from school. Her demeanor was infectious. Her friends were happy to allow her the constant revelry, for her smile gave them a sense of quiet peace. The dance gave her poise and grace which presented her with maturity beyond her years. She became a listener: her time given freely to classmates with stories to tell, fears to express, and wonders to imagine.

The little home at 14 Cottage Place remained their residence until 1932. Martin moved his sickly wife and growing daughter closer to her relatives in Pennsylvania. In the western suburb of Philadelphia along the Schuylkill River, Martin settled his family in Conshohocken. Some of the McNamaras had already moved to the borough, but they had changed their family name to Mack.

Martin's rough exterior gave little evidence of the depth and warmth of his inner demeanor. The people he met had to search through the cigarette smoke and sparse conversation to discern his true character. That was never the case with his daughter.

At home one Saturday morning, the ballerina found the sundrenched parlor perfect for her practice session. Her father had already chosen it for his reading room, but her entrance distracted him. Camille's first pair of toe shoes befuddled her father.

"Camille, you pop up on those toes like a Jack-in-the-Box," teased Martin.

"That's silly, Dad," reflected the dark haired lass. "My teacher wants me to practice with the tempo of the music." Her milky smooth skin flushed with color from her exertion.

"It looks very difficult, Young Lady," added her father with pride. He puffed on a Camel and watched her turn and prance to the melody on the phonograph.

Bright eyed with joy and wonder, Camille danced for her father. Her small frame still held to the childish build of a pre-teen. Her wavy tresses swayed from shoulder to shoulder mimicking the dance. "Someday you might watch me at the ballet in Philadelphia," she whispered, almost embarrassed by her own brash hopes.

"That will be the greatest day for Mom and me. You'll make it. I'm certain of that." He smudged out the cigarette in the nearby ashtray and met her in the middle of the room. The bows which they executed jointly were exaggerated and brought giggles of delight from the ballerina.

"You're the best, Dad," she complimented and reached her right arm about him in a playful embrace. "Just a few more minutes of practice, okay?" she requested.

Martin returned to his front row vantage point, took out a pad and pencil, and proceeded to form her figure onto the page. They finished together: her etude and his sketch. "Your work is better than mine, Hon," he volunteered.

"Let me see! Let me see!" she begged as she rushed to his side. The model was poised tiptoe. Her short length wavy hair floated outwardly ever so slightly. The frock, shaded gray, bowed with the effort of a turn. "I love it, Dad. I'll keep it forever," she beamed.

As Camille grew into her teen years, her parent's marriage began to shred. Mary's health waned, and Martin's drinking began to take a toll on the couple. At first, desperately in need of employment, he hired on as a laborer at the Conshohocken Borough Disposal Plant. The long six-day weeks erased precious family time from his schedule and left him tired and drawn at the end of each day.

With childhood behind her, Camille put aside the free spirited melodies that had danced her through grade school. By high school at St. Matthew's Roman Catholic High School, Camille was content to hum the ballet. Gyration gave way to the elegant carriage of a young, confident woman.

When Camille became interested in a classmate at school, Mary would have no parts of it. The lad was rough and a ball player, not one suited for her daughter. The young man mirrored the better qualities of Martin, quiet and reflective. Camille was drawn to his sincere, humble soul. This relationship, the parents' differing views about the boy, Martin's looming alcoholism, and Mary's deteriorating health were catalyst to the continued stress of their marriage.

Chapter Two

"The Pennsylvanians"

Timothy Lawrence Blanche was an anachronism of genealogical differences, typically American. Born on October 19, 1887, in Conshohocken, Pennsylvania, he claimed to be more Irish than French. His family name may have originally been "Blanchfield" from Clonroche, County Wexford, Ireland, but there were claims on his heritage from the Huguenots and from Alsace-Lorraine. He was the last of eight children born to Laurence Blanch (Blanchfield), who was, perhaps, brother to Arthur Blanchfield, also of Clonroche. He grew into a fair-skinned, narrow-faced man with a swagger and a dandy's air. The winter wind and the summer breeze treated him as badly as the sun on any bright day. The reddish heat would dissipate from his arms and face with the passing of an evening in darkness. He took to hard labor with a vengeance, hoping it would consume any inner turmoil from his soul. A granite quietness and stern rigidity marked his youthful demeanor. His frustration and intelligence led some acquaintances to believe he possessed a vocation to the priesthood.

His curiosity kept him in school longer than most of his peers. Machines, full of fire and steam, seduced him with their power and potential. With enough schooling to land a job at Alan Wood Steel Company as an engineer of a yard locomotive in Conshohocken, he took up adulthood at an early age with a confident swagger. His work attire was a denim shirt and tie. Private to a fault, Tim rarely spoke of his life with his brothers and sister, but he led a life filled with visits to them.

He managed to court a young girl of Germanic ancestry. At first, the encounters were more out of custom than passion. The affection grew upon him like an ivy vine on an oak, and he found himself committed to her with a growing and unfamiliar depth of feelings. A sense of possession overtook him.

Mary Catherine Heebner, born September 13, 1896, rose from a brewed cauldron of violence, poverty, and little education. The young woman grew up in Norristown, Pennsylvania, amid a hoard of devilish and sometimes felonious brothers. Her older brothers took to carrying pistols and living on a houseboat on the Schuylkill River between De Kalb Pike and Haws Avenue. They learned the construction trades and evolved into craftsmen with good skills. It was, however, their weekend lives that earned them a tempestuous reputation as fighters and drunkards. Mary managed to survive with a fun-loving personality that set her apart from the rest of her siblings. She learned to cook in the German style, but her ancestry placed her closer to Austria than to Germany. Her roundish figure and bright cheerfulness drew her in contrast to her thin, somber, redheaded beau.

Timothy and Mary attended "Picture Shows" and took walks on their dates. She enjoyed the time away from home, and Tim prided himself on finding inexpensive outings. Mary often wore a gumdrop-shaped chapeau. It concealed her waist length, jet black tresses. Later in life, she took to plaiting her hair painstakingly into double buns, tightly affixed above the nape of her neck.

On a casual weekend walk with Tim, her slightly bowed legs caused her to sway left and right attempting to keep apace of her companion's jaunty, beeline path. "You're in a hurry, Timothy?" she questioned with a child's coy smile.

"No, why do you ask?" mulled Tim as he turned to allow her to come to his side. A wide-brimmed fedora rested securely on his head. It hid his reddish hair from full view, but he had parted it with repetitive strokes meticulously down the middle. He dressed formally in tie and suit on these jaunts. "I'm at my train's pace, I guess," he stammered.

"Well, after cleaning and doing wash all morning for the boys, I'd like to walk a little slower," she shared with a touch of her feisty nature.

Unaccustomed to deviating from his own mannerism, he acquiesced, "I'm not in any rush to get anywhere." A stoic, unemotional countenance greeted her with his words. He was pleased to have done this for her, and it was betrayed by the slightest glimmer of a smile. Not willing to show that side of his make-up to Mary, he turned from her. Deeper within Tim, demons wrestled, hidden by his rigidity. These faults fought to consume his senses of morality, family, and caring. The mingling of black and white elements grew him into a man of gray complexity. He was a torn individual. Tim usually kept the darker traits at bay until he drank or he became absorbed in the pressures of work day life. Then they tempted and taunted him. The furies were viral and strong, for they often over-matched the more passive emotional facets of Timothy Blanche.

To Mary, Tim meant freedom from her rough upbringing, freedom from the ancestry of Bertha Halhauser and August Hubner, her parents. Like her sister Margaret, who found succor in her marriage to Roland Lauchbach, Mary saw marriage as her vehicle from the past.

On June 10, 1920, at St. Patrick's RC Church, the couple married. Mary became an obedient wife and a diligent homemaker. They started their family in Conshohocken in a row home in what locals called "Connaughtown." It was the neighborhood around West Elm and Fulton Streets where their relatives, the Kellys and Heebners had homes. Tim's sister Elizabeth, who had married one of the Kellys, was nearby.

By 1911, the two-hundred block of Spring Mill Avenue had become ninety percent Irish. The community took on names like "The Bowery" or "Frog Hollow" near West Elm Street and Sixth Avenue. Colwell Lane became "Whiskey Lane", Maple Street was "Cork Row", and "Irishtown" occupied Fifth and Wood Streets.

Life centered around Tim's work at Alan Wood Steel Company which sat on the eastern side of the Schuylkill River. Tim could walk to the plant, but he later took to driving a little black Ford coupe with running boards.

Sunday drives now replaced the easy promenades of the courting days. They would wend their way through Gulph Mills along Route 23 or into Valley Forge Park. Sometimes they headed toward Boyertown in Berks County or Souderton in the northern reaches of Montgomery County. They began a ritual of tapping spring water from a public spigot in Valley Forge. Gallon glass jugs nestled securely in the truck, ready to replace the drinking water at the house. It was Tim's luxury not to use the tap in his home. They would do so for forty years, and amass a collection of two dozen bottles.

Conversation was minimal, but the vistas of the region entertained the travelers. "Tim, one of these days I want you to teach me how to drive," asked Mary with little hope of an affirmative response. The idea was planted however, and she suspected it would someday flower to her advantage. She sat in the passenger front seat, and the fresh breeze wafted her thick, black hair forward and out the right hand window. As she turned to watch his reaction, she swept the impish threads aside.

On these ritualistic Sunday drives, Tim enjoyed the power of choosing where, how long, and when to go. "Humph! Now you know we have no time for such nonsense," he delivered, not considering any negotiation. The sun pricked his left arm as it rested on the bottom of the window jamb. An open bottle of Schlitz beer was wedged in the crook of his lap. He moved his arm into the shade of the cab. "Mary, I don't want you to go 'galavantin' around town like those floozies in Norristown," he crackled softly, but with a taut lip stretched across his slightly clenched teeth. He pried the beer from its mooring, took a quick draft, and returned it to his lap.

She was lighthearted still, for she knew he would take up a non-compromising stance. "It's just a thought, Tim! You never know if some emergency might happen, and I could help out." The bartering was going nowhere today, and Mary knew when to let him have his way.

"I can take care of those things. No need for you to fret," he cajoled. Then, in an attempt to change the focus of the conversation, he added. "Look there's a pipe coming out of that spring!" They had just passed the "Hanging Rock" in Gulph Mills. "We can come here and get some good water to bottle," he suggested, pleased to have a second location.

"Well, if the water dries up at the Valley Forge's spring, this is a good spot," agreed Mary.

With only an elementary school education, she was blessed with a keen insight into the inner workings of people's wants and desires. If the issue was important enough to Mary, she would exploit Tim's wants and gain acceptance of her wishes. He liked his beer and his bedroom privileges, and she was willing to barter and trade. On those rare occasions, Tim did not stand a chance.

The family grew in its little home in Conshohocken beginning with the birth of Francis on December 28, 1921. Margaret,

Anna Marie, and Joseph soon followed. When the second born son, Joseph, was born in 1929, influenza had again ravaged the East Coast. His death at nine months of age in the arms of his mother was a tragedy that cast a long and bitter pall upon the family. When Lawrence was born, they had outgrown the home. By 1931, they moved to a larger house at 614 Ford Street in Bridgeport. Tim felt it was close enough to his employment, and the daily trip by car presented little problems, even in the winter. The family continued to be frequent visitors to the Blanche relatives in Conshohocken.

He managed to work throughout the Depression. There was money enough for Mary to give food to the hungry. Her charity was marked on the curbing in front of the home. People in need, passing the residence, saw the message, "House that gives food," marked on the sidewalk.

Tim's drinking began to overtake him. He never managed to drive the outside world away or drown the inner turmoil of his soul. No one noticed the slowly escalating weekend binges; people tolerated driving and drinking through the post-war forties.

St. Augustine's Roman Catholic Church was an easy walk up a slight grade on a Sunday morning for weekly mass. The parochial school attached to the complex educated the parish children up to Eighth Grade. The Immaculate Heart of Mary sisters did a wonderful job of training – even left-handed students like Francis were moved to right-handed penmanship. Both Lawrence and Francis were left-handed. The graduates trekked to either Bridgeport Public, St. Matthew's in Conshohocken, or St. Patrick's High School in Norristown for their high school studies.

Francis's Sixth Grade teacher was Sister Vincent Gabriel who monitored her charges' progress in all academic areas.

She taught mathematics, history, science, reading, writing, and religion. The minor areas of art, health, and physical education came down to recess, craft work involving religious themes and a yearlong log of healthy eating recorded in a 100 page Parochial Schools Composition Book.

Work on the health log began with the Sunday Bulletin newspaper which provided color pictures of healthy children, fruits and vegetables, and dangerous products like a colorful ad with a pack of Chesterfield cigarettes. At the dinner table, Francis dutifully paged through the logbook to page five with its tag, "Do Not Smoke," carefully printed in pencil at the bottom. His feet dangled below him and brushed the knee of Larry who was playing with a set of metal automobiles under the table. Francis, intent on his project, ignored the mild rap on his shin from the little brother.

"Put something in there about the dentist, Franny," suggested Mary with a call from the kitchen.

"Okay, Mom! I'll use the false teeth guy." The eleven year old took the right-handed scissors in his left hand, quickly moved them to his right, and clipped the picture from the newspaper page with agility. It was second nature for him to live in the right-handed world. He moved forward to the next, unused page. Onto page fifteen, he pasted the wide-eyed, silver haired dentist peering at x-rays in his left hand. A set of upper dentures were highlighted, but seemed inappropriate for the youthful woman seated in his dental examination chair. "What's a good thing to say on the page, Mom?" wondered the young boy. He looked up from the dining room table and craned his neck toward the kitchen. The rumpled tablecloth was pushed out of harm's-way of his sticky flour paste.

Beneath him and under the table, Larry was busy pushing Franny's 1924 Keystone Packard Combination #49 Fire

Department truck back and forth toward an imagined hotel fire. The student had outgrown the toy, but Larry enjoyed its heft and bright red finish. The younger sibling was attempting to put the aluminum ladder up the shin of his brother. The small silver bell on the hood tinkled a muted alarm. "Larry! Come on, Buddy, I'm busy here!" ushered Franny with a firm annoyance. Larry scurried from the table to another conflagration by the floor model RCA radio.

Unaware of the student's distraction, Mary finally suggested, "Well, we only go to the dentist with problems, but I guess Sister would think that's not good health." Mary wiped her wet hands on her apron. "Better safe than sorry, I always say. Put down two visits a year, Franny."

Brown eyes rolled upward and the mouth leaned right and upward chasing the thought. As taught, he wrote, "Two years," neatly with his right hand. "Sister's going to be checking this tomorrow. Thanks, Mom!" he responded. The words, "See Your Dentist Twice a Year," framed the advertisement.

Mary arrived at his side. She had become a doting mother who favored her sons. The young boy shared a satisfied smile with her. "I have to check on the girls," she advised as she headed to the parlor. "Dad will be home soon, so clean up and I'll have the girls set the table. He'll want to eat right away," she voiced more to herself than to her son.

Lawrence exited the table-tunnel under knee power. He crawled into the path of Mame, as friends and older relatives began to call her. She doted on the boys and patted Lawrence's light brown hair as she passed him exiting the room. Franny and Larry already sensed an attitude of Tim's, one that was not shared with the sisters. He had time for the boys, but that meant that the boys needed to focus their attention on their father's presence more so than did their sisters.

Francis J. Blanche received an "Excellent" for his February 24, 1933, evaluation, but the health habits of his Sixth Grade log were lost on him. His teeth deteriorated, for his diet was too rich with German meats and fried foods. He later took up smoking as he modeled his sports' heroes of the times.

Chapter Three

"Being a Saint"

By the time that Franny went to St. Matthew's Catholic High School, Eleanor and Patricia, the last of the brood, had entered St. Augustine's along with Anna Marie, Margaret, and Larry.

Mame had taken a nephew into the house. Francis Hulmes, whom everyone called "Heebe," arrived one fall evening in 1934 from Maryland. His mother was one of Mary's sisters. When Heebe's parents both died of Influenza in 1927, the boy went to live with relatives below the Mason – Dixon Line. Stories of his mistreatment filtered northward. The family knew, but the facts were kept secret from outsiders. His care-givers locked the boy in storage rooms during drunken binges. When he caused some breakage in the kitchen, his foster parent threatened to throw him into the well in the back yard. Margaret Lauchbach visited the family with her husband Roland that fall. On hearing the boy's stories and seeing the condition of his situation, she hid him in the trunk of the family car as they prepared to leave. The Lauchbach's drove off with him. Not considering their family situation during the escape, they arrived in Pennsylvania with no resources to raise the lad. Shortly, the young man knocked on the Blanche's door and asked for room and board. He was fourteen. Heebe was older than Franny and was place two grades ahead of him at St. Matthews. The boys had different interests, friends, and ambitions.

Family life was a whirlwind for everyone but Tim. His job provided for them in earnings, social stature, and a close association with the church; but his work was hard, dirty, and demanding. He had little energy for family life. Covered in soot and diesel smoke from a day's labor, he came home to an easy chair, his beer, a bath, and dinner.

The high school student body to which Camille and her beau belonged was locally referred to as "The Saints". Some "Sister of the Right Order" or other denomination had prodded and cajoled the Mascot Selection Committee to choose a Catholic symbol for their blood and guts sports' teams. The artistic clubs too shared the mascot, so athletes and scholars became "The Saints".

The young, dark hair youth first came to the attention of his classmates when he won the lead role in a minstrel show. He took the role of the black faced Mr. Tambo. The event was well attended by students, parents, and members of the Conshohocken community. Many people and classmates had congratulated the teenage actor, but the one person who remained in his vivid memory was Camille Bernot. That began a high school ritual for him.

Franny bounded down the three steps of the green and yellow Schuylkill Valley Bus and onto the sidewalk at the front entrance of St. Matthew's Roman Catholic High School on Fayette Street. It was a familiar rite for him. His hatless head glimmered in the fresh morning sun. He used a nondescript cream to wrestle the dry morning hair into neat furrows with the ebony comb that he kept in his back left pocket. The eldest living Blanche son was taller than most of his friends. The lanky stride was athletic, self-assured, and quick like his father's. Light jacket, heavy coat, no jacket – the outer attire was seasonally prescribed. Always though, he wore dark or gray colored trousers, a white shirt, and the necessary tie. Within four yards of the bus stop, he was lost in the crowd of similarly attired male students rushing toward their side of the building through the double wide doors set in the large granite blocked façade of the building. The horde of bobbing heads climbing the staircase absorbed his height and shoulders as the multitude swept him up the steps.

Chatty pockets of navy blue uniformed girls began to form in the assent. Some coalesced along the sidewalk like beads of drizzle on a windshield as local girls who walked to school found their way into the student body. Others, likes magnetic parts, clumped by the bus stop and then in unison edged into the mob.

Petite Marie Camille Bernot beamed with spontaneous joy amid a group of friends as she approached the front entrance. Her wavy black tresses gently swung to her cadence brought on by a light, agile gait. The uniform frock was a combination of vest and skirt. It was freshly ironed and, like a theater ticket, admitted her to the Sophomore Class. Her white blouse was dutifully starched at the collar, for Mary Bernot wanted all to be well with her daughter's world. Camille, as everyone now called her, had done the touch-up on her saddle shoes. She easily blended into the throng.

Franny and she were classmates; and, over the last year and a half, Franny had designed a ploy to draw closer to Camille. The classes for boys and girls were separate inside the building. One of his two chances of communicating with her was this fleeting moment at the entrance way and a second after school before his bus arrived.

Hurrying to the left side door, Franny took his well-rehearsed post and awaited her approach. It had taken him months to garner the courage to impede her entry into the lobby. Over the past few weeks he had gained her attention, playing the doorman at St. Matt's. Camille now expected his presence. Her girl friends were impressed by his courteous gesture when he first swung the portal open for her. They had tittered in shy amusement at his act of chivalry.

The soft lilt of her voice rose in conversation amid her girlfriends. As he reached the top of the flight of steps, the lanky young man sprang to his position at the door. He was able to hold her at bay for a brief morning greeting. Now the moment stretched into minutes, and he was afforded lengthier idling with her.

"Mornin', Camille," he began. Her warm, roundish face peered upward to her taller classmate. He was overjoyed, but he tried to hold the mirth from his voice.

"Well, it's so nice to see you again, Fran," she greeted him coyly, directing her eyes at her traveling companions. The glance ushered them from her as if by some unspoken pact, and she found herself alone at the doorway with Franny.

He left the door unattended and focused on her playful presence next to him. Chaos surrounded the couple, and, at first, it was disconcerting. Time and frequency made the ritual common enough of an occurrence for the pair to be at ease. "Did you have time to dance with all that homework you got?" he wondered. His back found the granite wall, and he leaned easily against it. He took the role of a movie idol.

She was pleased that he showed such an interest in her lessons. With an endearing and natural smile, she responded, "I sure did, but I had to shorten my session."

"I'm going to start baseball practice next week. I guess we won't be able to spend time after school like we usually do," he noted with a tinge of sadness. The news was a contradiction for him, for he loved playing ball. He also cherished the after school moments with her. His head bowed, and she read the disappointment.

"Franny, I plan on staying and watching your games. We can see each other after them, I'm sure." She was on tip-toes, happy to have given him comfort.

The words filled him with expectation. The young man tossed the worries from his mind. "You're a princess, you know," came from him with surprising ease. Awkwardly, he stretched his right hand toward her bundle of books which were slung over her left shoulder, buckled with an old belt. The reflex confused him, for he was not certain if he wanted to take them from her or merely touch her hand. The confusion left the hand to fend for itself awkwardly in mid air, inches from her.

Camille saved him. "You don't need to take them. I've got to get to class now anyway."

"See you after school, then – okay?" His left hand on the door handle signaled her exit.

"Sure. Can't wait," she bubbled as she slipped past him into the inner sanctum.

Franny watched her proceed into the lobby and down the sterile hallway. A deep breath refreshed him, and he slid into the building.

Bridgeport and Conshohocken were separated by five miles along River Road, but they may as well have been universes apart. The couple was accepted by their classmates as a romantic pair, but they rarely dated. On weekend occasions, Franny could take a bus into Conshohocken, and Camille and he would walk downtown together. Hand holding became easier, conversation focused on their future plans, and life was their enjoyable companion.

The spring of 1939 before their class's graduation, Franny had a great season pitching for the varsity nine. The previous year he was side-lined for some of the season by a serious ankle sprain. He played, mindful of the weakness. On the diamond, he was permitted to be a left-hander, and the liberation from right-handedness exhilarated him. The athlete wore his baggy woolen uniform with distinction. It was gray with royal blue trim and a large number twenty-one in matching color. The dirt mattered to him. Grass and mud stains ground into the fabric and mixed with sweat. This badge of the athlete drew him from childhood, through his awkward teen years, and toward the labor of adulthood.

The field of play gave him great satisfaction: Camille witnessed his competitive nature and physical strength. In his mind, she gave him purpose, for she understood his goals and aspirations. Camille attended every home game possible.

One May day he pitched a close game against Bridgeport and won. Camille rushed upon him and threw her arms about him in a jubilant embrace.

Martin Bernot had walked to the field to support Franny, and the vision of his only daughter in such revelry brought a broad smile to his face. His head oscillated left and right in pleased disbelief of her spontaneity. Raising his right hand to inhale a puff from his lit camel, he examined the multicolored paints on his hand from his day's labor. The billboard advertisement he had done was completed earlier than expected, and he had the chance to see Franny pitch. The game itself held little interest for him, but this was a moment to share with his daughter and Franny. He waved at the couple, enjoyed their broad smiles, threw a "Thumbs-up" to Franny, and turned for home.

"Wow! Your Dad was here. That's great, Camille!" Teammates and well-wishers were gradually wending their way from the field toward the locker room, homes, and evening meals.

"He thinks the world of you, you know," she whispered, aware of the people still mingling about the field.

"What a day!" he exclaimed to the bright afternoon sky.

"You were wonderful, Zeke," she added to enhance his celebration. The nickname of "Zeke" became her pet name for Franny. Taken from the roster of a big league ball team, he wore it like a trophy. A few rapid, petite leaps accompanied her delivery. Her uniform hem leapt a half second late to her rhythmic pulses. He found it amusing.

"Your uniform can dance, too," he joked. His hand swept some perspiration from his cheek. A brown smudge of ballyard mud stained his face.

Camille giggled as she reached into her uniform pocket for her lady's linen handkerchief. "Let me get that for you," she volunteered.

"No way! Gees, Camille. Some of the guys might be watching," he fumbled. The demonstration of childish embarrassment was lost on Franny, but not on Camille.

"Oh, my! The big, bad pitcher, Zeke, wants to keep his dirty face," she taunted, laughing at her own playfulness. She took his hand flirtatiously, offering hers in apology, pretending she had offended him.

"No, I mean, I'm all sweaty, dirty. You don't have to go mopping up my kisser," he returned with bravado. He left her hand fall from his and picked up a baseball bat. He began smacking the sides of both his cleats. Sand, gravel, and dirt flew from them.

"Well! You take care of your own mess." She ran to the stands and, retrieving her books, scurried to catch up to Fran as he headed for the locker room. "I'll wait for you in front of school. Okay?"

"Sure. I'll be as quick as I can. We'll have some time before my bus arrives." Already, his back faced her as he jogged from the athletic complex toward the school facilities a few blocks away.

Graduations came. Francis Hulmes legally changed his name to Heebner. As an adult, he grew into a gangly scarecrow full of odd mannerisms and genuine good nature. After high school, Heebe displayed a keen awareness of mechanical principles. In 1940, he enlisted in the Army Air Corps. His pay checks came dutifully home to Mame, his Aunt Mary. This generosity endeared him during his lifetime to his adoptive family.

Camille settled into office work after graduation, remained a part time student of ballet, and kept close ties to dear friends like Anne Pieffer. Franny was listed as a laborer in the 1940 census. For some time he also worked as a pin setter at the local bowling alley. Gradually he moved into the automobile trades and evolved into a dependable brake mechanic. With his paychecks, he helped with the siblings and, by 1941, managed to purchase a used De Soto. He favored the big cars, ones with running boards, big trunks, and big engines.

This opened new horizons for the couple. Dating actually became an option. Franny always came to the Bernot front door to pick up Camille for their drive, or the trip to a movie theater, or a treat at the local ice cream parlor. The interlude in the front room of the Bernot residence was always tense. Mary was cold and aloof; Martin was sometimes inebriated, and conversation was difficult. Franny found these moments tedious, and the exit was a relief, especially with Camille at his side.

"I don't like that young man, Martin!" Mary stammered immediately as the door closed behind Franny. Hands rigid on her hips, she spun from the door to glare at her husband.

"Mary, he's a great guy," he delivered with his practiced patience. The syllables slipped too easily from his lips. His fresh cut, close cropped hair had begun to salt and pepper. He took a sizeable swallow from his Schlitz lager.

The frail woman before him mocked her physical weakness with her inner strength. "He'll bring no good to Camille," was flung through her gritted teeth. The white apron over her frock was attacked. She tore at the bow behind her back and pulled the top loop over her head. Mary swung the garment from her person in the direction of her ambivalent husband. "I want you," she demanded, "to do something for a change!" Her lean frame surged toward Martin perched now on the edge of his high back chair.

As if sensing the future, Martin prepared to flee, but his drinking betrayed him. She blocked any exit with an adept movement that placed her squarely at the toes of his slippers. He was her prisoner. "Oh, Mary, just leave the kids alone," he pleaded both for them and for himself. She would have none of it.

"You know what's right! But when you're drinking, you just don't care about anything." Humiliation was her weapon, but Martin's stupor was his defense.

"Nonsense!" he blurted.

She was incensed. Gasping for air, a fit of asthma was hurled before him. Numbed by alcohol, life, and an unhappy marriage, he stood, forcing her to retreat a pace. He spun himself with difficulty past the stooped, coughing woman and exited the room. He heard the spasms of coughing and gasping cease once he was free of her. A bitter smile led him to the refrigerator and another Schlitz.

As another war loomed, Franny was drafted into the Army on October 29, 1942. Before his induction into the army, however, on November 13, 1942, he committed himself to the U.S. Coast Guard. Franny scurried to obtain Martin's consent to marry Camille. The formal request to Camille was the easier task. She accepted his formal proposal, and their engagement was announced prior to his reporting for duty on December 9, 1942.

The future marriage plans put added stress on the relationship between Mary and her daughter and between Mary and Martin.

Chapter Four

"The U.S.S. El Estero"

The USS El Estero, moored at her Caven Point Pier slip, was fully loaded with munitions bound for the European front. The dockyard in Bayonne, New Jersey, was preparing for its departure amid escort ships from the US Coast Guard. Two additional munitions ships were loaded and rested at her right and left sides. A string of railroad cars were adjacent to the ships and held jet fuel and weapons. The Caven Point Pier held 5000 tons of high grade explosives. Bayonne and Staten Island fuel storage tank farms were nearby. It was April 24, 1943.

Acrid smoke began to ooze into the peaceful day as alarms sounded at 5:30 pm. The 325 foot ship was spewing black oily fumes from her bilge room. A boiler flashback had ignited the oily scum atop the pooled water. Chills rippled through the port. Firefighters from the Jersey City Fire Department rushed toward the El Estero while two Coast Guard fireboats arrived at water-side. Patrols of military personnel were busy evacuating the harbor near the ship, and a call went out for Coast Guard volunteers.

By 6:30 pm, sixty Coast Guard volunteers and two large fireboats, the John J. Harvey and the Fire Fighter, had joined the fight. Fear of the ensuing catastrophe mobilized the emergency responders. Manhattan and Brooklyn were endangered by a possible explosion of nuclear weapon proportions.

The Easter Eve fire caught the Explosives Loading Detail off-guard. The unit was preparing to go on leave when the call, "Ammo ship on fire!" came. As the sixty Coast Guardsmen scrambled to reach the ship, they flooded any conveyance moving toward the pier. White Coast Guard caps bobbed and tossed to and fro in the scurry of overloaded vehicles wending their way toward the El Estero.

Seaman Francis J. Blanche could see the plumes of acrid smoke pumping upward from the docked vessel. Home and his fiancée, Camille, flashed into his mind's eye, and he allowed the luxury of a daydream to overtake him. At this reflexive moment, the choice to volunteer surprised him. It was easier than he suspected, and he did not know why.

His basic training comrades were scattered about Bayonne this Saturday. They had met at New York's Manhattan Beach Coast Guard training center. Ralph McLaughlin had already taken leave and was in transit to South Boston for Easter. The wild haired, jolly New Englander had taken a fancy to Francis's sister Margaret. He sometimes traveled to Pennsylvania with him. Seaman Shea was in the mix of volunteers headed to the endangered vessel. His detail put him on the dock fighting the fire with land lines. Coast Guardsman Blanche spotted his friend rushing the nozzle head of a lengthy three inch hose toward the vessel. As it uncoiled from its nest dockside of the El Estero, Seymour Wittek monitored the unraveling and stood ready to open the spigot bolt when Shea reached the point of discharge.

Lapping tongues of flame spewed from the holds of the ship like taunting imps. Bathed in the blare of sirens and the staccato red and white sparks of emergency flashing lights from approaching vehicles, Blanche and his fellow Coast Guardsmen boarded the vessel.

Lieutenant Commander John Stanley led the volunteers onto the deck as Lieutenant Commander Arthur Pfister took command of the shore-side fire operations. It was Stanley's first day on the job. "Don't let any of the deck munitions get involved in this fire!" he shouted above the din of whistles, the roar of fire hoses from the harbor, and the evacuation sirens.

"We'll clear them off-deck, Sir!" came the response from Seaman Francis J. Blanche. The young lad had scrambled aboard alongside his Lieutenant and had already espied the ammunition canisters secured along the deck guns. "Come on guys; let's slide these off the deck." The crew emptied munitions lockers down a greased plank onto the pier, but were unable to clear the high octane fuel drums from the deck.

Twelve guardsmen were already onboard dumping water into the bowels of the El Estero. By 6:30 pm, fire fled from the skylights, hatches, and vents of the ill-fated ship. The crimson flashes of hot flame thrust through the pitch black, oily smoke. They jumped and cavorted toward the wooden containers that held the block-buster bombs, depth charges, and incendiary bombs on board.

Stanley moved rapidly to evaluate the fire fight. He watched the lean figure of Seaman Blanche struggle with a weighty metal case of anti-aircraft ammunition. "Two to a case," he shouted to the servicemen. "Nobody gets hurt here, Men!" bellowed the officer.

"Yes, Sir!" flew into the air from several of the volunteers on the deck.

Coast Guardsman Blanche moved athletically amid the ballet of chaos. The heat below him singed his black polished shoes as the deck absorbed the blistering temperature of the fire. When he took up a fire hose, his rush of movement was gone. He stood at a position best suited to throw water on the fire. Annoyance with the heat grew, for it made him dance, undulating side-to-side to keep from blistering the soles of his feet.

Tug boats were summoned to the vessel. Quickly the fire gained control. Crews of firefighters were driven from the hull of the munitions ship, but not before their efforts had put water at the source of the conflagration. Yellowish smoke broiled from amid the bowels of the ship, mixing with, and finally, overtaking the ebony fumes of the earlier fight. The immediate danger to Bayonne, New Jersey, and to the surrounding port with thousands of residents was evident to the Coast Guard Command.

Ironically, the El Estero's sister ships sat complacently alongside waving their red Baker flags, but "Hot!" was their message. Hawser lines were attached to the burning ship, but the fire had to be contained if the vessel were to be safely towed from harbor, past New York City, and into open waters before it could be scuttled. From the volunteers on board, seven Coast Guardsmen were called upon to contain the fire while it was pulled from its berth.

Coast Guardsman, Francis J. Blanche remained on duty amid all the preparations for the disembarkation. The scarecrow-thin Pennsylvanian, Francis now stood facing a threat of catastrophic magnitude. His mind filled with thoughts and images of the family back home in Bridgeport and Camille Bernot, the girl whom he had loved all through high school and who would soon be his bride. Deep within him, a sense of duty motivated his decision to step forward with six of his fellow Coast Guardsmen and fight the fire. He watched as Lieutenant Junior Grade McCausland was assisted from the hull, overcome with fumes and suffering burns and blisters from his encounter with the scorching flames.

Francis's jet black hair contrasted the white Coast Guard issue cap as much as his weak, light frame contrasted the task at hand. A worried grin of discomfort presented a mouth of sickly teeth. His would-be smile was tainted by discoloration from smoking and a mix of carries, some repaired and others unrepaired. Standing in muster with the other volunteers, he and his mates seemed the victims of some barbaric rite of passage; but, with orders and instructions given, Franny and his six companions transformed into the aggressors, scurrying to their assigned tasks on the vessel. At nearly six feet, he carried himself and the equipment with the ease of an athlete. Once in motion and under way, his speed and carriage presented a picture of confidence. All seven moved to assigned duties: some flooding the holds with drenching showers of water and chemicals and others liberating the vessel from anchor lines. The tugs began their relentlessly slow and steady pull as some of the men disappeared into the bowels of the ship.

The ranking boatswain's mate saw Francis headed for his duty station. "You're getting married in a few months." He flung after the young Pennsylvanian. "Get the hell off the ship!"

The answer came silently with a turn of the head and a continual movement forward. Seaman Blanche smiled wryly, shook his head and stepped to his duties. Like his fellow seven, Francis grabbed a departing volunteer and handed him his wallet and personal pocket contents. This ritual was spontaneous; somehow they sensed the magnitude of the ordeal.

Cooking fuel began leaking from a drum stored on deck. Blanche and his mates rolled it toward the opening where the ammunition cases were jettisoned onto the pier. As the drum left the deck, a trail of orange-crimson flame danced and cavorted after it. The hot liquid was snaking its way after the drum, aflame with anger. Seaman Blanche stepped aside, ran to collect a hose, and washed the steaming solution into the bay. The drum oozed its contents onto the surface of the salt water, and a fire began on the surface. The flames lapped at the El Estero, anticipating the ship's total consumption by the fire.

The population on the surrounding shoreline was warned of the danger by sirens and air raid wardens. Belching steam and flowers of black smoke with leaves and stems of orange flame, the USS El Estero was towed to pre-determined coordinates.

The seven Coast Guardsmen remained onboard working to neutralize and stabilize the progress of the incendiary. "We must be near the anchorage location," screamed one of Francis's mates.

"How do you know that?" tossed Seaman Blanche as he maneuvered a three inch flow of water into the maw of the ship. The fire had its voice, but the water spray spoke another language: the suffering ship wailed in pain. The seamen's conversations had to be shouted in defiance to the rumblings around them.

"A PT boat is approaching!" pointed the original speaker. His blue-draped left arm pointed to indicate the approach of a speeding vessel nearing the El Estero.

"They only have one reason to be out here!" reflected Francis. He watched the craft swing to the port side upwind of the acrid fumes that rolled from the hull.

No one ceased filling the hold with water. They listened intently to the rumble of the cutter motor as it throttled down and into neutral. "Attention, all hands aboard," rang the bullhorn with the voice of some unseen officer.

"Alright, Guys, this is going to get pretty crazy," ventured Coast Guardsman Blanche.

"On my mark, disengage the hawser line and immediately drop anchor!" spoke the electric dialect of the megaphone. The men on board busied themselves sorting out each person's new responsibility. The PT boat accompanied them a short distance more before the bullhorn shrieked. "Release the hawser and drop anchor!"

Seven volunteers reeled from their hoses in a mad assault on their newest duties.

The sense of being towed, then adrift, and finally anchored presented a mystical silence and calm to the men. In a matter of moments, they were held fast, but safety still remained aloof for them. A thunderous explosion on the starboard side ripped their momentary hope from them. Turning, Francis saw a pillow-shaped cloud of angry black smoke rising above the ship. One of the drums had exploded.

Another notion entered the sensory synapses of the volunteers. "Your water line has risen!" reported the voice on the megaphone. "Prepare to abandon ship!" Somehow they already knew or rather felt the El Estero was sinking.

With pumps still running water through the hoses into the hull, the seven Coast Guardsmen threw lines over the port side, and scurried onto the rescue boat. There was no celebration, only the business at hand – the crew getting the boat at a safe distance from the scuttled ship. With exploding drums, a pulsing orange-hued light, and visible deck fires, the El Estero went to her rest. White steam rose from its bowels entwined with coffee colored smoke. The ship settled on the bottom with most of its decking still visible just above the water line. With the USS El Estero as a backdrop, the men celebrated their safety with the crew of the rescue boat.

Mayor Fiorello La Guardia arrived on scene at 9:45 p.m. and noted that the ship, although partially submerged was still afire. By 11:30 pm, the all-clear was finally sounded. For fear that German U-boats or spies would learn the full extent of the near disaster, no public celebration was planned. These "Subway

Sailors," as they were affectionately named by locals, were now beloved heroes.

For Francis J. Blanche, the events to follow were full of promise and hope. His wedding day was set. It was Easter weekend, and he had leave to be home for forty-eight hours. On Tuesday, he would be back on duty.

Chapter Five

"Blossoms of Summer"

By August of 1943, the family needed larger quarters with the children growing older. Anna Marie took the lead in searching for a suitable rental property that could house the family members. She considered the number of occupants: Margaret, Ralph McLaughlin and other Coast Guard friends of Franny, Larry, Eleanor, Patty, and Heebe who still frequented the Blanche household for long visits. They moved abruptly to a residence once used as a way station hotel at 700 De Kalb Street. Located at the junction of Seventh Street and Route 202 in Bridgeport, it kept them in their familiar parish of St. Augustine's. The schools, friends, and church would all remain. Eleanor already attended grade school, but Patricia, who turned three, roomed with her. Anna Marie and Margaret were young women and sought more privacy. Lawrence with his tinkering had his own room since Franny went into the service. His brother bunked with him when he was home on leave. Airman Heebe still required a bed and board when he was in town. The crowded conditions of their smaller home were alleviated by the old way-station hotel on De Kalb Street.

Tim and Mame rented the hotel. It featured huge, high ceilinged rooms in its three stories. The sizeable lot featured an array of fruit, berry, and nut trees. The entire third floor was a family sized apartment. The home featured one hundred and twenty-three doors.

The wedding on August 14, 1943, of Camille Bernot to Francis J. Blanche was a hurried affair. The Best Man was Richard Stone and the Maid of Honor was Anne Pieffer; they served as witnesses at the St. Augustine Church ceremony. The parish priest, Father Christopher J. Gidney officiated. The new family residence was the site of the reception.

Martin Bernot, Timothy, the groom, and his Coast Guard friends, Ralph McLaughlin, Shea, and Stone managed to return to the 700 DeKalb Street residence for the reception with some trepidation. They had stopped briefly at a pub on Fourth Street, and Stone and Shea dragged the party south on De Kalb Street up the hill to Seventh Street.

The party spilled onto the large L-shaped porch which caressed the southern and western sides of the old hotel. The beer inspired stories and manly banter kept the female participants at a distance. Tim became somber and stoic amid the well-wishers, but Martin joined gregariously into the mix of seamen. His adventures on the open sea at wartime impressed the young men.

"Why, I was the meal fisherman for the crew!" expounded Martin with little coaxing. "We'd pull into a port, and the guys would hand me a stout pole and reel, and I'd set out to catch us some fresh fish. The galley was always ready to cook up my catch." continued Martin.

"What's the biggest fish you ever landed?" ventured Ralph.

"Must have been that big grouper I landed off Cuba," boasted the father-in-law. "Could have been one hundred and eighty pounds, I guess."

Shea saw a chance to change the subject and voiced, "So how were the Cuban ladies?"

Martin looked about at the eager faces of the sailors and the scowl from Tim. "No, I'm not going to go there, Fellas," he apologized. "I'm sure you have your own stories and you don't need some from World War One."

Mary Bernot stood at the kitchen doorway with disdain etched into her demeanor. The Blanche family and acquaintances took to calling her Mary "Mack". Her family had shortened the "McNamara" of her heritage. Martin caught sight of her countenance peripherally. He waved an open hand in her direction and forced a smile to acknowledge her.

Timothy became uneasy, stood and began to pace with a list and a swaggering gait. He left the group and pushed his way into the kitchen.

"Mary, Mary, where are you?" he called with force and determination. "What are you up to?" he yelled into the hubbub of meals, dishes, and scurrying women dutifully at their tasks of supplying the guests with any provisions available.

"Tim, I'm here putting some food together," she responded from amid a cluster of ladies.

"Fine, just don't come out onto the porch, you hear!" directed Tim with cold purpose.

"Tim, you're an 'old fuddydud'," she tossed at him as she shooed him from the kitchen.

The women were milling about the ground floor rooms in small cliques. In the sitting room, toward the front of the inn which faced Route 202, the bride sat with Anne Pieffer and the Blanche daughters. Francis entered the room without fanfare and took a seat next to his bride. Dressed in his Coast Guard dress whites, the groom chose an official air rather than a more romantic carriage. The day, however, suited him. His joy, happiness, and peace were evident. Before he covered her left hand with the touch of his right hand, he noted the wedding band and small engagement ring. He smiled. His exhale sounded his inward satisfaction, and Camille leaned into his shoulder.

Anna Marie approached the couple, leaned forward, and kissed her brother on the cheek. "You both make a wonderful couple. Congratulations, Brother, you did well," she prompted, touching each with a confident hand. Camille received her joyous smile, and Anna Marie departed toward the kitchen.

Patricia romped about with her curls bobbing up and down, yoyo fashioned. Her frail slender torso easily found space amid the chat of the ladies. Her six year old sister, Eleanor, had found a safe haven on the settee across from the bride. She sat alone.

"Eleanor, come here and sit with me," invited Camille, patting the seat next to her. The soft, smiling face of the bride presented no threat to the young child. With a bashful stride, the young girl approached Camille. The child was struck by her kindness and beauty. Camille embraced the child, for she seemed lost amid the festivities. "Are you having a good time?" she moved to address Eleanor.

"Uh, huh," began the child. "There sure are a lot of people here today."

"That's because this is a special day for your brother Franny and me," reported Camille, placing her right palm on the girl's shoulder. The threesome sat like old friends, comfortable with each other.

It was the first meeting of Camille with most of the family. She had known Anna Marie and Margaret from school at St. Matthew's High School. Lawrence was a budding scholar with much promise. There was talk of his going on scholarship to St. Joseph's Prep School. His brown topped head could be seen searching out an adventure for himself. Larry, wedged between the older men's conversations and the women's dialogues, moped about the scene with some indifference. Mame found him and gave his presence justification by making him a delivery boy for the guests.

Francis made a point of complimenting his younger brother, "Larry, thanks for helping my buddies out. You're doing a great job." Then he added, "But don't work too hard. This is a party, you know."

"Sure, Franny," he stammered, and, as he hurried on another errand, he echoed, "Mrs. 'Mack' wants some cake. Yep! This is a party!" The remark erupted like a cheer from the bleachers at a ball game.

Patricia found herself shooed from the porch by the firm directive of her father. Timothy rarely addressed the girls; they were the domain of his wife. Mame nurtured and directed her daughters until one of the boys' issues took priority. At those times, an emotional indifference toward her daughters sometimes emerged.

Francis's commitment to the Coast Guard meant that the wedding and honeymoon would be dampened by his orders to return to Bayonne, New Jersey.

Camille came home to stay with her parents during Franny's Coast Guard tour. Mary Bernot did not conceal her dislike of her daughter's new husband, for she vocally disagreed with her youthful daughter's decision to marry. She seemed distraught to share her only child with "that hooligan". Mary's dread of being alone in the near future with an alcoholic husband nagged at her being.

The new Mrs. Blanche remained a jovial breath of life to all who knew her. She carried a bubbling, magnetic personality in her small frame. Her round, almost angelic face was always afire with a beaming smile that depicted her heartfelt joy of life and people. Wavy black hair bounded around her attractive face and magnified her perfect complexion and milk-white skin. Everyone loved Camille, and now, by extension, they all accepted her husband. Like Franny, she possessed an athlete's balance, for years of early training in ballet and dance had honed her movements to a perceivable grace and dignity.

By late October, Camille suspected that she was pregnant and hid it from her mother, fearing a larger confrontation. She avoided seeing a doctor to protect the truth of her condition. She yearned to tell her father, for he would have been elated with the news. Too many disagreements ensued, and Camille sought refuge with her Aunt Ruth and Uncle George Spare who lived upstate. By the time the young bride left for Lebanon, Pennsylvania, she was expecting her first child to be born in April.

It was difficult leaving her father and her friends in Conshohocken, but she wished to avoid the chance that things would be said that would forever ruin her relationship with her mother. She asked her mother to ship a large suitcase with her worldly possessions to her aunt's residence. So she embraced the community of Lebanon and found others to ingratiate.

Mrs. George Spare, by a series of favorable events, had garnered a secretarial position at Lebanon Valley College. Her employment and that of her husband, George, afforded them the rental of a single house. Ruth Spare enjoyed the nearness of good neighbors and the college. That prompted their decision to occupy the residence. The narrow, two story brick building echoed the architecture of the street. The upstairs bathroom divided the rear and front bedrooms. On the ground floor, the living room sat adjacent to the front door. A dining room and rear facing kitchen completed the first floor.

Bayonne and Lebanon became connected by the travel of the United States Postal Service. Franny penned a letter almost weekly, and she cherished them as much as the rare phone calls. Camille kept contact with her friends in Conshohocken and her new mother-in-law, Mame.

Just before Thanksgiving of 1943, Camille penned a letter to Mary Blanche. From the onset, the young bride was conscious of sharing Franny with a doting mother and worked to endear herself to her. That Mame did not consider her an "outsider" was proof of Camille's success. Her beautifully hand written letters worked magic.

11/19/43
Friday

Dear Mrs. Blanche,

Perhaps you think that I have completely forgotten you – since you haven't heard from me in all this time – but really, I haven't. I've meant to write at least a little note many times but something always seemed to come along. You know how those things are. Golly, anyone would think that I was an important business woman the way I can never find time for things. Maybe I should hire a secretary.

Franny was here yesterday and there is no need to tell you how happy that made me. Just knowing that I'll see him again soon cheers me up. He is a pretty wonderful person –as if you didn't know.

(2)

It has always been so hard for me to put into words how much I think of that son of yours, but I did want you to know for such a long time. Really, I'll try so hard to be as good to him as you have been. A girl would have to be pretty mean not to be good to him – he is so sweet and thoughtful. I consider myself pretty fortunate to have Fran for my husband. Please don't think I am being silly, Mrs. Blanche, because I mean every word. After all, you deserve to know.

Fran said that it would be all right for me to send you the receipt book for our wedding ring. The payment was due last week but he forgot to bring the book with him when he went…

(3)

home. I am worried that they will be sending a bill to my house because it is in my name. You see, my mother doesn't know how we had to get the ring and I'd rather she didn't find out. Would you mind very much if I'd send you the money when it is due each month? I don't mean to impose on you.

Hope you have been well and aren't working too hard. Never in my life did I see anyone work so much. Tell Marie (Anna Marie) and Margaret and the little ones that I send my love. Goodness! You'd better not tell Larry that I called him a little one. Fran says that Patty is bigger every time he sees her. Hope she isn't a grown-up lady by the time I see her again. Have you heard…

(4)

from Heebe lately? Remember me to him in your next letter. Guess he will mind being away from home this Christmas. It is hard to be so far from every one you like – especially around the holidays. Guess I'll close now – and sometime soon I'll send you another few lines.

By the way, I gained a few pounds since you last saw me. My health is perfect but I'll sure be glad to be thinner again.

Love to all,
Camille

The letters drew Mame and Camille closer just as her relationship with her mother drifted farther apart. Mary remained despondent with her daughter and with her husband and fell into poorer health. Martin worked his trade as a commercial artist for Ardway Sign Company in Ardmore, PA. He was not one to write, but Camille relished the occasional sketch from her father. Some of the drawings depicted her with an imagined grandchild and others of a sailor that he had fashioned. Words did not come as easily as did the drawings. Her world was loosely knitted together.

Chapter Six

"Lebanon, Pennsylvania"

The cedars of Lebanon are ancient; their aroma, presence, and history span the hours of our yesteryears, our todays, and our tomorrows.

The house was quiet when the Spares were out. These moments became productive to the young bride, and she spent time penning her reflective thoughts. Camille had several favorite writing locations: the dining room table, the kitchen breakfast table, and her bedroom. Her correspondence to 'Zeke' usually originated from the quiet of her upstairs bedroom.

10:30 am.
Monday

Hello Honey,

Here it is Jan. 24 and I am still waiting – and probably will be this time next week. I see no signs of going very soon – looks like someone got their wires crossed or something, huh!

It sure was sweet of you to call last night. Maybe it doesn't make a gal feel good to know that her husband cares so much. You are always doing things that prove your love for me. Someday I hope I can show you just how much you mean to me.

My suitcase still didn't come, Zeke. Mother called on Saturday night asking about it. She said she hoped it wasn't really lost 'cause practically everything I owned was in it. But it sure looks as though it has disappeared to me. Ain't it a shame? start praying…

(2)

To St. Anthony real hard, honey, so he finds it for me.

Did Ralph have a good time on his last liberty? Does he seem to be making any progress – or won't Margaret give him a tumble?

Golly, that is too bad about Shea. He should have been glad that he found her out before he married her instead of fighting. I don't see how a girl could be engaged to one boy and run around with someone else. Seems to me he is well rid of her. Or maybe they really aren't through.

Honey, don't forget to ask someone how I am to get you up here when Jr. decides to be born. Maybe I won't have to know for a few more weeks, but then again, maybe it will be before you come up again on liberty. One never can tell about such things it seems to me.

(3)

By the way, Zeke, I've been thinking that you should spend your next few liberties at home, not that I don't want you to come here – I live for the day you have off and we can be together – but I feel it is best. In the first place you have sort of been neglecting your mother lately – taking your wash home + running right away. There is still another reason, Honey, I think this trip is too much for you. When you came up on Friday night you looked completely worn out and I worried about you more than you imagined. I don't want you to think I am a natural born worry wart, honey, I just think too much of you to see you let yourself wear down for me. Please try to understand that I am only thinking of...

(4.)

your health, Zeke. You will need your strength when I send for you. In fact, I'll have to borrow some from you. That will be one of the many times I'll have to depend on you even more than I usually do.

Honey, I love you so much and want you near to me. It gets worse all the time – my wanting to be near you. Wonder if that will ever change – don't tell anyone but I hope it never does.

Must leave you now – no more to tell you. Think I'll go for a nice little walk. – as it is a bee-u-ti-ful day.

Lots of love + Kisses
Your wife,
Camille

The basement gathered the usual extraneous debris of life, but nothing of value was horded there. Lebanon had a history of flooding, and the residents knew and respected its nature. Laundry was hand washed in the basement tub and could be hung to dry in the small backyard or in the cellar during the colder months. This became a weekend chore.

The following Sunday, Uncle George had gone to the neighbors to help with a small renovation project. Ruth was steeping a pot of tea for herself and Camille, who decided to sort her laundry in her room.

"Auntie Ruth, are you doing any wash today?" The question sang through the upstairs and gravitated to the first floor kitchen.

"No, I'm not, but you take it easy today. It's Sunday," she shouted backward toward the yawning mouth of the stairway.

They had just come from mass. Aunt Ruth looked like family. The women shared complexion, body shape, and the black wavy hair of the McNamaras. Ruth had developed a pleasant, endearing personality. Her older sister, Mary, had stolen all of the least favored characteristics of civility. Somehow Camille understood the reasons for the contradiction, and loved both without question.

Camille wrestled with the issue of her pregnancy and her mother's moods. The youthful mother-to-be, now residing far from home, opted not to see doctors on a regular basis. Aunt Ruth had little success prodding Camille to seek help with her occasional headaches, shortness of breath, and blurred vision. In her naïve inexperience with pregnancy, Camille merely attributed these annoyances to her condition.

"I'd rather do it today. I think the basement will be a little warmer," she bemused. The weather of January 30, 1944, was still, and the lower arching sun managed to provide some welcomed radiant warmth. "Besides, I prefer that you're here when I'm doing chores. I still can't find everything I need."

"So you think I'm hiding things from you, Camille?" The good humor was not lost on the young wife.

"Yes, and you're stingy, too!" she retorted with an audible giggle from the upstairs bedroom.

"Three can't live as cheaply as one!" she countered. The banter was short lived, and Ruth added, "Wait 'til I come up and help you with the hamper, Camille"

"I'm okay. I can handle this little load, and then we can have our tea together," she reported.

She exited the bedroom with the step of a ballerina, but the hamper before her was an awkward partner. It fretted like a pouting child before her. Blood pulsed at her temple with the added bother and rebellion of the laundry basket. The elongated, woven basket bounced into her pregnant frame. She booted it forward in annoyance, but it stubbed its base on the carpet of the hallway. It impeded her progress again. Camille prodded it onward with the toes of her right foot. A smile traced her face; her grace of movement was lost to a clothes' hamper. With a shake of her head at the contradiction of happenstance, she waddled toward the descent. At the turn, the basket wedged under her refusing to assist her attempt to swing its weight into the downward space of the stairwell. Lifting the hamper brought her shoulders over the stationary container. A flash of dizziness and double vision caught her off her guard.

"Whoa…!" shot from her in a rifle crack of surprise and tenuous fear. Head first, past the first few downward steps, Camille screamed a long drawn, "No!"

The vacant air sent the words magnified as if from some sportsman's field megaphone. The fall took on a swoosh quality as the hamper remained beneath the young woman. The pair sledded atop the treadles, and she gained speed downward toward the right angle landing. Her feet beat the wall uselessly, leaving black scuff marks as their signature. The hand rail caught the top of the basket and tossed her head first from the hamper into the wall at the bottom of the landing. The heavy thud of flesh and muscle driven into the plaster wall was followed by absolute silence. The building was indifferent to her safety. The wall remained fixed against shoulder and head, leaving no indentations only a painting done in streaks of blood.

Aunt Ruth's senses piqued at the two words, the "swoosh" of woven cane on stairs, and the impact of body against building. She felt the house stir, move against the force, but it was the silence which brought paralytic fear into the heart of Aunt Ruth.

"Oh, my God! Camille! Camille! Oh, my God!" exploded from her in transit to the landing. The young woman lay crumbled like rolled, discarded newspaper in the elbow of a passageway. No movement, silence, a fetal position. She lay, cradling her abdomen – both arms wrapped securely around her child. "No, no, no!" The aunt shouted in horrid rage. The tea pot was screaming its siren wail. Aunt Ruth fled in rescue to the neighbors where her husband was visiting. She needed their immediate assistance and their automobile.

In the waiting room at Lebanon Sanatorium Hospital, Ruth Spare was allowed the use of the hospital phone. In reflex action, she telephoned her sister. The young husband had not entered her mind. In shock, she leaned on thoughts of her family. The news would destroy hearts in Conshohocken when word came that there had been an accident. Ruth fought to put aside the memory that Mary had groaned in sorrow and anger at the news. It was Martin who gave her the number to reach Francis in Bayonne. Martin reached a nephew, James McNamara, to drive him to Lebanon, but the doctor refused to allow Mary to travel under these circumstances of her ill health.

The message relayed to Seaman Francis Blanche twisted his dreams and life into a nightmare. The young bride had fallen, tumbled down a flight of steps, and was in a coma at the Lebanon Sanatorium Hospital. Francis could not hurry fast enough; a bus took him to New York City's bus terminal off Forty-Second Street. There he had to transfer on an agonizingly slow local toward Harrisburg. Despondent, he spoke to no one, stared vapidly into the darkening evening, and prayed. The connecting bus would arrive in Lebanon at 4:30 p.m., and the cab dropped him at the hospital entrance one-half hour later.

The notification at the Blanche family home in Bridgeport ripped the quiet complacency of their lives into chaos. The duty had fallen into the hands of Ralph McLaughlin. With Francis already in transit, the anguished husband had to depend on either Shea or McLaughlin to carry out his request. Ralph called Margaret and relayed the details to her. Tim had not begun the heavier drinking that usually marked his Sunday afternoon, and the sobering news put Mame and him on the road by 2:00 p.m.

At the reception desk, Francis was hurriedly ushered from the lobby by an aide. Passing the waiting room, Aunt Ruth and Uncle George spotted the pair and scurried to join them. They caught them at the foot of the stairs.

"Franny, I'm so, so sorry!" Aunt Ruth whispered in muted respect. She was wearied, her face drawn in a frown, and her eyes reddened with salted tears.

"What do you know?" jumped from the seaman. His eyes were flared wide, energy poured from them. It was a question he had carried throughout the entire trip. It leapt from his being without permission at Ruth's greeting.

"Camille is still unconscious," she began, and then, as an afterthought, she stated the obvious, "You have to see the doctors." She could tell that he wanted more from her.

"How serious is it, Aunt Ruth?" The aide stayed behind as the party of three ascended the staircase off the main lobby.

"She looked like she was trying to... Franny, her hands and arms were hugging her child. I don't think she tried to protect herself in the fall." Aunt Ruth drew a calming breath.

"Broken, everything's broken!" he muttered.

They were ushered into a small room on the second floor by the operating rooms. Four leather seated chairs dotted the interior, but no one sat. The doorway filled with a tall figure draped in a white lab coat. Insignia from the hospital was embroidered on the pocket, fitted with pens and a thermometer. The buttoned smock dressed the man with a formality that matched his demeanor.

Dr. Henry Van de Water entered the room with his right hand extended to greet Seaman Francis J. Blanche. Atop the cordial handshake, he ventured, "I'm sure this has been a very difficult day for you and your families. I am Dr. Van de Water." He continued as if the words had been carefully prepared beforehand, "You have my utmost sympathy." The phrases sounded dire, and no one moved with any words of interruption. Silence occupied space for an awkward moment. Releasing Francis's hand, he saw the young sailor shuffle uneasily and drop his eyes to the floor. He waited politely.

"What can I do?" stumbled from Fran's mouth. His eyes now sought solace from the doctor before him. Aunt Ruth turned quietly and took a seat in the nearby chair alongside George.

"At this moment, Camille is stable, but her vital signs are a concern." A left hand patted the right shoulder of the young husband. "We are very concerned about the babies," he delivered with a firm, serious tone.

"Babies?" gasped Aunt Ruth, "what do you mean 'babies'?" she gasped.

As if the new information had not been spoken, Francis muttered, "Will she be alright?"

"Mr. Blanche," he addressed calmly in an attempt to frankly present his next directive in the hope that the husband might respond with clarity to the issue at hand. "What you need to do is to make a decision, the most difficult one that you will ever have to make."

"I want her to be better, Doctor. What has to be done?" he finally managed with some control and poise.

"Your wife has a head injury, but the Toxemia is more of a concern to us. Only five percent of young mothers with multiple children can develop this serious infection. When this goes undiagnosed it can be fatal, even for young, healthy patients."

There was an audible sob from Ruth as she understood the doctor's diagnosis.

"She'll be alright, though, Doctor – right?" he wished the best.

"I must be honest with you. At this point, your wife is struggling to overcome this infection, Mr. Blanche." His necessary bluntness pained him, but he knew he could not change the events unfolding. "We want to take the children from her as soon as possible before her functions deteriorate and the infection affects the children. I need your permission to perform a Caesarian Section to save them."

Functioning on an emotional level unfamiliar to him, Francis asked, "Will that improve her chances?"

"In all fairness to you, Mr. Blanche, I'm sorry but we do not believe Camille will live beyond the next forty-eight hours."

The words pushed Franny backward, and he fumbled for a seat next to Ruth and George. She grasped his hand tightly.

"If I can't have Camille, you can do whatever needs to be done," defeated, he sobbed. Tears flowed freely now. His guard was down, but he sensed Aunt Ruth's touch. He wanted to be away from this, but the only place he found was deep within his being. He sent the pain and sorrow somewhere and vowed to endure the horrors that he must face.

Camille's vital signs took a turn for the worse, and the staff scrambled to operate to save the children. Before anyone else arrived that day, Francis was the father of twin boys. His wife was in critical condition and had not regained consciousness.

Tim and Mame arrived after the surgery. They made a stop for a meal and drove into the hospital parking lot around 6:30 p.m. Their son's travail filled them with anguish beyond life's expectations. To be grandparents without joy, to be parents without happiness, and to hold quiet vigil with Francis was their only comfort. While he sat at Camille's bedside, they supported him with their words and their presence. Aunt Ruth was a stalwart, for she had had more time to absorb the events of the day. George felt like a bystander but focused on his wife's need to comfort the family. Ruth, Tim, and Mame made brief stops to the nursery where the boys were placed in incubators. Francis never ventured to that section of the hospital.

Martin did not arrived at the hospital until nearly 11:00 p.m. that night. His travel left him weary, and the unfolding events would give him no rest. He did not find the strength or the courage to call Conshohocken, and James McNamara was left the task of notifying the family and friends. Jim first made a phone call to arrange a companion for Mary. Then he drove home and called on her early next morning.

Camille Marie Blanche died peacefully with her devoted husband, loving Aunt and small community of family by her side on Monday, January 31, 1944.

Francis had, in a brief span of ten months, gone from hero to husband, from husband to father, and from husband to widower. He took that time, those memories, and his feelings and locked them tightly into a coffin of unspoken dreams. No one who knew him, whether family member or friend, would ever traverse that dark abyss or open for question or discussion any of the events of those days. Eventually, Franny began to "unbelieve" them - the events which had transformed his life forever. He struggled to salvage his life and to escape the cruelty that fate had dealt him. In the harsh simplicity of his deliberate plan, he had set into motion a means of protection, a buffer, from the turmoil of emotional pain that would haunt him throughout his life. Out of reverence, remorse, or perhaps bitterness, he never again mentioned the name, Camille.

The children, birthed two and a half months premature, remained in Lebanon Sanatorium Hospital for three months, gaining strength and weight. The nurses and staff loved and nourished them. So began the doting on the youngsters, twin boys taken from their dying young mother.

Chapter Seven

"Where Do We Go from Here?"

Camille was laid to rest in St. Matthew's Cemetery in Conshohocken on February 4. The Bernot plot rested roadside on Fayette Street in the St. Joseph's Section. The newly turned earth lay naked in the cold winter breeze. Traffic along the highway was choked by the number of vehicles parked near the gravesite. The funeral rite gave little or no consolation to the family and friends of the young wife. All their questionings went unspoken, and Franny maintained an agony of silence.

Many paths diverged in these woods surrounding Philadelphia. Francis trudged back to the service and his duty in and around Bayonne, NJ, after the services. Tim and Mame returned to Bridgeport. The adult world awaited the rest of their offspring.

In the beginning of April, Francis received a registered letter from Lebanon Sanatorium Hospital from the head of the pediatric ward. The twin boys had gained sufficient weight, growth, and development as to be released from the hospital's care. Franny at first petitioned Martin and Mary to bring the infants to their home and rear them until Franny was discharged from the service. He felt encouraged and relieved by the phone call with Martin, but the father-in-law needed to speak to Mary before he could guarantee any help. The initial plan was shattered a day later when Martin returned the call to the Coast Guardsman.

"Hello, Franny! It's Martin," chimed the friendly voice on the line.

The young serviceman was elated with the call, for it meant that the children would be with Camille's parents until he left the Coast Guard. "Yes, how's everything in Conshy?" All the locals shortened the town's Lenape name to its briefest syllables.

"I had a long chat with Mary yesterday," he began, and his spirited voice at the greeting dwindled and waned in power as his conversation grew. "She's a stubborn woman at times, Franny. Her health is still not good, and, well, she doesn't want to take on the physical responsibilities of raising two infants." Martin was recounting some truths and some lies. He edited Mary's assessment of the situation and retold it as a health concern. He did not report her actual words of despair, "If only she hadn't gotten pregnant!" Kindly, Martin wanted to convey to the beleaguered father not only his desire to help but also his inability to tackle the obligation with his wife's refusal.

"Gees! Martin, I was hoping this was all settled. I've got to be in Lebanon Easter week to pick up the boys. I knew it was short notice...and my Mom and Dad already have a full house." The dilemma flattened his voice to a monotone.

"I'd gladly do it in a minute, Franny, but I really don't have a partner in this," he confessed as mildly as he could, trying to save his wife from the young man's disdain.

"I understand." He conceded. "Look, I've got to get on this, Martin. I'll keep you posted, okay?"

"Sure...Let me know when I can come visit the kids," some elation slipped into the latter comment, for Martin ached to have the grandchildren become a part of his life.

The phone call put Francis on a hurried series of maneuverings. Married friends, family members, and even public agencies could not offer an immediate solution to his impending trip to

Lebanon. He phoned his family in Bridgeport. Mame answered and listened intently to the pleadings of her oldest son.

"Franny, we've taken in Heebe and raised him. We can certainly take in your two little ones," she pledged. Her sincerity issued from the comment spontaneously.

"What about Dad? Is he okay with this, too?" queried Franny, considering what had happened with the Bernots.

"Are you kidding!" she blurted without hesitation. "Your father will do whatever you and I ask. If he was willing to take in my nephew, he'll certainly agree to have your boys here." It was settled.

"Okay, Mom, but only 'til I get out of the service." He placed the small print into the contract to ease her commitment and ensure his.

Once Francis Bernard Blanche and Bernard Francis Blanche arrived in Bridgeport, the most obvious and pressing issue became their care. The large hotel/home was now flooded with the paraphernalia of infants: gifts, clothing, furniture, food, and people. Family, neighbors, and friends wanted to support and assist the family whose lives had been so tragically affected. This added necessary stability and eased adjustments being made by everyone, except Francis.

Despite the activity in the home on most weekends, one lone figure sought the fringes, the edges of the group during those days filled with friends and family. He sought out a vacant room; and, seated on the small sewing machine bench, the uniformed Coast Guardsman slumped over the covered machine in a weary embrace. His back heaved in muted sobs. Somehow young Eleanor and Patty found him. Side by side, they stood in quiet respect, bewildered by the scene before them. Eleanor ushered her sister from the room, and gently touched her brother's shoulder as she exited.

The goings-on were also traumatic for the young three year old, Patty. Her childhood as the "baby" ended with the arrival of the twin celebrities. The two youngest daughters banded together for survival against the barrage of attention foisted upon Mame and her little boys.

Martin and Mary parted – he to Norristown, and she to the inner circle of her Conshohocken family and friends. Martin drifted into a hobo's existence. He wandered from town to town and from job to job, eventually returning to freelance sign painting. He settled with Kunda Sign Company, and lived in a boarding house just off Swede Street. It was September of 1944. His visits to De Kalb Street often took on the appearance of a standoff between warring factions. He never knocked on the huge front door sober. The single granite step at the threshold presented a formidable obstacle to him. Mame always checked the front door from the front sitting room. It was always a weekend and Timothy was home. Being a heavy drinker himself, he seemed to tolerate the appearance of the "In-law." Mame, perhaps remembering her own brothers, did not. She set into motion a rite that would occur during all of Martin's visits to his grandchildren, sober or not.

Once into the home, Martin was ushered to an upright parlor chair. Mame would leave the room momentarily and return with either Francis or his brother in her arms. The caretaker stood before the seated Martin and showed the child to him. She then carried the child to Timothy, place him in the man's lap, and left for the twin brother. Mame presented this sibling to Martin in like fashion before she sat on the sofa holding the baby in her arms. Strained conversations ensued. Martin usually assented to the treatment imposed by Mame, for his emotions were dulled by the inebriation. To a casual on-looker, the theater was cruel.

60

Alone with his alcohol Martin endured life, forced from the family that he yearned to embrace.

Ownership loomed its menacing head like a medieval dragon, and Mame took loving possession of that which was only partially hers, the twins. She succumbed to the notoriety, the attention, the praise of townspeople who filled her with pride for her dutiful sacrifice in rearing, "Those poor motherless boys."

Seaman Francis J. Blanche received a letter from the Coast Guard Command in New York, the details of which he sent on to his parents.

COTP Office
Room 10, Barge Office
New York 4, New York
"Instructions for City of Bayonne, N.J. Presentation Ceremonies"

25 September, 1944

1. On Monday, 25 September, 1944, the City of Bayonne, New Jersey, is honoring the Coast Guard officers and men engaged in fighting the fire aboard the munitions ship S. S. EL ESTERO in April, 1943. Individual medals will be presented to all hands by Rear Admiral Charles A. Park, Chief of Operations, U. S. Coast Guard, on behalf of the City of Bayonne.

2. Preceding the presentation of medals at the civic ceremony at the Senior High School Auditorium in Bayonne, a dinner will be tendered to all hands, to be followed by a parade to the high school. The dinner will be at 1715, the parade at 1900 and the presentation ceremony will start at 2015.

3. You are one of the men to be honored at this celebration and you are directed to read carefully the following instructions concerning your participation therein:

(a) The uniform for officers will be Dress Blue B (Blue uniform, white shirt, white cap covers). The uniform for enlisted personnel will be Dress Blue B (Blue uniform, white hats, no leggings).

(b) You will report to Chief CROWLEY at Jersey City Barracks promptly at 1500 on Monday, 25 September. Further orders concerning your participation will be issued to you at that time.

(c) There will be a limited number of tickets in a special reserved section at no cost for relatives of the men being honored, should they want to attend the ceremonies at the high school. Make your request to your Commanding Office, but do not request these tickets unless you intend to use them.

(d) Transportation for officers will be available at the Barge Office, departing promptly at 1615.

R. L. Jack

Francis ordered two tickets for Mame and Tim. Neither Mary nor Martin were contacted or invited. It should have been a glorious day. Their son was one of the honorees in a parade and medal ceremony in Bayonne, New Jersey. The parents learned of the event and its dangers from the Admiral when he introduced the medal winners. They had little inkling from Franny of the magnitude of what he had done. They were proud to be with him on that day, to meet his officers and fellow seamen, and to share stories of his youth with other parents.

The three tugboat captains were awarded medals and commendations. The seven Coast Guardsmen received the Naval Silver Star for valor. Lieutenant Stanley received the Legion of Merit, and members of the Ammunition Loading Detail were awarded a medal especially struck for the occasion. Rear Admiral Charles A. Park presented the medals. From the ceremony, all the travelers went their separate ways.

Timothy and Mary Blanche went home to recant the marvels of their eldest son. A few papers were beginning to release the news of the event once security and secrecy were less important issues. The bit of joy carried them into the Christmas season.

Francis found it difficult to make a positive and healthy emotional connection with his offspring. His weekends with them in Pennsylvania were bitter sweet. The visits magnified the distance that began to separate him from the children. In his nightmare, they were dropping into some dark place. No guilt followed the indifference he felt, for he did not care that he was a weekend parent or that his parents usurped his parental role with the boys. He made fewer and fewer trips home and began to spend weekends with sailors and nearby families who offered home meals and comforts to the seamen.

He met a tall, thin, energetic woman with black curly hair in East Orange. Florence Winters was a fun-loving distraction to him. Lebanon, Pennsylvania, and the twins did not spice the conversations of those early meetings. Later, as Franny gained confidence in the relationship, he confided in Florence. She admired his sensitivity and enjoyed his notoriety as a local hero. Mr. Stanley Winters made his friends and relatives aware that his daughter was seeing the young Bayonne hero. The spring of 1945 came and the romance of Franny and Florie blossomed.

One evening, Florie visited her local parish Rectory to seek the advice of her priest. She had some pressing issues concerning her relationship with the young seaman. His previous marriage, the twin boys, and the courtship were on the agenda.

"If you're getting that serious with this young man, Florie, I suggest the two of you start thinking about marriage," ventured the sage. He remained behind a rather large mahogany desk, took out a cigarette, and lit it with a flip-hinged Zippo lighter.

"He's not ready for that step yet, Father," she offered, a bit reluctant to deepen the importance of her meeting with the cleric. "He needs my support, but there is a fear and reticence in him. It's like he's running from his pain."

"I think a stable home life can support him until he learns to deal with the issues he has." A long, voluminous cloud of billowing smoke poured from his lungs.

That idea had lain in wait like a stalking cat. Florie remained quiet, for she knew that might be a daunting task. Her head bowed; she fingered the flounce of her dress.

Father left her free of an obligatory response when he followed the statement with his own answer. "Well, you're a bright girl, and you could offer him your care. That would even be more reason to walk up the aisle." He was pleased with himself. Church logic was on his side.

The relationship with which the priest dealt on this occasion was more complex and troubled than he has surmised, but still the good counselor pressed for their wedding.

One Friday in the fall of 1945, Franny appeared unexpectedly in Bridgeport. He had chosen to spend this particular"leave" weekend at home rather than in New Jersey. He tossed his knapsack in the foyer, and it rolled with a thump onto the oaken floor with a softer fall than normal. He was traveling light this time, and there was no extra laundry to do. Everyone at home rushed to greet him just inside the front door. Embraces and smiling faces warmed the chilly air that had pushed its unwelcomed presence into the room.

"Dad will be very pleased to see you when he gets home," announced Mame. The girls stood nearby playing with the hems of dresses and frocks admiring their big brother in his uniform.

"Good, Mom. I didn't miss dinner, then?" said Franny considering a home cooked meal.

"No, you haven't, Son," responded Mame as she led her sailor into the confines of the sitting room. Spot, Larry's mixed breed dog, ran up to the sailor and wagged his welcome, sniffled about, and scurried over to Larry's feet.

The welcome waned, and the children soon busied themselves with chores, the radio, and any conversations that they had abruptly interrupted with his entrance. When Tim returned home, he was permitted a private audience with the Coast Guardsman.

"You doing okay up in Jersey, Franny?" he wondered. The dirty clothing reeked with the smell of burned diesel fuel. He continued his normal routine upon his homecoming. His jacket and shoes were removed. He placed the shoes neatly in his favored storage location. Tim continued the conversation as he hung his coat on a separate hook, far from the other outerwear of the family. His coat was covered in oily soot.

"Nothing new is going on. We had a quiet week." advised Franny. "I thought I'd like to see everyone for a change." It was evident that he had traveled light, but a shrug, like he had left something unsaid, gave the hint of another agenda. Tim let it pass.

"Good to see you." Then, he added. "Well, let's get cleaned up and have some dinner."

The meal was noisy, and Dad and Franny had their fare share of Schlitz beer, fried and breaded veal cutlets, stringed beans, and mashed potatoes. A salad was a rarity at the table, but dessert always followed. It was mandatory. A milk pie was finished without leftovers.

The following morning cigarette smoke and brewing coffee awakened the children well after Mame, Tim, and Franny had risen. The tenor of the voices drifting upward to their second floor bedrooms provoked a stillness and inactivity in the stirrings of the children. None ventured beyond the doorways of their quarters.

"No! No, no, you are not going to do this!" resounded in echoed force upward through the double staircase. Mame's shout crackled and reverberated with her anger and rage.

"Calm down, Mary!" hushed Tim in an undertone in his attempt to suppress the tension of the moment.

"I will not calm down. This will be the ruination of me... and him, Tim," she retorted still holding to the energy of her admonition. She moved side to side, in hurried thought and rebuttal.

"Look, Mom, it's time for me to move on," countered Franny in a prepared delivery. "I've got a little over a year of duty left, and I want to be settled when I'm discharged."

"Not with that woman!" shot Mame without hesitation.

"You really don't know her, Mom. She comes from a good family, and they treat me fine." Franny motioned toward her, but fell short of placing a gentle hand on her shoulder. Mame looked sharply toward his father, but found no immediate ally in his posture. Franny prodded him to speak with a flick of his head.

"Mary, maybe she'll grow on you," Tim shrugged in dismay.

"All these women are after my boys. I have to watch even Larry and who's interested in him," issued from her torment. A deep basal wail arose from within her, uncontained and mournful.

Faces could be seen frozen in doorways along the second floor. Anna Marie waited transfixed, expectant of more chaos.

Crying with bellowing frustration and consternation, Mary yelled, "No more foolishness!" The words left her breathless, but she attempted to flee up the steps toward the first landing at the turn of the grand staircase. It divided into two approaches to the second floor. On the tier, she pivoted to face the men below her. Both full arms grasped at her chest just below her neck. Silence poisoned the air. Mame reeled backward, struck the wall, and slid downward in a cascade of apron, frock, and legs. Her head heaved back and forth struggling for breathe. A rush of footfalls from the men below and the older children above thundered onto the landing. Eleanor and Patricia ventured onto the second floor landing and clung to the railing with frightened concern. The eighteen month old twins toddled in the entrance way of their room.

Gulps of hysteria oozed from the seated parent as she made no effort to regain her footing. When the family reached her, she had succumbed to her emotional exhaustion and begrudgingly rested. The words were gone from her, but the family's vocal concerns rose in a cacophony of incomprehensible chatter. The family guided its queen bee in a cluster of activity. The colony pushed slowly into the confines of her bedroom. The day was spent without compromise; and, in her silent resolve, Mame forced everyone into retreat. The leave voluntarily ended in the afternoon. Franny returned early to New Jersey.

Chapter Eight

"The Jersey Side"

The three Coast Guardsmen sported winter formal blue uniforms with dark kerchiefs looped around their collars. The January sky was gray and still. By 1947, Ralph McLaughlin, Jack Shea, and the groom had just months before their tour of duty would finish. They were under orders from their officers, the parents, and the bride to behave. The bridal party consisted of Seaman Shea and the bride's sister Dolores, Guardsman McLaughlin escorted Miss Anna Marie Blanche, and the bride, Florence, and her father, Mr. Stanley Winters. The small affair did not lack for "Pomp and Circumstance" for the trappings of the service and reception remained formal.

A long, white train of expensive lace followed Florence throughout the day. The scalloped neck line of the bride's gown was duplicated on her maids-of-honor dresses. The motif of embroidered flowers over the netted sash and bodice also decorated Anna Marie and Dolores's gowns. Each woman donned a white lace veil and carried a full bouquet of white roses and lilies.

The Winterses reveled in the day and celebrated with joy and enthusiasm the wedding of Florence. The Pennsylvanians rather played at the semblance of happiness. Much history marched into the Jersey City proceedings, but no words spoken dampened the excitement of the day. Franny appeared solemn during some of the still moments of the celebration. Like Tim, his father, Franny generally avoided a broad smile on pictures. He preferred to conceal his poor dental health behind a stoic expression.

When life settled into routine, Florence worked as a secretary. Franny made the weekend trips from Bayonne and began to seek employment upon his discharge from service. Stan Winters was well known in the area and promised immediate work for Franny when he was out of the service.

In the spring of 1947, Franny found work at a nearby pickling factory. He drove deliveries from the factory to the distributors and stores in the area. He took on the extra tasks of maintaining and repairing the trucks which the small company owned. He enjoyed that there were no bends in his road or bumps on the highway. Life was a friend, and he wished to keep it that way. He became pliant, giving way on issues before they could solidify and shatter his neat New Jersey world.

Florence again brought up her pre-wedding, New Year's resolution for 1947 just after a Saturday morning breakfast. Their apartment was flooded with sunlight, but it falsely promised warmth on a cool late winter day. The little kitchenette held a chill that necessitated slippers and a robe.

"Are you doing any truck repair today, Franny?" enjoined Florie. She stood her ground at the sink, back towards her husband, and hopefulness in her voice.

"No, why?" reflected Franny as he finished his second cigarette of the morning and sipped the sweetened black coffee in his cup. "You have something that needs to be done?" he inquired.

"Nope!" she fired with resolution. "I'd like to talk to you about something that I've been mulling over since New Year's Day." The delivery was a slow and easy draw. No hint of urgency or threat fell into the tone.

Franny heard the words almost like a passing remark, one of little importance and something easily settled. "Sure, I'm all ears," he sighed with a rare broad smile. He had begun to have dental work, and his countenance showed the results.

Florie turned while rubbing the wetness from her hands with a cotton kitchen towel. The chair growled like the warning of a dog as she slid it from under the small table. Franny watched her maneuver to the table, and he put his newspaper aside. He left the crossword puzzle page open and facing upward on the table. "I'd like to visit your parents next weekend," she suggested.

Franny nodded at first, and then offered, "That's nice. I'm glad you want see them. I haven't seen Lar…." A cough and a raised hand halted him mid-thought.

"Not that kind of a visit, social I mean. I'd like you to ask your Mom for the twins."

He saw her head tilted and her facial muscles press upward and toward her right eye. Then the idea of her words trapped his consciousness. "Whoa…I wasn't ready for that!" He pled for time, time to twirl the idea around, let it dissolve a bit, allow it to take on the warmth of his mouth. "They're three years old." He did not know why he had even uttered the fact, but he sensed it signified a long journey for him.

"Yes, and your Mom and Dad have been troopers," she complimented. "They're getting older now, and Patty and Eleanor are still little girls. You've sent money every month to Mom and Dad. You deserve to have them with you."

He was not ready for this. Franny wanted to be free of the decision, this bump in the road. His young bride presented both hands to him with palm upward in supplication. "You've thought this out, Florie?" he offered, but he knew the answer.

"Certainly! All the obligations, the responsibilities, and the duties. Franny, you are their father, and they deserve to be raised by you. Mom and Dad could spend more time on your younger brother and sisters." Her delivery's precision marked a great deal of thought about her resolution.

Franny stood and marched to the counter where the coffee pot puffed its percolated steam. He poured another cup of coffee. "I'm willing to take this on, Florie; but it's not in me to ruffle feathers, yours or anyone else's." Sugar and spoon swirled about in a tempest of hot liquid. "We have no idea where this might go," he reflected almost in prayer.

"I think we still have to do this. You'll be a great Dad. And I want to see you assert yourself." Her hands had moved to her lap, and she spun to face him at the counter where he stood with hot coffee at his lips.

Franny was not sure from where the last statement originated, and it threw him off his guard momentarily. "I'm okay with this instant family idea. Mame, though, she's the unknown here. If you still are willing to take this on, I'll call and see if they're going to be home next weekend. Then, we can bring it up with her and Dad." Franny considered the calmness that his concessions brought: Florence has what she wanted. He did not have to deal with the issue until the weekend. The idea that he could comply with the conditions of rearing two boys and easing the burden on his own parents consoled him.

Timothy and Mary would be home next weekend and were anxious to see Franny. The fact that Florence was also coming seemed to have little import in the planned visit.

The light crust of frozen "onion" snow crunched under the De Soto's tires as the Francis Blanches turned into the stone driveway at 700 De Kalb Street in Bridgeport. Franny and Florie rushed into the front door to an energetic and enthusiastic welcome. Eleanor and Patty, who were interrupted at play, scurried into the lobby off the front sitting room. They held a family of dressed paper cut-out figurines. The twins were underfoot, pushing their presence into the mix. Tim stood behind the youngsters and guided them from the mayhem of coats, hats, and gloves. Florie embraced Eleanor, knelt to hug Patty, and reached for the nearest twin boy, Bernard. Her quick motion startled him, and he flew to cover behind Tim.

"Daddy," he pleaded for shelter from the woman before him. Francis, the other twin, stood his ground, and allowed the woman's touch upon his shoulder and then his cheek.

"The boys are beautiful," sang Florie as she stood to greet Timothy. "Where's Mother?" she questioned of the patriarch.

"Where else? – the kitchen," he reported with a matter-of-fact indifference. "How was the ride, Franny?"

"No problem, Dad. There's no snow cover until you get into Pennsylvania." The young husband was moving Florie into the sitting room. "I guess Margaret and Ralph are settled in by now?"

"Yep! They have the entire third floor set up as a full apartment. Margaret is putting together a little room for the baby." He sat in his usual comfortable chair, and the two little boys immediately joined him. Francis, the taller of the two, shinned onto his lap.

Ralph McLaughlin had married Margaret with the normal haste of marriages occurring around the war. He had taken a sales position selling furniture in Norristown at John's Furniture Store. The couple was busy in their apartment improving the accommodations for their seven month old Gregory who arrived on September 3, 1946.

"Call us down for lunch, will you, Eleanor?" was Franny's request as he ushered Florie up the winding stairs to the third floor apartment. The visit was back-slapping friendly for the old mates, and it afforded Florie a chance to test the pair on the issue of taking the twins. The practice run gave some encouragement to the young bride, but Franny was taking the proceedings in stride. He gave the allusion of one confident and calm in the face of doubt and uncertainty. Margaret shared her concern that Mame did not usually consent to life-changing events. She was easy with the mundane and usual, but unpredictable with weighty decisions.

The luncheon brought Anna Marie and Larry from their studies and diversions in their rooms. The twins and Patty ate first, accompanied by watchful adults and siblings. Their meal finished, they were cleaned up and sent to play. The adults had the dining room table to themselves. Sporadic interruptions infiltrated the lunchtime chat as the children would wander into the room for advice, complaints, and attention.

"Mommy, Mommy, Bernie took my car," wailed young Francis as he scurried to the comfort of Mame's chair.

"Uncle Franny will help you," suggested Anne Marie.

The name "Uncle Franny" pricked the senses of Florie, for the boys had been taught to speak of their father in this manner. Timothy was "Dad" and Mame was "Mommy." Franny got up and followed the young twin into the sitting room to resolve the problem with the car. Larry excused himself to attend to school business at a friend's house. The wiry brown haired teenager had set his sights on a private preparatory school, and he held to his dreams of a college education. Anna Marie remained at the table. She, too, had goals and aspirations, but the situation with her parents trying to raise Heebe and the twins pre-empted her choices. She gave the family her time and her talent in exchange for brief moments of indulgence. She enjoyed sports, classical music, Kent cigarettes, and a salad of fresh tomatoes, garlic, and olive oil. Tim and Mame permitted her all of these.

Uncle Franny returned to the dining room and sat next to Florrie. She placed her hand on his which rested on his leg.

"Mom and Dad, Florie wants to make an offer to you. It's kinda one of her New Year's resolutions," he began. The message satisfied him, but Florie was hoping for a more mutually agreed upon approach.

"Well, actually, Franny and I have both spoken about this, and…we hope you agree that it's a great idea." That said she only had to bring the matter to air.

"So what do the two of you have cooking?" prodded Mame. She pushed her chair back and readied herself for enlightenment.

"Well, we want to start a family," she began with a soft shyness, "but we already have one." Silence greeted the speaker. No one wished to address the possibilities of what she had implied.

With a naïve simplicity, Anna Marie voiced her heartfelt wish, "What! You two are expecting?" The couple shot looks of surprise toward one other.

Franny seemed more flustered than his wife. He stammered, "No, no, no! That's not it!" His head swung to and fro like a clock pendulum. Florie's comment rescued him.

"Franny and I think it is a good idea and the right time for us to bring the twins to New Jersey with us," interrupted Florie with courage beyond what she thought she possessed.

Either not wishing to believe what was said or having misunderstood her daughter-in-law, Mame contributed, "The twins are welcome to visit both of you any time."

"No, Mom!" her son blurted, but, sensing the curtness of his words, he added, "Florie didn't mean for visits; she means permanently."

"Franny, that's crazy!" The mother blurted without a second of thought. Her weight shifted uneasily in her chair. Mame was uncomfortable.

"I know it's kinda sudden… after all this time, but Florie…" he was not allowed to complete the thought.

"Sudden!" Mame thundered with strength to her voice that surprised everyone at the table. "You're talking about ripping this family apart. My God! Those boys are like our own," she stammered with a slight emotional falter in the force of her delivery.

Florie tried calmly to bring her logic to the table. "Mom, we know how difficult these last years have been for you and Dad to take on the added pressure of raising the twins along with the girls." The titles of Mom and Dad still rang with awkwardness in her address.

"They've been no trouble at all. My heavens! The girls haven't suffered. The twins fit right in," she summarized with a calm and clear delivery. She had set her mind to the task at hand, and her determination gave her unbridled assurance in her position.

Franny looked downward trying to find the right words to pursue the debate. Florie gave him the moment to take the lead, but Anna Marie spoke first.

"Florie and Franny are their family too, Mom. You have to have known that this day would come," she offered as a measure of sanity.

"We take the twins everywhere. All our friends and relatives know that we took them in after their mother died. They know we're doing the right thing. They're used to being with us," spun from her like a web, entrapping present and up-coming arguments. Tim remained silent. He finished the beer in front of him.

"It's tough on Franny, Mom, when his children call him Uncle Franny," mumbled Florie with an air of trepidation.

"It's very natural for the boys to call us Mom and Dad. They belong here; they're comfortable here and sheltered from all the trials and hardships that have been part of their lives. They shouldn't have to face all of that now!" Her shoulder went back; her posture erect and solid.

"That's why we should do this now. Mom, it will be impossible later," appealed Franny. He sensed the attention of everyone at the table directed at his mother. Her pain throughout his troubles echoed sadness; he felt her somber thoughts simmer with this fresh view of the proceedings. Turning to face Florie, he saw her pain, too. The key to any resolution was his affirmation of either Florie or his mother's position. The choice had to be his; the sacrifice had to be his; and the consternation of Florie or his mother would always rest on his shoulders. A realization that he had acclimated to the anguish of his own feelings in the past permitted him to accept what might be lost or gained at this juncture in his life. In the end, the children either stayed or came with him to New Jersey. Either way, the future carried a burdensome plight, an onerous weight, etched with tragedy and despair.

"This will be the death of me," slipped from Mary like the dirge from an opera. Those who heard the comment believed it, for her demeanor plunged into defeat. The result of her woeful comment brought guilt into the conversation. It lay open and vulnerable like a damp piece of sod, newly uprooted and homeless.

Florie pondered this turning point. If her husband took the offensive, the day could be won. New to the marriage, she knew little of the darkness in the man. The sacrificial habit he had taken to himself clothed him in an inner loneliness that was unreachable by others. She was a stranger to his psyche. His ability to endure any consequence was a certainty to him, but the other players bore their own insights, fears, and expectations. Franny sensed their turmoil and his, and these feelings he evaluated against all possibilities.

"Mom and Dad, you can't ask something so unnatural of us. Everyone has needs and has invested so much love and made such sacrifice in these last few years." He threw this plea into the winds. The hearts and minds of the others would make his decision for him.

"I can deal with it, and the rest of the family will accept it after time," ventured Tim as the empty bottle rocked under his touch.

"The twins can be your wedding present," interjected Anna Marie, sensing a favorable outcome now that her father had given his approval. Florie pressed her hand tightly onto Franny's, excited by the support from her sister-in-law and Dad.

"I will not stand to have these little boys ripped from the only home they have known…to be taken from the mother and father they have grown up with. No, no, no – that's my final word! No!" Mame stood, took a belligerent breath, and exited to the kitchen.

"You might have to take Mom to court, Franny," came the verdict from Anna Marie.

Fran swung his head from side to side in response to the suggestion.

The ride homeward to New Jersey was marked by periods of argumentative prattle, deadly silence, and no clear solution.

Francis J. Blanche waited and pondered his dilemma, willing to absorb the disappointment of his wife or his mother. As time moved into a future of indecision, his wife lost the twins and her admiration of her husband. His quiet pain initiated longer bouts of drinking after work and on weekends. Florie was soon pregnant with her first child.

Uncle Franny and Aunt Florie continued the charade on visits to the "nephews" in Bridgeport. They were less and less frequent, centering on holidays and special events. Uncle Franny generously gifted Bernard and Francis on their birthdays, and the twins relished the visits from their Uncle Franny.

Dennis Blanche was born on September 20, 1947, a blond headed, well-proportioned little boy with sad but sincere eyes. Father and son marched through infancy, through the toddler's years, and through the drudgery of diapers and messy feedings. Florie tended the child's needs with a growing love and attachment to her son. The same doting toward Franny, however, began to wane. The fire of their relationship ebbed with his mood swings, and Franny settled into the mundane work of mechanic and driver. With the youngster still at home, the couple decided to have Florie enter the workforce. The Winterses agreed to assist with Dennis on days when both parents worked.

Florence found the outside world as a secretary at the local air base refreshing once again. She put aside the tedium of routine at home and enjoyed her new found independence. The issue of the twins became less irritating to her sense of fairness and her respect for Franny. A passive demeanor settled upon her at home, but vitality grew within her among the adults at the base.

Mame had taken the initiative to learn to drive under the pretext of transporting the twins and the rest of the children to St. Augustine's Catholic School. The trip was fourteen blocks round trip, but it was a whole new universe to her. When she telephoned Franny one winter morning in 1950, he supposed she had a driving story to relate to him. Instead she announced the death of Mary "Mack" Bernot. The news brought the family back to Pennsylvania, but this time to Conshohocken.

The viewing was anticlimactic and somber for an Irish wake. None were surprised by her passing. The mourners slumped quietly in small clusters reminiscing with relatives and friends about the shared fate that marked their lives. Three common threads marked the evening. The mourners conversed about the tragedy of Camille's death. The relatives and friends praised the upbringing of the twins under the goodly and saintly care of

Mame and Tim. Lastly, all possessed the discipline not to discuss those issues with Franny and his new wife. The couple sat in plain sight, touched by polite conversation or social exchange. Mame and Timothy garnered most of the attention from the mourners with the arrival of the twins. The boys, whom the Bernot and McNamara clans rarely saw, remained in the back sitting room where they became a focal point for the curious crowd. The families and friends were paraded before the two lads.

From the mourning parlor, Mame reported to those nearby, "I just love my two little boys."

The mourners arrived in waves, paid their respects to Martin and the family, but soon sought out Tim and Mary. "It must be so difficult to keep up with two little children," bemused one attendee.

"No, not really," Mame offered, "they are no trouble at all."

"Are they here, Mrs. Blanche?" queried one mourner.

"Why, yes. Tim and I left them with my nephew, Joe Heebner, out in the back sitting room. We don't think the viewing parlor is a proper place for them, being so young."

The listeners agreed and admired her protective doting of the children. "Isn't it wonderful of you both to make the sacrifice to raise them as your own," voiced one.

When Mame excused herself to check on the youngsters, she passed a solitary pair seated in her row of folding chairs. Uncle Franny and Aunt Florie were mourning another loss, the loss of his own children. Franny's brother and sisters made the evening passable for him; but, for Florie, it was a constant reminder of his lack of initiative and his submission to his mother.

In the back room, Mame was greeted by a rush of miniature arms and legs. "I missed you, Mommy," caressed Bernard as he wrapped his arms around her portly waist.

"Me too, me too!" echoed Francis, joining the embrace with his brother.

"You boys are being good, aren't you?" she asked playfully. Spotting her nephew nearby, Mame directed softly, "Don't let the boys go in to see the body. I don't think that's necessary." Her tender concern was met with universal approval.

"I'll keep them entertained, Aunt Mary," asserted Joe Heebner. The mourners respected the protection she desired for the twins. The twins attended their grandmother's viewing without the slightest knowledge of her or her passing. They were six years old.

Martin, alone again among his wife's family and the Blanches, managed to quietly commune with a glistening flask of Canadian whiskey. He remembered being fifteen again and orphaned. The pain was deeper now, for Camille's death was what he mourned anew that evening. The death of Mary "Mack" Bernot had dredged up much pain and heartache. Her passing blended with the tragic losses which preceded her. He never visited the twins in the back room. The mourners went away in a blur of sights and sounds.

During the ride to New Jersey, a debate ensued. Florie's point came down to one clear-cut issue. "Fran, you have to stand up to your mother for us and the boys, and... that's it!" she flung at him. Throughout the trip, she delivered the ultimatum gently, again and again with varied words and gestures.

Franny spoke his final appraisal of the argument with common sense and a moral edge. "You don't think it takes a lot of strength to give them up, Florie. She is tender, caring, and loves them just as I do – maybe even more." This was the kernel of his thoughts and actions. He wished it away, but the facts stood stubbornly and unflinchingly before him.

Chapter Nine

"The Gift Wrapping Comes Undone"

The New Jersey life of the Francis J. Blanche family possessed all the semblance of average America. On the stage from afar, normalcy prevailed. Behind curtains and the lit stage, there lurked the lines and acts of life which the cast members shared, feared, and disliked. The extras heard the story with curiosity but feared delving too deeply into the history of Franny's agony. So, he worked with peers on an inert level; they shared the trite and mundane of their lives. His in-laws knew the surface, but their relationship was tepid. The passive and, at times, sacrificial decisions regarding his twins did not invite anyone to share his pain. Florie drifted from him. At first, the held hands departed, then the embrace of greetings eroded, and then the intimacy became a play. The spontaneity gone, the young wife migrated to the diversity of experiences that her work brought.

The pages of memory flipped back in time on occasion, and a visit to Bridgeport on May 13, 1951, for the twins First Holy Communion brought about a compromise of sorts.

The formal pose in the photograph on the side lawn of the De Kalb Street home depicted Franny and Florie side by side, standing tall behind the three children. Uncle Franny wore a starched long-sleeved shirt and gray trousers, despite the warm spring afternoon sun. His tie dangled crisply in a "belly-warming" swath just above his waist. Aunt Florie wore a blue suit coat and matching skirt. The jacket was form-cut and trimmed with a corsage of orchids that the "twins" had given to her. Three year old Dennis stood shyly between the twins with his blond head aimed downward to the ground before him. His three button lightweight brown and maroon jacket rested neatly over brown pants. His fidgeting did not disturb the cleanly parted blond hair. The white powder on his saddle shoes remained untarnished by the shuffling of his feet. He rocked back and forth. Two pillars of white were his bookends. Francis, the taller of the twins, stood on the right, held at bay by Aunt Florie's left hand upon his shoulder. The smaller, but older brother Bernard was anchored by Uncle Franny's left hand. They wore white jackets, white above-the-knee shorts, white socks and shoes. Bernard took on the appearance of a formal welcome, for he placed a firm left arm around his "cousin" Dennis. His small frame leaned into the toddler. The forced contact left Dennis in some discomfort and he played with his hands at his waist.

"Smile!" shot Anna Marie. It was the family photograph that almost everyone wanted. Mame milled about, generally at peace with the day.

"I can't wait to get that one developed," she wished aloud as she walked toward the picnic table where the family and guests had gathered.

"Can Dennis and us play now, Uncle Franny?" sprang from the voice of Bernie.

Florie reacted in response before her husband, "Watch you don't get all dirty!"

The trio was off down the embankment of the yard. Her words seemed to have given permission.

"Thanks, Aunt Florie," shot Francis over his retreating shoulder. A five year old awaited them at the level ground below the picnic area. Little Gregory Mc Laughlin skipped toward them in gleeful excitement. The foursome, busied in play, sometimes moved as a unit of gun fighting cowboys. Other games merged the boys in multiple arrangements of partners and even singles in tag. The boys had no difficulty orchestrating their own amusement.

"Dad," offered Franny to Timothy, "Florie and I were hoping that you and Mom might let us bring the boys to Jersey for a week – for our vacation?"

The gentle delivery fell on his attentive ears. The minimal smile which formed on his flushed face pleased Franny. The plan was to get all of the family behind the idea before Mame heard the suggestion. "We'd take them on Saturday and bring them back the following weekend. It looks like the third week of July works best. What do you think?"

"Franny, that would be wonderful for you and the boys," agreed Tim.

"Daddy, Daddy!" shouted a voice to Tim. It rose from the communicant by his knee. It was young Francis. "Dennis just wants to play with Greg, but he's s'posed to be with us." The sadness of his feelings mingled with his annoyance with his cousin Gregory.

Mame had just arrived from her duties in the kitchen. She stepped amid the youngsters and directed, "You boys go up on the porch and take turns riding them pedal cars of yours. Greg and Dennis can share with you two." Her presence disrupted Franny's plans.

"Too soon! You're here too soon!" thought Franny to himself.

"Mary," offered Tim, "Franny and Florie have a vacation coming up. They'd like to treat the boys to a week in Jersey – maybe time at the shore, I guess."

Amid the preparations of the picnic, the events of the day, and the arrival of the local priest, Mame was caught off her guard. "My, my!" she stammered with the realization that the offer was meant in good faith and reasonable. "Sure, I guess that could be worked out."

"Mom, this is great, and the kids will have a great time," he rattled quickly. The mention of the itinerary cut the discussion short, and the plans solidified before some unknown force shredded them into confetti. The wink and smile from Florie buoyed his spirits. "What a great first step!" he thought.

Mame shuffled off to greet Father Christopher J. Gidney who stopped on the porch to congratulate the First Communicants. He and the Pastor, Father James Mc Enery, felt a responsibility to them. Keenly aware of the twins' background and the pain of this family, Father Mc Enery acted as the "parents" advisor at St. Augustine Parish and became their spiritual mentor. Mame especially confided in him. In good faith, he supported Mame's decision to hold onto the twins in Bridgeport. The younger parish priest also backed Mary and Tim, for he felt the Jersey couple had much to work out regarding their new marriage and Franny's past. The Father Mc Enery, although well-meaning, usually comforted Mame emotionally when he dealt with her. Unfortunately, the deeper issues and their significances continued to boil unnoticed beneath the surface.

"The boys will have a great time, Dad," sparked Franny, content to have made headway.

A tap on the back of his wrist from Florie gained his attention. She leaned in upon him trying to indicate a private word with him. "I wish the children wouldn't call you 'Uncle Franny.'" She whispered with her head on his right shoulder. She straightened after the delivery. She required no response from her husband.

The picnic and celebration continued; and, the overnight guests, Uncle Franny and his family from New Jersey, left after Sunday mass. Dennis went home with his mother and father;

Uncle Franny drove home to his work; and Aunt Florie stepped into a world of unmade choices.

Back home, neutrality reigned. The twins came for a week that summer, and Florie wondered if their presence would turn the dilemma in her favor. Franny realized, however, that the two seven year olds could not fully comprehend the complexity of their parentage. To him, the ramification of any decision had to rest with the adults involved and not the children. Dennis had to be considered as well. How would he take to sharing his parents with his two "cousins"?

Ice cream cones in hand, the three boys hovered about the little circular table outside the Sundae School Ice Cream Parlor. It was the Tuesday of their vacation week. Florie wielded a fistful of paper napkins, adeptly catching and wiping the running rainbow of chocolate, vanilla, and raspberry that gravitated toward the Asbury Park tee shirts of the children.

"How do you like the ice cream, Boys?" cajoled Florie.

"It's really good, Aunt Florie," chimed Francis as his tongue swung sideways to lap his chocolate cone.

"Mine's yummy!" added Dennis. "Daddy, where's your ice cream cone?" questioned the youngest.

"No, I've got my cigarette, and ice cream doesn't go well with it," instructed Franny.

"Well, you can have a lick of mine when you're done, Uncle Franny," volunteered Bernard. He shoved the lavender dollop upward to the adult as if to allow him to preview the sample.

"Thank you, Bernie, I just might take you up on that 'cause I do like raspberry," he said with a smile.

"When are we going home, Uncle Franny?" interjected Francis abruptly.

"Why you'll be here for another four days," responded Florie, a pang of concern on her face.

"Oh…okay!" mumbled Bernie. "I kinda miss Mommy and Daddy," he mustered with a shy, whispering voice. In an attempt to sound "grown-up", he added, "A little bit."

"We're going to do some really fun things. The week will fly by." Franny's effort appeased the youngster, but Bernie's comment left a bruise.

Once the twins returned to Bridgeport, Franny found artificial solace in a few extra beers and martinis over the weekends. He gradually left the lagers for the stronger spirits and always insisted on gin, not vodka, in his cocktail. His nature evolved into a more reclusive mien which often left him curt and impatient with Dennis and his childhood antics. Florie played the buffer, protecting both father and son. She applied the salve and dressed the scratches and scrapes.

Mame and Tim had their share of visitor; and, later that same summer, Martin appeared at the front door. It was a sober Saturday for him, and Ralph and Margaret eased the awkwardness of his arrival with their sincere happiness in seeing him. Fran, Bernie, and Gregory were busy pushing trucks through the dirt pile under the massive oak tree in the side yard. Martin joined them after a brief skirmish with Mary. He sat like a Native American chief cross legged amid their revelry. He shared a brief comment that he had grown up out west and had seen many Indian teepees.

The trio of lads ran from him in an explosion of dirt from their trousers. "We'll be right back, Grandpop," shouted Fran over his shoulder. In a flash of time, they were upon him, dressed in full cowboy attire.

"Maybe we can put up one of those teepees, Fellas," he mused.

"Yeah, can we?" shouted Bernie. "Let's do it, Grandpop."

Martin went into the house; and, after some serious negotiations with Mary, appeared at the kitchen door dragging a large carpet with some difficulty. The twins recognized the rug as the floor covering on the storage room adjacent to the front parlor. "Get me some poles, Boys," he ordered.

The three cowboys rustled up three of Mary's clothesline stanchions, leaving a wet sheet to brush the grass beneath its pinning on the line. In thirty minutes, Martin had the cowboys occupy an eight foot high, cone-shape prairie dwelling. Martin, Fran, Bernie, Gregory, and Larry's dog frolicked on the plains of Bridgeport until Martin left. The twins fought the razing of the edifice for a week before Mary ordered Timothy to take it down. She was in need of her clothesline poles.

***

Over the passing holiday visits, Franny permitted the "Uncle" and "Aunt" titles. Florie learned to tolerate titles, for she had abandoned hope of ever having the twins with them. She also found herself struggling in the marriage.

Franny also sensed a growing distance between them, and his attempts to reduce the gap were exacerbated by his moods. Florie recoiled even more. She fought the loss of her new found freedom, and his requests for her to shorten her work hours and other base duties sapped her independence.

The following winter over Franny's objections, Florie accepted a full time position. Dennis could be cared for on the base or by the Winterses. The extra income did not lessen the stress in the marriage. Other concerns arose with both parents in the work force.

In the middle of that summer, the Francis J. Blanches were headed to Asbury Park, New Jersey, for their vacation. The addition of Francis and Bernard was an easy sell to Mame after her compliance a year ago. The twins arrived in New Jersey with many subtle and some surprising changes to their behavior and mannerisms. Then, as eight year olds, they were athletic, competitive, and curious. The couple was surprised by their entrenchment with daily habits. They beleaguered Florie with requests to have things the way they were at home. "Fluffernutters" for lunch, matching clothes all day, and baseball cards and catches that lasted for hours. At the beach, the marshmallow and peanut butter sandwiches became lava runs of warm brown and white ooze.

Dennis found it difficult to be a threesome. The twins constantly vied for his sole allegiance to one of them alone. Bernard wanted his attention for a catch, but Francis pulled him to flipping baseball cards. Uncle Franny took up refereeing.

With Franny's concerns about his marriage belaboring his waking thoughts, this constant ebb and flow with the boys simmered like fresh sunburn. It wore thin.

The family had secured a boardwalk picnic table outside of a deli-styled eatery. The boys still refused any sandwich selection from the café. Florie ordered a club sandwich to share with Dennis who enjoyed a diverse palate. Franny was waiting for his order of a lobster roll and Florie's club sandwich as he paced to and fro near the table.

"Hey, you Guys! Sure you don't want to try some of the club or lobster?" he suggested. He watched Florie maneuvering the tote bag searching for the rest of an acceptable meal for Bernie and young Fran. Negative nods swayed from both heads. "You're on vacation! It's great to try new stuff," he urged. Swaying heads again greeted this request.

Florie busied herself with the preparation and unwrapping of the twins' lunches. The pressed contents of the sandwiches made at home oozed onto the crisp wax paper.

"Nah! Aunt Florie found a baloney sandwich," reported Francis.

"I'll have the jelly sandwich, Aunt Florie. That's what I like." Bernie did not pick up the taut smirk of annoyance on his "Uncle's" face.

"Number twenty-three!" rang out from a strange voice inside the deli counter. Uncle Franny checked a piece of paper in his head. "That's us, Florie. I'll get the sandwiches." He turned and crossed the boardwalk through a shower of bright warm sunlight. His button down short sleeved shirt fluttered in the mild breeze. The loose fitted trousers mimicked the shirt when the wind struck his legs.

Bernie had watched his departure, stood, and picked up his jelly sandwich. Magnetically, he retraced his Uncle's steps, drawn to him by some invisible cord. Franny was already on his return to the table when he met the twin mid way on the boardwalk. The boy's white bread sandwich looked antiseptic in the glaring noon sun. He had jet black hair which complemented his uncle standing next to him. The child's deep summer tan, however, contrasted the adult. Franny had a pale indoor quality to his skin. The garage and the cab of his truck had sheltered him from too much direct sun.

"Want to try a bite?" he tempted, thrusting the lobster roll down to the boy.

Bernie waved his pristine white sandwich at the request. "I don't think I'd like it, Uncle Franny," reflected the boy. He stood, giving no indication that he wished to leave.

Caught in the middle of a moving vacation crowd, Franny was anxious to deliver the food to Florie and Dennis. His impatience like another child tugged at his sleeve, but Bernie held him at bay by some unseen force. "Look it's not going to kill you!" he shot out with more energy than he expected. Frustration marked his movements.

"I don't want to, Uncle Franny!" was the boy's retaliation.

"Fine! Then don't!"

The child heard the anger. His body stiffening and tense, only the child's head moved – upward and searching. His feet became concrete on the wooden planks.

"And... stop calling me 'Uncle Franny'! I'm not your 'Uncle'; I'm your father!" Wrapped in a crush of strangers, the pair was alien. The eight year old and the twenty-nine year old did not touch. The distance was just a short span to cross, but the relationship loomed too far to reach. No gravity was present to pull them together. Like similarly charged magnets, the two floated side by side in repelling orbits.

Bernard thought he was being scolded in the schoolyard. "Timothy's my Dad," he wanted to say, but one does not sass an adult or argue with one. He desired his twin by his side, to share this confusion, this punishment. Knowledge of the crime he committed was beyond his awareness. Fear was present, doubt ran furious, and a step needed to be taken. Any thought might take him from this terrifying catastrophe. "Can I try your lobster roll, Unc..." rained from his lips. The roll came to his mouth and he pecked at the sandwich.

"No more 'Uncle Franny', okay?" his father reiterated and waited. The child nodded. "From now on, it's 'Dad', Bernie. You'll call me 'Dad'." It was not an invitation, but an order.

Bernie wanted to ask, "What do I call..." he had no word in his vocabulary for his question, but he thought, "'Timothy'? Do I call him 'Dad', too?" But the adult world overtook him, and he fell silent. He swallowed the lobster roll.

Fran saw the reflexive gulp. "So, did you like it?" stumbled from him awkwardly. Too late to withhold the sandwich question, there it was – out in the open, a silly, irrelevant question. It wedged into the chaotic reality that he had just thrust upon his innocent son. Not waiting for a reply, Franny turned the boy gently and lead him to the shelter of his brother.

At the picnic table, Bernard sat, pinned to an unusual silence like a piece of patchwork about to be attached to the knee of some used dungaree. Franny related to Florie what he had said before he directed the same message to little Francis. "You and your brother are not to call me 'Uncle Franny'. You may continue to call Timothy, 'Daddy' and Mame, 'Mommy', but I am your father. You will call me 'Dad'." No history came to light. No mother's name or her death was explained. No coercion to move to New Jersey was put into play.

Dennis was safe from the effects of the revelation, content with the club sandwich. Franny hoped that the unearthing of this buried data with the twins might forestall the deterioration of their marriage.

Florie, although impressed that some progress had been made, had little or no change of heart. "It's probably 'too little too late'," she mused.

"Maybe it's a start, Florie?" he proffered.

In the end, the event did not heal the marriage. The twins never joined them in New Jersey. The new status quo was as mired in unspoken truths as any other event for Francis J. Blanche.

***

Late in the summer of 1952, Anna Marie had taken a very profitable position with a realtor. Margaret and Ralph had their second child, Colleen, and moved into their own home in Audubon, Pennsylvania. By then, Larry, who had survived a serious illness and graduated from high school, enlisted in the US Navy. The massive inn was deemed impractical for the seven remaining Blanches. The rental on the De Kalb Street house equaled the monthly mortgage for one attached, double home Anna Marie had seen in Norristown, and the family would be owners. Tim, Anna Marie and Franny, whose monthly support of the twins continued, would help to defray the monthly cost of the home at 631 West Lafayette Street in Norristown, Pennsylvania.

The twins began Fourth Grade at St. Augustine's, but after much discussion, the Blanche family moved across the Schuylkill River to their new home. By Halloween, the boys were registered in St. Francis of Assisi Catholic School.

The new residence was cramped: Eleanor and Patty occupied the third floor attic bedroom, Tim and Mame had the large front bedroom on the second floor, the twins shared the small middle bedroom off the stairs, and Anna Marie, who now wished to be called "Marie", had the rear second floor bedroom which faced the small rectangular back yard. The twins had many adjustments to make to acclimate to Fourth Grade as new students.

A cold rainy work day in early April of 1953, greeted Franny with difficult brake work, a shop with a short staff of mechanics, and numbing fatigue. At home, he began his martini respite before Florie and Dennis arrived. Familial chores and requests assailed his attempt to empty himself of the labor and the life of the day. Florie settled into the kitchen with a quiet reminder to Dennis, "Leave Daddy rest, okay?"

Spotting a toy metal delivery truck under the table beneath his mother's workspace, the lad grasped it securely with the thought of sharing it with his Daddy. The child sensed a mission to bring it to his father. "It's just like the one Daddy drives," he appraised. Bolting from the undercarriage of the table, Dennis made a dash into the living room.

Where're you going?" Florie blurted. "Oh, no you don't!" followed the blond haired boy into the adjacent room.

Dennis was upon the seated, tranquil man in a flash. The father saw the youngster approach and abruptly threw his left arm out to parry the charge. Dennis fell in a heap. Florie screamed before the child reacted in sobs of disbelief. Uninjured, Dennis was swept from the floor into her embrace. "How could you? How could you be so careless? You could have hurt him badly," she challenged.

"Florie,… Son, I'm sorry. I didn't mean to knock you down. You caught me out of sorts – that's all," he pled in his own defense. He rose and began to follow the pair into the kitchen, but stopped abruptly. Florie had thrown a backward glance of prohibition into his attempt to reconcile his actions. He slapped both hands downward against his thighs, did an about-face, and retreated to his lounge chair.

Returning from work that Thursday, Franny found no one at home. In the bedroom, he noticed space in the wall closet. Fear drove him to the phone, rather than to Dennis's room. He dialed Stan Winters.

The conversation was terse and awkward. "Franny, I'm sorry I can't tell you anything. Florie said she left you a letter on the kitchen table. That's all I'm supposed to tell you." The silent pause shrieked its painful truth before he added, "I'm really sorry, Franny - really sorry!" The receiver dropped with the click of a trigger and the droning, monotone hum of the dial tone blew mournful taps. He picked up the sterile white envelope.

"April, 1953

Fran,

There is more to life than waiting for things to happen. Dennis and I have taken another course, and I am sorry to hurt you this way. I do not want you to know where we are. A lawyer will be in touch with you for us.

Florie"

A month of emotional pain and crushing guilt followed Fran's call home. Anna Marie, Margaret, and Ralph arrived with a moving truck to console him and uproot him. The yellow beech wood bedroom set went to Norristown when Franny abandoned his New Jersey home. He told the Winterses to do what they wished with the remaining household items.

Florence and Dennis went to Nixon, NJ, for awhile and later returned near her family in East Brunswick. She worked as a single parent at the Raritan Arsenal. The distance in miles and spirit presented a chasm not to be crossed. In Franny's mind, his presence in New Jersey could only hurt Florie and Dennis by bringing up the unresolved issues that had torn them apart. Franny walked away from his wife and his son.

Chapter Ten

"Martin and Timothy's Demons"

Martin Bernot was finished with Conshohocken and the Philadelphia McNamaras. They were indifferent to him and to his travels. Alone, his companion became his addiction to alcohol. On Jacoby Street above the county courthouse, he roomed and eked out his subsistence with odd jobs, painting free lance and for local agencies. His sobriety determined the length of employment at any given time. He took to wanderings of varying lengths. He was at sea without the guidance of the merchant marines of his early years. Destinations did not concern him, for it was the process of travel on which he survived. It was his happenstance to run with some of the Heebner boys, and they informed him of their sister's move to Norristown.

One Friday afternoon in the late spring, Martin made his way down Swede Street toward the Philadelphia and Western elevated trolley station. Without purpose or any particular place to go, he decided to forgo the trolley into Sixty-Ninth Street. He had finished a signage job early and began drinking around three. He reeked of stale cigarettes and rye whiskey. Listing to starboard he swung himself west up Main Street, crossing the Stony Creek at the railroad station. The climb up the western slope of Main Street began to clear his head and sober his thoughts. There was direction to his walk, and he remembered the address on West Lafayette Street. It did not feel right to him.

He paused at the curb, reached into his sport jacket hip pocket, took out a tin flask, and drew a large swallow of rye.

As he approached the Blanche residence, his gait wobbled and weaved along the sidewalk. Toward the end of the block of twin homes, a small band of five boys dissipated, scurrying in many directions before him. He reached number 631 with difficulty. Above him on the porch, two black headed nine year olds stared down toward the sidewalk at him. He had to negotiate three cement steps, a landing, and then four wooden stairs onto the porch. They entered the vestibule as he approached. The closer he came to the front door, the farther the faces of the boys dropped along his frame. He was vaguely familiar to them, but his disheveled appearance left them in doubt.

"Is that Grandpop?" volunteered Bernard as he nudged an elbow into the side of his brother.

His twin answered with a grimace of sorts. Caught with the uncertainty, he called, "Mom, some man's on the porch!" The comment had a sense of urgency.

The figure stepped to the screen door, but Martin made no effort to knock or ring the buzzer. A roundish woman with a white apron pushed past the youngsters and filled the doorway. Her salt and pepper hair was pulled hard into two buns behind her head.

"Martin Bernot!" she forcibly barked, "you look a disgrace!" She flipped the latch securely into its eyelet on the screen door jamb.

"Yeah, I know, Mary," he cowered, "just wanted to see the boys."

Two curious lads pressed into her back and craned their necks around her to see the man at a closer distance. She held them at bay with her flailing arms by her side. When Bernard tried to slip by on her left, she swung her generous hip into his path.

The boys settled in defeat awaiting the outcome. "I'm not going to allow you to visit when you're drunk, Martin!" Authority and strength wailed in the comment. "Tim's not home yet, and you'll cause a lot of trouble if he sees you like this." For a brief moment, a thread of fear entered her throat. Some dark nightmare had encroached into this daylight drama. "You better leave now!" she stammered.

"I understand," succumbed Martin, "but can I come back to see them?" He was fumbling for a kerchief in his back pocket. Inebriation magnified his efforts. He wiped spittle from his mouth and returned the handkerchief to his coat pocket where it rested with the empty flask.

"Only if you are sober and cleaned up. Tim will be furious if he hears you came here like this." The second statement affirmed for her a right to place demands upon him.

She reflected on another recent visitor. Timothy had argued vociferously with Mary the day one of the Heebner brothers had visited. His drunken, loud, and crass language put Timothy into a tirade. Tim refused to let him enter the house. The request to use the bathroom was denied, and the rude brother-in-law proceeded to urinate on the front concrete steps in broad daylight. Tim had given her a stern warning that he wanted none the likes of her brother in the house with her or the children.

Martin was tottering forward and backward and had difficulty making the one hundred and eighty degree turn to the head of the steps. "It won't happen again, Mary," he promised in the voice of a school boy, his back turned to her in retreat.

His grandsons had run to the front window of the sitting room and watched his descent with bewilderment. "That's Grandpop Martin. Isn't it, Fran?" wondered Bernie aloud.

"Yep! You think he might come back?" offered Franny's to the situation.

"Guess so?" The brevity of the answer as a question spoke volumes about the amount of interest that they held in the visit. They rushed out the back door with gloves and balls in hand. The dirt of the back yard awaited them.

Martin left with a singular kernel planted in his mind. His self-respect and pride ached, wounded by the foolishness of his actions. Mame's direct refusal to admit him into the house fed the growing determination in his heart and soul.

Tim arrived at home that day weary, hungry, and covered in diesel soot. He wanted rest, but the twins were upon him as he passed through the house. The threesome trod by Patty who was busy with homework at the dining room table. They encountered Eleanor in the kitchen with Mame. The dutiful wife had dinner well underway while the daughter related her day at school. Mame had no intention of mentioning the visit of the afternoon, but two impish youngsters had a different agenda.

"Grandpop Martin was here today, Daddy" reported Francis with bubbling enthusiasm.

"What? How come he was here on a Friday, Mary?" despite his fatigue, a spark of energy flicked throughout his being.

""He was just passing by. Wanted to see where we were living, I guess," she stammered. "But he was only here a minute – and he stayed on the porch, Tim," she confessed.

"Yeah, well, I don't want the neighbors getting any crazy ideas 'cause some stranger comes to the door," reflected the father with more concern than seemed necessary.

"I'm sure he'll only come around when you're home, Tim," she countered, hoping this might smother and cool the heat that had risen in Tim.

"Too many unsavory characters around here, I think," bemused Tim. In Bridgeport, the location of the home had given to isolation, produced a fortress-like defense against intrusions.

Now, the family shared space and a fence with the family next door. Now, the once spacious interior of an inn was reduced to side-by-side attached bedrooms. Tim had to deal with the discomfort of proximity. The loss of privacy eroded his peace and contentment like battery acid onto the frame of his automobile. A dark storm, which impinged upon the peace of the family, arrived in the gray clouds of physical closeness. The gale brought thunder and lightning flashes into their lives, revealing the tormented mind of Tim. That night, the walls began to speak in ominous and frightful, Freudian tongues.

"No! No! Tim, I don't!" came in a muffled pitch through the walls. Disturbing the quiet of the house, Mame's plea awoke one of the twins.

Then the father's voice rumbled with muted anger from the adjoining room, "You'd better not. 'Cause I'll kill the bastard!" Bernie sat up in his bed and checked the other bunk. Fran had pulled the blanket around his ears.

"Nobody's doing anything like that," pleaded the second voice from the front bedroom. Bernie rose and shuffled toward the closed door of his room. He stood attentive to the dialogue coming from the master bedroom.

"Yeah, you think I'm dumb! I see them passin' around here, lookin' at this place." Fran waved his brother back into the shadows of the room.

"That's not true, Tim!" denied the wife. "No, no, you don't have to go and do this. Tim! Tim! Stop, please. I'm not going anywhere. I'd never do that to you and the family and the boys. Please!" A sense of danger and peril sickened Bernie, pulling him again toward the parents' bedroom door.

"Umph! Thump. Grrr!" noises filtered through the interior walls, dying in the twin's room. The moans that chased after the sounds of struggle drew the boy to touch the door. The sudden waft of air in the black space before him terrorized and paralyzed the child on his rescue mission. Only the dull light from the street lamp lit the figure of his father who stood rigidly before him. The gaunt man wore only a sleeveless tee shirt as he walked by the boy at his feet. Bernard felt invisible at that moment of terror, for his father passed him with no recognition of his presence. The stark figure, nude from the waist down headed to the bathroom at the end of the hall. The child's eyes followed his gait until the door shut behind him. Turning mechanically toward the open doorway, Bernard saw the whiteness of twine and rope knotted over the foot of the bed.

"It's alright, Bernie! Everything's okay. You don't need to come in. I'm fine. Daddy just got a little upset. You go back to bed, okay?" The rapid fire pieces of information and the quick, sharp directive held the boy at bay. When Mame heard the shuffle of his footfall, she added. "I'll see you in the morning."

The mornings and the nights were never the same again. The twin's room buffered the rest of the household from the psychotic ranting and unfulfilled desires of the tormented man. The dutiful wife became participant and managed to dull the sounds, ravings, and actions of her husband. She shielded the twins and family from the outbreaks. Even when peace ruled the evenings, the threat of disaster and evil loomed like a carrion bird on the second floor. The psychosis grew. Tim moved farther and further into his world to seek out the offenders. At first, he had searched the room, but found none of the intruders he suspected. Later, his illness sent him throughout the house to uncover the perverted gigolo who would ruin his family. Then, the front door and the sinister darkness of the street became his haunts. As Tim wandered beyond the bedroom, the older children too took on the efforts to assuage Timothy's demons. Tim left the house bare footed and in his familiar night dress on his occasional crusades. Each child took his turn scampering into the night to recover their half naked father on his wild escapades. The twins gained knowledge of his sickness and, over time, recognized reality through the calm of their mother and the care of their siblings. Daylight fought back the madness and became its nemesis. Father, mother, and family became exorcized by the blessed morning sunrise.

Martin did return to his grandchildren. Mame had placed the germ of his recovery into his desire to see the twins. A series of fortuitous events shaped the development of their relationship. A painting job in Doylestown brought Martin into the lives of the Van Sant and Dalton families.

Fran Dalton was the son-in-law of Lydie Van Sant. She was a well-situated widow and spent most of her dutiful time with her daughter Betty. Lydie worked as a volunteer for patriotic groups and enjoyed extensive travel. Her only son had perished in World War II. Since his loss, she worked as a dedicated "Gold Star Mother." Her charity and volunteerism lead to a fateful meeting with Martin Bernot.

Against the flow of his life, Martin became her sober companion after partaking of their church rite of acceptance. Lydie's dilettante society brought Martin into clean living, rich wardrobes, and seasonal travel to various vacation sites in Florida. The couple frequented St. Petersburg, St. Augustine, and Sarasota.

His history fed his new acquaintances with wonderment and a strong urge to give him a better life. Lydie took over the communication reins in dealings with the grandchildren: fruit baskets and tee shirts arrived at Lafayette Street during each southern excursion. She promoted regular visits to Norristown, even when Martin set up housekeeping at her residence on Bustleton Avenue in Somerton. He commuted to Norristown on the train at Somerton, then by elevated from the Frankford section, and finally the P&W into work or to see the twins.

Martin picked a warm summer day for a visit to the twins. Prompted by Lydie, he prepared to offer his new, best side to the Blanches. He wore a short sleeved silk shirt with neatly creased tan trousers, brown belt, and brown, well-shined loafers.

The family had just finished lunch on this particular Saturday. Tim was reading the Norristown Times Herald in the front parlor when the door bell rang. Mary dutifully left the kitchen and walked to the front door, passing Tim in his easy chair. The twins trailed behind her, driven by the curiosity of the door chime. It rarely announced a visitor. Knocks and voiced greetings were the norm

"Oh, my God!" she exclaimed, "It's Martin Bernot, Tim." She could not admit him into the room without Tim's approval. Her words brought the father to the door for his inspection of the visitor.

Impressed by Martin's carriage, Tim nudged Mary, "Well, let him in to see the boys, Mary." He did not see any need to address Martin at first. Once in the parlor, Tim volunteered, "Sit there on the sofa, Martin." With suspicion still picking at his sentiments, Tim signaled young Fran to come to him. Tim and Fran sat on his easy chair. Bernie had been corralled by Mame onto the settee by the front door.

"Where are you staying now, Martin?" remarked Mary as she placed both arms around the lad as he slipped onto the floor before her.

"I'm living in Somerton in Northeast Philly," he answered with more comfort than normal. "Did you get the fruit we sent from Florida?" He swung his hips to the right and dipped his hand into his trouser pocket. Mame thought he was going to take out his cigarettes, but two large coins emerged instead.

"Yes, we did get the citrus. Thanks so much. It was a great winter treat," she said politely.

"I enjoyed the grapefruit, but the boys didn't care for them," added Tim, catching the twins by surprise. It appeared to give them voice also.

"I liked the gumdrops," flung Bernie without hesitation. "You know… those little, itsy-bitsy oranges." The subdued laughter surprised him.

"You mean the cumquats, Bernie," corrected Martin with a tender smile. He pushed his right hand into the room. "Would it be okay if I gave the boys each a silver dollar?"

"Certainly, Martin," approved Mame with eyes reading Tim's bearing. "Go to your grandfather, Twins," she delivered, ushering Bernie toward the well-groomed visitor. Tim released Fran to receive his gift.

"Thank you, Grandpop," rang simultaneously from the duo.

"Now, you two save those in your banks. They're special," suggested Mame.

"Wow! These are too big for my bank," apprized Fran as he fingered the weighty coin.

"These are a whole dollar, huh?" asked Bernie.

"Yes, they're silver. If you keep them, later they might be worth more," advised Martin. Coffee and the leftovers of their lunch were offered. The conversation brought recent histories to light, and the hours passed cordially. As Martin bid his farewells, he surmised that the primary run to Lafayette Street was a success.

Visits progressed beyond the earlier sheltering, and Martin finally "earned" the right to hold and touch his grandchildren. He petitioned and obtained visits from the twins on New Years' weekends in Somerton. This became a pre-teenage rite of passage.

After Christmas, Martin arrived in Norristown for the twins. The trio headed for the Philadelphia and Western Trolley into

Sixty-Ninth Street. Laden with the travel bags of the boys, Martin still managed to keep them snuggled about him in the heavy transit traffic. Once off the trolley, they boarded the subway which was elevated at Sixty-Ninth Street for the trip cross-town to Frankford. The twins had a multitude of questions during their excursion amid the public transportation centers of urban Philadelphia.

"Where's all the trees, Grandpop?"

"Nobody plays ball around here?"

"There sure are a lot of stores!"

"Grandpop, how come it's so dirty down here?"

Martin's responses were generally brief and to the point. The twins accepted any answer, for they were enthralled by the activity before them. Their senses, like sponges, gorged on the stimuli that streamed upon them. The "clickity-clack" of the rails and the rocking of the cars wore into their memories like rivulets of spring run offs.

At Frankford, the Magi impersonators picked up the north bound train into the Greater Northeast and Somerton. The young boys anxiously stretched their legs upon departure. Their Grandfather impressed them with his energy and rapid walking pace as they traced the incline along Bustleton Avenue, called "The Pike," toward Lydie Van Sant's home. Martin cautiously kept curbside, allowing the twins a little freedom along the property lines. Running over manicured lawns, through hedgerows, and darting down driveways, the boys cavorted like frisky colts.

"You, Boys, get rid of some of that extra energy before dinner," he mused to the two impish lads. Taken over by their revelry, they heard the sounds of his words but not the sense. "We still have a ways to go," he announced more to himself than to the pair running beside him. He felt the weight of the valises, filled with double sets of every piece of clothing for the weekend.

After a fifteen minute hike, the party reached the residence. The walk had succeeded in transforming the vitality of the youths into the semblance of decorum and calm. Lydie was pleased with the boys; Martin was quite satisfied with himself.

The boys learned to play canasta, did thousand piece puzzles, and picked up extra table manners. They would pass on his wisdom in the expressions he favored: "Never put more on your plate than you can easily eat," or "You can always take more," or "That napkin is to keep you from wiping your fingers on your pants."

In summer, they also traveled to Wildwood, New Jersey, where Lydie dressed Martin and the twins in summer jackets and lightweight shirts and trousers for their promenades on the local boardwalk.

In Bustleton and Bucks County, the twins spent time with Lydie and her daughter's family. Fran and Betty Dalton had two gentlemen for sons, Billie and Bobby. The twins at first were suspicious of the two boys, one their age and one younger. The Dalton's had a calm ease about them. Bernie thought they were dull, but Fran pointed out that they seemed to enjoy being around the adults. The family represented a normalcy of home life to the twins. Their presence around the twins succeeded in enlightening the Blanches to the inner workings of a typical family.

Martin doted on his grandsons who grew to enjoy and appreciate his company. He sketched them one summer day on the porch swing that hung suspended from the ceiling. The boys swayed back and forth counting Fords and Chevrolets on Bustleton Pike as Martin caught their profiles in charcoal. Encouraged by Lydie, Martin took myriads of pictures, but he most prized his sketches of the grandsons. He was their magician; they were his sanity.

Chapter Eleven

"Parenting and Buses"

On West Lafayette Street, normalcy took a vacation. Tim continued his late night tirades often venturing into the lighted street half naked. An emotional numbness settled over the twins, and they began to deal with these episodes with calm, practical actions. They felt anger then complacency, but understanding and the need to be of assistance guided them as interlopers in the nightly drama. Bernard and Francis allowed the repetition and frequency of these occurrences to blur their memories. The trials were so personal that one sensed that none of the other siblings were participants. In fact, the children shared, in turn, the battles with Timothy. Each, in the enormity of the psychological storm, saw himself or herself alone. The daylight did not bring these escapades or any conversation about them to light.

It was into this cauldron that Francis returned after his failed marriage in 1953. The front bedroom became his haven, crammed with too much yellow beech wood furniture. His twin boys were moved from the middle bedroom and put into bunk beds in the room with their father. Mame and Tim took up temporary residence in the smaller bedroom vacated by the twins. The rest of their set of bedroom furniture went into the basement.

Franny's turmoil became the family's peace. During the time that he spent at 631, the nightly escapades stopped. Tim's pride, humanity, shame, and concern postponed his psychosis.

Young Larry never spent much of his adult life living with the family. Handsome in uniform or street clothes, he was a hand shorter than his older brother. His dark brown hair set him apart from his siblings, but he carried the same physical trimness as the others. He served in the U.S. Navy on the Destroyer Gatlin in the Formosa Straits. Three things initiated him into manhood: a tragedy on board the Gatlin, the near invasion of Formosa, and his battle with Mame over his choice of a bride.

During practice maneuvers, one of the Gatlin's five inch guns fired into its own deck killing and maiming many of Larry's best friends and shipmates. His letters recounting the event were woe-filled and brutally graphic.

As a radioman, Larry was responsible for monitoring the radar for vessels in the area of the Straits. On one occasion, his screen filled with blips, too countless to number. An attack squadron made up of every flying contraption possible was headed for Formosa. In the air, there were jets, by-planes, single winged private aircraft, commercial planes, and helicopters of every shape and size. The seaman concluded the account, "If the U. S. Navy had not spotted them at that time, there would have been a full-fledged invasion...all-out war!"

Independent and in love, Larry announced his intention to marry Helen Reed of West Conshohocken. Mame countered with piqued emotion and anger. This particular snit took place amid witnesses, but she never let that deter her. At these times, she never budged: Franny's marriage to Florence, the couple's petition to have the twins, or Larry's desire to marry a non-Catholic. The young ex-sailor held his ground and wed his first love, Helen Reed.

He went to work for Schuylkill Valley Bus Lines, driving the yellow and green local in Norristown. When his brother, the mechanic and truck driver, came to West Lafayette Street, Larry saw him as a good fit for the company. Franny was hired because of his service and his experience driving trucks in New Jersey. He became one of the regular route drivers

The twins knew that shouting and raw emotions were part of family life; but, with Uncle Franny now "Dad" living in the same house with them, a lull settled upon the household like an easy sluggish fog on a warm summer morning. The pressing issues now were more like pushes.

The father, who worked at the Allan Wood Steel Plant, had a regular schedule to follow. Like clockwork, he would return begrimed with diesel soot and smelling of machinery every afternoon around five. The train engineer never spoke of personal issues. He kept a number of padlocked lockers in his mind and heart and soul.

The father, who worked for Schuylkill Valley Bus Lines, had an irregular schedule to follow. The twins often caught the aroma of a freshly lighted cigarette upstairs. Wandering into the room unannounced, they would find him sitting, propped up with a pillow behind his back doing a crossword puzzle in ink pen. He was genial in the morning, and the afternoon, and in the evening. The bus driver did not betray much of his inner workings to the boys. From the chaos of work on the bus line, he would return in clean uniform, pressed, neat as a pin and smelling of Old Spice cologne any time of day, night, or morning. Often, the twins would be off to school as their father headed upstairs to bed. At times, he quietly eased himself up the steps and into bed without awakening the youngsters. The household had become very pliant and adaptable.

One particular fall afternoon, Bernard and Francis scampered through the back door, muddied from a pick up football game with their neighborhood friends. They tried to play at the Moose Hall's horseshoe-shaped center lawn or the Christian Science

Church lawn, but their troop was always abruptly chased from those premises. That did not deter their frequent incursions onto those hallowed grounds.

Mame did not ask where they had played. Fran pulled the refrigerator door open and Bernard grabbed glasses from the kitchen cabinet. Each poured a large volume of milk into his glass. Humid sweat dripped from their brows, reddened faces pocked by cool weather splotches peered up at Mame. This title, which almost everyone used in reference to Mary, now was paired with "Nana". The grandchildren, Greg and Colleen Mc Laughlin, began to address her that way and the endearment took hold. Both "Mame" and "Nana" suited the twins.

"That was some great game, Mame," shouted Fran, forgetting his inside voice. He trumpeted the news as if she stood across the field from her.

"Yeah, I wish," the woman shouted loudly back to the boy, comically mocking his tone "I could have been there! But...I'm busy getting dinner." As she spoke she slithered downward toward the startled face of the twin.

"Heh, heh!" giggled Bernie, understanding the challenge that she made to Fran's boisterousness. "You're funny, Nana," he added as he attempted to pour a second glass of milk.

"Oh no you don't, Young Man!" hurled Mame. "You'll ruin your dinner!"

"But we're really thirsty. We'll eat everything! Won't we, Fran"

"We promise, Nana!" contributed Fran moving toward the refrigerator along with his brother.

Turning serious, Mary countered, "No, I told you, 'No'!" The threesome hovered by the refrigerator. Bernie's hand rested on the handle, Fran moved to back up his brother if needs be, and Mame strode to the forefront. Her strategic position prevented the door from swinging open even if Bernard tried.

Bernard looked defeat in the eye and walked toward the kitchen sink. His glass went into the basin. When he turned around, Fran wandered through the same journey. "Let's get out our chemistry sets!" Fran's invitation to his brother lived only a moment, for Mame had other plans.

"No, you won't!" she imposed. "You both are filthy! Get yourselves upstairs and clean up before your father gets home!" Her tone dictated compliance – for a half second. Both youngsters had stepped from the kitchen upon hearing the directive, but immediately they halted as one person.

"Which 'Dad'?" Francis wondered. The question left Mary momentarily still.

"Yeah! Nana, is it 'Black Dad' or 'White Dad'?" added Bernie.

"What are you two talking about? 'Black Dad' or 'White Dad'! Where did this come from?"

"Bernie and I were trying to figure out when two people have the same name…," began Fran's explanation.

"Sure, like 'Dad' and 'Dad'," finished Bernie.

"I didn't think the two of you had a problem with it," pondered Mary. She pulled a chair from under the kitchen table and sat by the doorway. The conversation had captivated her.

"You have a bunch of names, Mommy." The thought spilled from Fran like a distraction.

As usual, Bernie saw fit to finish the idea. "You're Mommy, Nana, Mame, and Mary," he enumerated.

"Okay! But where did this 'Black Dad' and 'White Dad' come from?" The inquiry found voice as she sat eye level before the twins.

"I said how Dad comes home from the busses all clean and neat." This evaluation arrived from Fran as he ambled toward Mame. The sentence ended when he reached her side. He put a rough and soiled hand upon her apron as it covered her knee.

"And I said how Dad comes home all dirty and smelly from the trains." The thread of logic was beginning to strengthen. Bernie had one hand in his pants pocket fingering some pebbles that he had collected and the other tugging at his brother's shirt. The conversation for him had ended. That had been everything that needed to be said.

"So, the two of you have been calling your fathers by these names," she figured. Then, her curiosity peaked. "For how long?" This she mouthed almost with a growl, as if they had some devious plot afoot.

"Don't know, Nana. Maybe, since a couple weeks," calculated the taller of the pair.

This stimulated the need for more conversation from Bernie. "So, who's coming home first? Black Dad or White Dad?"

Caught between reverence and irreverence, Mame held a thought for a second. She relinquished this chance for an educational lesson to expediency. "Black Dad," fell from her tongue in a mixture of comedy and befuddlement.

"When is White Dad coming home, then, Nana?" probed Fran with indifference, not realizing that they held the upper hand now, for Mame had bought into their nomenclature.

"He's in New York City today. I don't think you'll see him tonight, Boys," informed the adult before them. "Now, you git up those steps and clean up!" When they heard the word "get" pronounced "git" it signaled the firmness of her intention.

Neither left immediately: each circled back briefly, long enough to throw an embrace around her plump torso. Both of her arms cradled a boy reeking of the sod and the out-of-doors. They left hurriedly, but the smile on her face lingered in timelessness.

***

A hoard of street urchins raced up and down the back alley of the West Lafayette Street home one sunny day early in Easter week. Some of the boys were "Publics" from Chain and Pearl Streets; the others were Catholic school classmates of Bernie and Fran from St. Francis of Assisi Elementary School. It was a friendly riot of activity, mostly challenges of feats of athletic endeavor. The lads carried no balls or gloves, no kites or marbles, and no baseball cards. The lack of gear and sports' equipment brought out the need for creativity.

A wall separated the Moose Hall and the FOE Elks buildings from the alleyway. The clubs parking lots bordered the Main Street side of the alley.

Tin cans appeared from a neighbor's trash and a rousing game of "Kick-the-Can" ensued. No clear cut winner emerged from the half hour duel of Eastsiders and Lafayette Streeters. The competition switched to "Kick-the-Wicket" with a similar outcome. Fate stepped in as Johnny Vasile and Jimmy Zollers hefted some alley stones in their throwing hands. The games moved into the adjacent parking lots. The two combating teams became individuals: Billy Stevenson, Bruce Weideman, Joey Montabano, Billy Spangler, Kenny Quinter, Mike Early, Matt Cory, Harry Riggs, Jimmy Zollers, Johnny Vasile, and the twins. The lone tom boy, Lois "Loey" Troutman, left when the stones were hefted. The curmudgeons began to randomly select and target various signs, paper bags, and debris in the alley and Moose parking lot. Stones hailed down upon any inanimate object picked to demonstrate the hurler's prowess.

"Hit that metal box on the Moose wall!" yelled one of the competitors. The invitation was universally accepted without comment, save the fusillade of exploding stones against the mortar of the building. The large ten foot by four foot windows at the back of the building were invisible to the hurlers. So determined to strike the electrical box between two of the tinted glass windows, the boys vied competitively with youthful tunnel vision.

"What the hell is ya doin'?" rang fiercely from a voice sprinting around the corner of the Moose building from Haws Avenue. An individual clothed in a bartender's apron was quickly approaching the army of brats in the alley. One against so many! "Damn it! Yous rats is ruinin' the floor in der!"

In an explosion of diverse movement, the eleven boys disappeared like the spray of a firework rocket in a millisecond. Some raced directly passed the enraged attendant onto Haws Avenue. Others darted toward Main Street between the two club buildings. The third group headed east along the alley to the Veterans of Foreign Wars post at the next corner, off of Main Street.

The ravings continued from the man. He netted no rascals, too caught up in his fury to single out and collect one of the perpetrators. "Thems bowlin' alleys next to dem winders! Yous kids is splatterin' glass all over them alleys!" The town crier was announcing to anyone the damages inflicted on the Moose Hall bowling lanes.

Adults from the neighborhood were inching closer to the scene, roused by his vociferous ranting. Up the alley from Haws Avenue came a black and white squad car. The "jinx" was up!

Easter Sunday brought Detective William McKernan to 631. He found the family home from morning mass. Officiously, he served papers addressed to Mr. Francis J. Blanche with warrants against Messieurs Bernard and Francis Blanche for damages to the Moose Hall. The court date was set on the documents. "I'm not taking them," announced Tim to the detective.

"Well, they're juveniles. They have to be accompanied by their parents," retorted the officer with authority.

"Bill?" questioned Marie, who knew the detective from her high school days, "couldn't this have been done tomorrow. I mean, your news is ruining the family's Easter." Her plea fell on deaf ears.

"Look, Marie," he defended, "I have family, too, and I'd like to be with them right now, not here. This is the best time to catch all these families at home."

"How many families are involved here, Detective?" wondered Mame.

"Ten...eleven boys were named in the damages, Ma'am." That information provided, he promptly left, and the home was in disarray the entire day.

"Franny will have to take them," contributed Mame. White Dad was out; and, by default, the task fell to him.

Standing in front of the Montgomery County Court House with ten other sets of parents, Francis J. Blanche paced anxiously amid the strangers with whom his boys had involved him. The sunny, late afternoon warmth helped to dissipate the anger and disappointment of the parents. With the fines paid, $29.95 for each boy involved, and with the lads rescued from a trip to the youth detention center for the county, most adults felt relief. The nine to eleven year olds huddled together and mumbled their elation to each other that they had been spared a trip to "Monkey Hall."

Franny pulled his two sons from the midst of their companions in crime. Desiring to leave this awkward civil ritual behind, he sensed an obligation to offer some lesson to the pair. "This is just great!" he began, "I come home finally to be your parent, and the first thing we do together is come to jail. After all these years, I'm still the one footing your bill!" It was the first dent in his armor that the boys had witnessed. At that moment, this present of his words of wisdom did not seem like the message that he should have left with them, but the timing was perfect. The package was not tied in a bow or a ribbon; it was more of a knot.

Bernie feared White Dad; the quiet demeanor of the man was often accompanied by an unsmiling face. Bernie also enjoyed White Dad when he took off his armor in lighter moments. The twins rarely faced discipline from Mame or Black Dad. Sometimes one of the aunts would stifle their independence and spontaneous actions. Bernie was more volatile and gave into verbal outbursts and reckless acts.

The Mc Laughlins arrived one Saturday and parked up the street from the house. Mame and Black Dad were on the porch and young Fran ran toward the car to greet Gregory, just three years his younger. With archery bow and arrow in hand, Bernie saw a target advancing toward Fran. Without hesitation or thought, he armed the bow, pull the string taut, and let the arrow fly. The missile struck Greg in the left knee cap, sending him screaming to the pavement. A mass of people rushed upon the wounded child, leaving Bernie on the porch to observe the havoc of his senseless act. His ears highly focused on the reports coming from the sidewalk.

"He's going to be okay."

"The arrow hardly got through his dungarees."

"Hit the bone: he'll have a good bruise."

A De Soto came up Lafayette Street. Mame turned from the scene and shot her face toward the porch, "Here comes your Dad, Bernie. Wait 'til he gets a hold of you!"

The imp-boy turned and disappeared into home, abandoning his weapon on the porch. Terror urged him to hide: first under the kitchen table, next the pantry, but finally he drove himself up the stairs. Alone and without any idea of his pending punishment, he cowered behind the front bedroom door. The endless minutes of self-imposed confinement waiting for White Dad to find his hiding place drew in his mind a sentence of countless and severe retributions at the hands of his father. He did not know the man; and he did not know his discipline; and he was sickened by the anxiety.

"I know you're up there!" preceded the footfall of White Dad as he ascended the stairs. The boy hunter's body quaked uncontrollably. His respiration was in gulps, sucked through his clenched teeth. The door flung open. The boy sat in fetal position spasmodically quivering with both arms wrapped around his head. He sobbed and peaked upward at the tower of a man back lighted against a setting sun which flooded the bedroom.

White Dad stood silent evaluating his course of action. He stood unmoving. He stood for many long agonizing moments. He stood over this second wounded child. He turned and left the room without saying a single word.

***

When Franny first secured the position with the Schuylkill Valley Bus Lines in Norristown, he generally ran one of the local routes to Conshohocken, King of Prussia, Collegeville, or Lansdale. His dependable, friendly manner endeared him to the company, and he soon was given charters that took him to New York City, Atlantic City, and Washington, DC.

On one particular charter, Franny was assigned to take a men's social club from the East End of Norristown to Atlantic City on a day trip. The group was comprised of African-American men who sometimes took these day trips to the shore. The itinerary was a ritual: early departure, beer and finger food on the bus, arrival at Atlantic City before noon, a day spent on the beach, and a dinner stop in Atlantic City before the return. Mr. Hank Saunders, who had a tailor and dry cleaning shop on Swede Street, just below

Main, organized the party every year. He also coached a teenage baseball team in the local Connie Mack League.

The trip began smoothly as the men loaded the supplies onto the green and yellow charter bus. Hank introduced himself to Franny, and they chatted as the supplies came onboard.

"So, you have that tailor shop right across from the Main and Swede Street terminal?" quizzed Franny.

"Yeah, I've been there eighteen years or so," answered Hank in a low-pitch, matter-of-fact delivery. His close cropped hair had patches of gray along his temples and down along his collar line. He spoke with a raspy basal tone, worn masculine by hours of loud coaching instructions from the sidelines. Franny liked him immediately.

"How long have you been doing this trip?" continued Franny. The two men climbed the three steps onto the center deck of the bus. Franny had his seat before Hank responded.

"Guess this is the sixth trip to Atlantic City. We used to go to Washington, but that was too long of a round trip." Hank took a seat behind his driver as Franny accelerated, turned east on Main Street and headed toward Philadelphia.

Bits and pieces of conversation came and went along a broken path of turns, stops, and pauses through the Northeast, into Philly, and across the Walt Whitman Bridge. Franny occasionally caught Hank's walnut colored eyes in the rear view mirror as the conversation continued. Hank took the monotony from the ride. Franny enjoyed the stories and the warmth of his client. Franny could smell the sandwiches when they were unwrapped and eaten. The hops aroma of Schlitz beer mixed into the meaty air of the rider's on-bus picnic. Conversations ebbed as the food was consumed. Hank had moved to the rear to participate in the festivities. "Hey? Franny, you want something to eat?" shot forward from Hank's new post in the rear.

"Nah, thanks anyway," said Franny, glancing into the center mounted rear view mirror. Then he continued, "Not while I'm driving, Hank. But if there's anything left at the end, I'll be happy to have a little lunch."

"I'm goin' to try to save you a bite," came up the aisle in response.

Twenty minutes over the bridge, Franny sensed a muted change in the travelers. The meal was finished, but the keg of beer still drew the passengers' attention. Franny caught a glimpse of a figure rising and approaching from the rear of the bus. He recognized Hank, who worked his way up the aisle with a little difficulty, fighting the pitch and roll of the moving vehicle. The crowd was quiet enough that Franny could hear the hum of the diesel engine droning toward Atlantic City. They were just reaching the Pine Barrens when Hank slid into the seat behind him.

"Franny, hate to interrupt you…but the guys need a rest stop." The word arrived apologetically. "The beer's taken its toll." The words rode on a path of laughter.

"I hope this isn't going to be a problem for you," advised Franny, "but Schuylkill Valley doesn't have a layover stop set up for you." It was a polite way of addressing a more serious issue.

"I know from past trips that none of these local Jersey places want us to stop," posed Hank. He spoke the information without emotion. "Look, maybe you could just pull off the roadway a bit. Any little patch of pine trees should give us enough cover." An air of desperation tinged with discomfort nestled into the softly spoken plea.

"I'll see what I can do," reflected Franny from his vantage point.

Miles of flat, sandy soil filled his panoramic view. Low-lying pines inched their growth toward the road bed from both sides of the highway. Ahead, an arc of yellow-white terrain appeared just off the tarred surface. A quick calculation told Franny that the bus would easily rest in the space. He began to decelerate as the bus neared the site. Immediately, a riot of activity commenced behind him. Each passenger in need of relief shuffled into the aisle to set and define his pecking order in the queue that formed instantly. A voluminous "Whoosh" from the brakes, accompanied the opening of the front door. Hank led the party into the sunlit wilderness of the Jersey Pine Barrens. Franny watched as their heads bobbed left and right, up and down searching for a suitable place at which to urinate. Almost like a committee consensus, the social club gravitated toward the side of the bus. Franny could see from the side mounted mirror the line of men along the bus trying to remain secluded from the highway and any oncoming or trailing vehicles. Franny glanced through his front window and then left into the side mirror. There was no traffic anywhere to be seen. A few men had remained aboard and were enjoying their adolescent jokes at the expense of their comrades. Then the impulse hit Franny.

A spasm wrenched his right arm toward the door lever. He pulled it closed with a jerk. He saw the men next to the door react when their heads shot right. His right foot pressed the accelerator firmly and the bus began to roll forward. With his eyes fixed on the right side mirror, cautious of his passengers' safety, he guided the tour bus just forward enough to reveal to the entire open highway every paralyzed rider standing in mid urination. Dead silence filled the interior of the bus as he again pulled off the tarmac fifty feet ahead of the disembarked passengers. From the center mirror above him, Franny saw five sets of faces inside the bus glued onto the back of his head. He could read the questions running through their heads. Laughter exploded, attached to thunderous pounding and slapping of the faux leather covered seats. Any doubts Franny may have had about his instinctive escapade were abruptly dispelled.

Through the right side mirror, he detected the men in various degrees of urination. Some busied themselves with their zippers; some wanted to run after the bus but had not finished the task at hand; and some raced up the highway in pursuit of the green and yellow coach. He opened the door, admitting the first members of the rest stop crew.

"What the hell was that?" "Stupid thing to do!" "Could' a killed someone!" rushed into the bus as the men ascended the steps. They were greeted by Franny's friendly smile and the roar of laughter from those already inside.

When the second group arrived, the laughter shook the bus as the first set of rest stoppers now joined in the scene. By the time Hank boarded with his remaining companions, they were already doubled over in laughter. They had heard the earlier responses and laughter that the first two groups received as they re-embarked. Men passed Franny slapping his shoulder, his hand, and his back. Their words to him were laughs and guffaws. Some passengers rubbed the cap on his head as if massaging a friendly old dog.

Hank stood, transfixed, "Man, Franny, that's the best prank that's ever been played!" He stood swaying gently for Franny had already engaged the clutch and was headed up the road, east to Atlantic City.

"I just couldn't resist, Hank!" he admitted. Then he confided, "Something just came over me."

"Well I'm glad it did. These guys will never forget it. Man, what a hoot!" he mumbled as he worked his way into his seat. The gradual secession of laughter and conversation marked the time as the tour group approached its destination.

The bus company had a regular debarkation site at one of the beaches a block south of the famed Atlantic City Convention

Center. Franny navigated the streets northward so as to allow for the passengers to exit safely in the beach-side curbing.

When he stopped mid block, Hank tapped him on the shoulder.

"Ah, Franny, we don't usually get off down here," he advised with a kindness that acknowledged that an innocent mistake had been made.

"What do you mean?" pled Franny.

"Well, we generally can't use the beaches down here near the center of town." Hank had accepted this situation during his last few trips. His friends and he were not about to let this ruin the good times that they had planned. As if he also felt a responsibility to his driver, he added, "Franny, we have a favorite spot in North Atlantic City. We'd rather get dropped there." He stood next to Franny and guided him north to a familiar parking lot where other busses had already parked. Coaches from churches and companies dotted the sand lot. Franny realized that these companies were African-American owned. As Hank left for the beach, he handed Franny a paper bag with a neatly wrapped sandwich and sides. He presented the driver with a cold soda that he had garnered from one of his non-beer drinking friends.

Franny thought about his African-American Coast Guard friends and Hank. The thought went with him on his leisurely stroll around the city while he waited for the departure time.

There was the scheduled restaurant stop in Atlantic City before the return. After that break, most of the men dozed and rested quietly, spent by a day of frolicking in the sun. The return trip followed the late setting sun westward.

Nearing Norristown, the group began to stir to life; a noticeable disturbance moved some object from seat to seat up the aisle like a hound dog on a scent. It stopped at Hank's seat in the form of an okra-colored envelope. Back home at the Arch Street pick-up location, Hank's social club went their separate ways.

"The guys wanted me to give this to you," voiced Hank in the quiet of the evening. He was the last to leave.

"Aw, what did ya do? You didn't have to do anything," stammered Franny, sensing that it was a gratuity.

"We always give the driver a tip," was his officious reply. "But you were the best; I mean the very best we've ever had."

"Thanks! Hank, I had a great time. Your friends were good sports, and I'm glad they weren't offended by my prank."

The men shook hands, and Franny watched with a sense of somberness, mingled with joy, as Hank disappeared into the shadows beyond the streetlamps along Arch Street. He felt the weight of the envelope in his left hand. Opening the flap, he discovered the biggest tip that he had ever received. The following week, Hank had a new customer appear at his shop. The dry cleaner's had Schuylkill Valley Bus Lines uniforms to do.

***

On October 28, 1954, Florence Winters Blanche filed for divorce in Middlesex County, New Jersey, on the grounds of "Abandonment". Uncontested, the court proceedings continued until the final divorce decree was granted on January 28, 1955. Franny had no contact with Dennis during the three months of legal dealings. He never discussed the divorce with the twins, and they remained unaware of any intrigue. His older siblings and parents supported his decision to allow the divorce without contesting any of the issues. Franny learned that Florence had begun dating Douglas Crane, who was serving in the U. S. Air force in New Jersey.

With that door shut, Franny now carried only the lingering questions of Dennis who was left in the custody of his mother. The ex-husband found himself allowing time to pass without making any efforts to reopen or renew his relationship with the child. In delaying any contact, he opened no old wounds for Florie or Dennis, and his sadness over the separation began to wane. It became easier to remain silent and detached.

Chapter Twelve

"Deepening Pools"

Late in the fall of 1956, Franny returned home from work in the afternoon. The twins were slamming a rubber ball against the concrete step mimicking a baseball game. He did not address them but strode into the house with determination written on his face. The tension was obvious to the boys who threw a few more fielding chances into the steps before following their father into the house. Voices tumbled from the kitchen. Mame and Marie spoke in tones of counsel. They pled for Franny to reconsider some matter.

"It's something you can't take back, Franny," advised Mame.

"Make sure in your own mind that you won't regret it later," added Marie.

The twins could not hear their father's responses, for he sat on a kitchen chair facing the back yard. Mame spotted the pair approaching the doorway.

"You two go outside and finish that game of yours," she ordered with a firm slow delivery. Franny turned briefly toward the boys, and they saw his tear-reddened face. The sense of being interlopers overtook them, and embarrassment and sadness moved them to the front door. Before they exited, the sons heard Mame utter the words, "Florie and Dennis."

The stale air in the parlor seemed to crackle with the words. The twins felt anger that someone had hurt their Father, and they sought relief from its grip. The game drew them. The energy went into the hard tosses of the ball onto the steps, the vocal "grunts" to retrieve the grounders, and the speed of play.

A car passed them on Lafayette Street, a limousine. The driver parked the black Cadillac against the curb just up the street from the curious boys. Enthralled, they watch the driver exit the car and head toward them. He carried a thin leather briefcase and wore a dark brown, three pieced suit. He nodded to them as he ascended the three steps of their playing field. Mame admitted him into the house immediately and waved the boys to remain outside. Waiting for the stranger to leave the home, the twins found the car a distraction. As they approached, they noticed a woman seated in the back seat, curb side. They heard voices on the porch behind them and turned to witness the visitor leaving the porch.

"Florie has only her 'Thanks' to offer you," bade the man turning to descend the stairs.

The words added up to sadness, anger, regret, and action for the twins. They raced to the car ahead of the driver.

"Why are you doin this to my Dad?" screamed Bernie.

"You're Florie, aren't you?" yelled Fran.

The woman's head turned toward the approaching driver in the street. She did not confront the boys as the chauffeur deftly started the engine. Rapidly, he pulled from the six hundred block of West Lafayette Street, leaving the twins without answers. Once in the house, Fran and Bernie felt shunned. No explanation was forthcoming. They never learned that their father had just signed adoption papers for their half-brother, Dennis.

***

The Schuylkill Valley Bus Company made White Dad and Uncle Larry fixtures in town. Larry ran the loop and regular routes, but Franny now drove more of the prestigious charters. During Franny's local run, a young widow from Bridgeport began to frequent his trips on the Norristown State Hospital route. The thin, black haired woman cooked at the mental facility and became a familiar presence on Franny's trips. She was raising two sons on her own, and that coincidence brought conversation into the daily treks from downtown Norristown up to the northwestern site of the hospital.

Bessie Pastino, nee Bessie Carfagno, lived with her parents in the southeast end of Bridgeport. Her mother still cooked at the Friendship Grill, a favored Italian restaurant located just at the exit of the borough into Swedeland. Her sons, Albert and George, were her total universe, and their family experiences prompted a deep and lasting relationship. Bessie listened intently to the little bits and pieces of Franny's life and, eventually, the couple began dating. The warmth and the attention of her family drew Franny from his hermitage on Lafayette Street. He began to frequent the Friendship Grill and the Carfagno residence.

Albert, who was born on March 31, 1942, remembered his father George Pastino only in youthful flashes of wonderful family times. George, Jr. was not as fortunate. The death of their father in February, 1947, occurred before the child was born. George's birth on September 17, 1947, left him to be raised by a single parent. Bessie encouraged them to have an open acceptance of Franny and his relationship with her. Mr. and Mrs. Carfagno knew Franny's Bridgeport history and welcomed him into their lives. Franny was content and at peace with the budding romance.

Bessie had a traumatic childhood of her own. Diagnosed with cancer at age twelve, she fought hard through high doses of radiation therapy, which at that time was highly experimental. The treatment would leave her with a life of continued physical problems. Nerve damage caused her constant pain which emaciated her. She was blessed with an unbridled energy that directed her through her pain, the medication, and the daily activities that supported her sons. That same ferocious determination and activity that had pulled her through her childhood illness created a productive and caring woman whom Franny admired and grew to love deeply.

Mame and Tim knew the Carfagno family from their days on De Kalb Street, and Al had known of the "Twins" from his time spent at St. Augustine's Elementary School. The growing relationship between Franny and Bessie raised the stress level for Mame. She battled Tim during his now increasing fits of rage, and now the issue of Franny's future left her with little surcease. Bessie's frankness, her energy, the two sons, and dynamic personality were seen as eccentricities by Mame. Franny's siblings held to views that were either supportive or neutral concerning the relationship. When marriage became a paramount consideration for the couple, confrontation again reared its ugly head.

It was infrequent that Franny would be home for dinner, especially if Bessie were not accompanying him. He planned it as a courtesy call to share his decision about Bessie and himself with his parents. The twins had shuffled away from the table to the television until they were called back for dessert. Eleanor and Patty sat patiently waiting to clear their father's plate and utensils from the table. Franny noted his mother's edginess. Tim was content to sop the residue of beef stew at the bottom of his plate with the last piece of Wonder Bread.

"Mom...Dad, I've made a decision." The statement was etched with certainty salted with a calm, but firm tone of voice. Tim simply acknowledged that he had heard the words, but Mame leaned forward, shuffling her weight in her son's direction.

"And what is that?" she reflected, almost copying her son's delivery.

"I'll be moving out soon. Bessie and I are going to get married." The words rang as if practiced, a dialogue for the stage.

"How's that possible, Franny? The church won't let you marry." Mame spoke the tenets of her faith with unfailing conviction. Somehow she expected that fact to end the conversation. She was surprised when Franny volunteered more of his plans.

"I know that, and so does Bessie. We're going to a JP as soon as…"

"No one in my family has ever been married before a Justice of the Peace!" rolled from her like a boulder down a steep incline.

Without any apparent reaction from Franny, he continued, "As soon as we can make arrangements to buy a luncheonette we've been looking at. We'll settle George and Albert in schools after we move into the business."

Tim heard the exchange like a television news item. He pushed his plate and service away as if sated. The two girls grabbed the utensils and plate with sharp, crisp raking motions across the linen tablecloth. They ushered themselves into the kitchen, glad this time to have dishes to clean.

His German mother gathered her thoughts as the chores offered a brief cessation in the conversation. "If you're going to take a step like that, don't expect Dad and me to condone it," she countered.

"That's okay. We kinda expected that. The Carfagnos offered to help us out anyway they could." Franny had been down this path before, and the result had been a confrontation. He was determined to prevent Mame's emotional response from escalating and causing her any harm. Once before it had ratcheted into a tirade that almost put her into the hospital.

"The Carfagnos don't speak for the church, Franny," she stammered as her hands rolled over each other as if she were kneading dough. Then she turned to her husband, "Tim, we can't go to this wedding!" Then turning to face her son, shot, "Why... Franny, you'll be excommunicated!" Her soul was broken. Tim finally realized the seriousness of the moment and languished in muted sadness on his own. He had no tools to assist his wife.

"Franny, I'd like you to do what you want, but Mom sees no other way." The words placed him clearly on neutral ground: he was actually supporting both Franny and his wife.

"Bessie and I would like to have the twins live with us, but..." he hesitated, knowing that this extra issue would surely light a fuse in his mother. "We will talk about that after the wedding." He saw that she was relieved not to have to address that question.

"You're going down a lonely path. I mean our friends, the relatives, the church.... My God, Franny, it's like you're going away again," she negotiated.

"Mom, I want you to know that Marie, Margaret, and Ralph are going with us as witnesses. We're going to have a small reception at the Friendship Grill afterward."

These revelations did not comfort her. She feared that the "tag" of excommunication would cripple his adult life, isolate him from her world. "I hope you don't expect to have the twins there. I don't want them involved with this si..." she agonized over the word that she had almost spoken, "I mean... this ceremony."

"We won't be taking George or Albert either, Mom," he uttered in an effort to console her before the argument escalated beyond her control. Both of Bessie's sons knew of the plans, and they were disappointed that they would not be permitted to attend the ceremony. "Mom and Dad, I'm sure you anticipated that something like this was going to happen. I just hope that someday you'll have some peace with it. I've applied for an annulment from my marriage to Florence. Keep praying for it to work out."

That night, with the table cleared and chores done, the family retired, leaving a solitary figure dressed in housecoat, rocking rhythmically back and forth at her familiar place at the dining room table. Her hands cupped a wooden set of Rosary beads.

One day Franny left Lafayette Street dressed for church with Marie, and they were on their way to meet Margaret and Ralph. Bessie's sister Rita and Bobby Mc Arthur were there also. The bridal party had a small reception at the Grove Street home of the Carfagnos. The twins had no indication that White Dad and the entourage left for a wedding. In fact, they were never privy to the announcement of the wedding.

Soon the Lafayette Street home had an extra room again, but the space soon filled with angrier and more uncontrollable bouts of rage, jealousy, and physical confrontation with Black Dad and Mame.

By late 1957, the evenings and nights grew tense with Tim's pacing, checking the windows, locking the doors, and grumbling with clenched teeth and fisted hands. Then, a singular, icy and dark drama came upon the household.

The usual ever-increasing crescendo of voices from whispers to spoken tones, to shouts of rage never happened. On this silt black night, an explosion of shrieks and commands tore the dreams of the twins into shards of unwanted reality. Hurriedly racing from their bedroom to the front master bedroom, the boys expected to find death. One flipped on the hall light as the other pushed through the closed door. As if awaiting them, but looking past their startled figures, Black Dad stood. His lean, gnarled body, rigid and statuesque in the shaft of hall light, reflected the yellow pale luminescence. Sobs and gasps of deep breaths assailed the three male figures standing in the doorway. The elder male was catatonic, clothed in only his sleeveless tee shirt. A thrashing of movement below them on the bed drew Francis toward the woman as he placed himself protectively between the bed and the man. Bernard put both his hands up to the man's chest in anticipation of a flurry of violent movement. There was a momentary hint, a flexing, a glance shot toward Francis. As Black Dad's hands moved slowly upward, Bernard touched his chest gently. The adult's feet shuffled, but sensing the hands of the young boy in front of him, he halted, still rigid with anger and rage, but somehow compliant with the open hands upon his tee shirt.

"What's this?" stammered Francis with his head turned toward Mame. She lay on her back dressed in a full slip. The covers and blanket were strewn about the floor. Two pillows supported her flailing head as it swung to and fro; her body heaved left and right. "She's tied to the bed, Bernie! Gees, she's tied to the headboard!"

"Dad, what are you doing?" Bernie successfully prodded Tim a few steps deeper into the darkness of the room. Now faint glimmers of the street light could be seen backlighting the elderly man.

"She's not getting out! No, Siree, and they aren't getting in!" burst from the man as he stood draped in yellow. Bernard had expected no answer, for Black Dad had appeared entranced. The words moved the lad backward, requiring a new awareness of the situation.

"Nobody's trying to get to Mame, Dad!" he tried to speak logic into the chaos.

"They're always out there skulkin' about, trying to take her away!" He gritted the words with fixed, unmoving lips. Spit misted through his locked teeth.

"I gotta get Mom out of here," shot Francis as he struggled to free her. "Keep Dad back and away, okay, Bernie!"

Shrieks and screams resonated into moans and sobs. Francis rushed to the far side to undo the bindings on her left wrist. The hallway filled with the daughters: Marie, the oldest, pushed through and pulled her mother up from the bed and delivered her to Eleanor and Patty in the hallway. "Twins, you try to get Dad dressed!" she ordered as a second thought as she followed her mother and sisters into the hall. They worked their way down to Marie's room with difficulty. Mame's stout and short frame became weighty and awkward. Frail and limp, the emotional turmoil had drained her strength. Francis found the pajama bottoms.

During the labor to dress Black Dad, the girls' voices became a divergent audience of plans, soothing pleas, angry reaction, and compassion. "That's it! Tomorrow he goes to the doctor!" "Poor dear, Mom, are you okay?" "How could he…we let this happen?" "Has he been doing this kind of thing all along?" Out of the frantic conversation, the twins could hear Mame's exhausted plea for understanding, "No, no, Dad's just very jealous, that's all."

Marie had made the irrevocable decision, and there would be no turning back, "Dad's going for treatment, Mom. No one is safe anymore. You understand?"

She wept and cried her answer of agreement. Quiet began to filter through the early hours, but Francis and Bernard struggled to put the pajama bottoms on Black Dad. They moved his unbending torso to the bed, placed him gently upon the sheet and slid the trousers onto his lower trunk. Suddenly, great fatigue overcame Tim, and the twins rotated him on the bed, covered him, and watched him fall to sleep. The statue before them began to inhale with soft, long breathes and deep, soundless exhales. The arms and legs bent, relaxed, and sunk heavily into the mattress.

132

They stood over the bed, fearing to leave him at this moment. The pair exchanged nods of disbelief. "It's ten to three." Francis said matter-of-factly.

"We're probably gonna flunk that math test tomorrow," added Bernard.

"Hey! This has happened before and we managed. Right?"

"I hate these nights!" Bernard sat on the floor, and Francis found the small changing chair by the window. They sat as at a wake and did not depart the room until summoned by Marie.

Tim was scheduled to be admitted to the Norristown State Mental Hospital. On a beautiful afternoon, the family finished lunch and left the kitchen to Mame and Black Dad. Everyone was busy with home work at the dining room table or chores in their rooms. Some conversation erupted in the back of the house by the kitchen door. It burst into the quiet work of the children like a black wall of weather, threatening, ominous, and howling. It dressed itself in icy fury.

"You can't go out there like that! Tim! Tim! There's no reason to bother that man!" screamed Mame. Alerted, the girls ran into the kitchen followed by Fran and Bernie. Their mother stood transfixed, facing the back yard, a broad shadow blocking any view of the yard.

"What's up?" shot Eleanor to Mame. The question demanded an immediate response, but none came. A huddled mass of children gathered behind the woman. Still there came no response from Mame.

Loud and inaudible words pierced the group within the house. The children waited in doubt and confusion, reduced to impotence by their mother's trance. Fran pushed forward, followed by his brother. The jostling touched Mame and she pivoted, prompted by the physical contact. A shard of light from the yard flicked into the kitchen and opened a visual pathway from the home. Standing erect with hands raised, Black Dad shouted angry words that shook and tossed his head back and forth and side to side. The silent on-lookers sensed his rage, but their horror focused on the knife which he held firmly in his right hand. He pointed with the weapon, forcing the audience to travel to the visual target which he had selected in the alleyway outside the back fence. Words tumbled in ravings, inarticulate and fierce from his challenging posture.

"My God, Mom, Dad's got one of the kitchen knives!" blurted Patty.

"What's he doing out there? And...who's that guy he's yelling at?" sputtered Bernie.

"He got all worked up when he saw that man coming out of the Moose Hall," reported Mame with a dire sense of the need for a quick resolution of the events. "We have to get him in here before he goes after that man," pleaded Mame.

Tim took an abrupt step forward: Franny pushed the screen door outward. The girls rushed onto the back porch; Bernie followed his taller twin down the two short steps onto the walkway.

The lone figure in the alley had turned in a face-off with Tim. His manner showed a degree of inebriation as he swayed to-and-fro, seemingly unaware of any danger. He was a roly-poly, squat figure dressed in blue jeans and a short sleeved plaid shirt. He fumbled for an item in his pocket, and scanned the area as if searching for something.

"Dad! Dad! Hey, Dad!" sounded Franny in an attempt to pull his father from his single-mindedness. Bernie hustled alongside his brother as the pair rushed to take a stance between Tim and his prey.

"There's nothing you should concern yourself with," he managed with an unexpected calm amid the turmoil.

"Dad, you have to relax and listen," added Bernie. Apparently the figure in the alley had moved, for Tim's head and eyes swung to the right, up the alley toward the Veterans of Foreign Wars parking lot. The boys slithered to their left attempting to impede Black Dad's stare. His eyes shot left, then right, as if momentarily distracted. "Let's walk back to the porch. Okay?" Bernie wanted him away from the innocent catalyst in the alley.

Fran moved a half step back toward Tim, but Bernie remained fast, holding a second line of defense in case Black Dad bolted for the back gate. The knife remained outstretched as if awaiting a handshake as Fran approached. "How about I take that knife before you hurt one of us, Dad?" negotiated the young teenager.

Tim looked upon the weapon he gripped in his hand as if it were foreign to him. He appeared surprised to see it there, and bent his right arm as if to get a closer look. Then he eyed the two boys. The question on his face signaled his first true recognition of the twins who stood before him.

Seizing the instant, Fran stepped confidently toward Tim, reached out his hand, and received the weapon from Black Dad. It was a brief, quiet ceremony that mocked the severity of the moment.

After admittance to the hospital, the doctors placed him on medication for the first time. He was in abject misery there. Sadness filled every visit with the feeling that your best friend had been forced to move out of town.

After Sunday mass at St. Francis of Assisi church, the Blanche entourage drove north on Buttonwood Street up to Sterigere Street, turned right for one block and entered the grounds under a massive rough iron gate on the left side of the street. Mame maneuvered the Buick through a maze of large brick buildings. Pat and Eleanor sat in the front with Mame on the bench seat, and the twins were in the back seat with Marie. Some of the buildings had heavy metal or screen guards over the windows. There was a tunnel system that sprung to the surface on occasion but returned below ground like roots on an ancient oak. The tunnels connected each building, allowing egress and entrance without surfacing. Like a human torso, all the vital organs were sharing this lifeline. The Buick stopped alongside a two story building with a sign marking it as "The Social Hall."

Margaret, Ralph, Gregory, and Colleen were standing at the doorway nearest the parking lot. Margaret, who worked at the Eye, Ear, and Nose Clinic at the hospital, entered the building before anyone else. She made her way to a reception desk, asked a few questions, and dutifully announced, "They'll bring Dad down to the sitting room."

The large sitting room presented three clusters of chairs, sofas, and benches. The furniture arrangement facilitated each visiting family to meet with their relative with only distance as a privacy screen. People visiting a patient waited in the room as an orderly ushered the patient into the room and eventually into the circle of family already seated in its own cloister. Black Dad entered benumbed by medication, assisted by a middle aged nurse. She left after directing Timothy to one of the leather lounge chairs set amid the family. The older visitors struggled with conversations with their father. A half hour passed before any of Tim's younger children became comfortable or talkative. No one tried to leave the huddle of chairs. The stark surroundings and the unfamiliar mannerisms of Tim disconcerted Patty, the McLaughlin children, and the twins. Each of the children approached the man as PopPop or Dad, touched his hand, shoulder, or thigh, but returned to a seat with little spoken except customary polite greetings. The patient seemed to look beyond and through each of his guests, except for Mame. When she took a position on Tim's right, he pivoted the upper part of his body toward her and trained his eyes upon her.

"You have to get me out of here...let me come home!" he pleaded.

Mame took the petition in silence, looking to Marie and Margaret for words.

"Dad, the doctors need you here for further observation," reported Margaret. "They need you here so they can get your medicine right." A visible uneasiness marked the Blanche group. Light and encouraging conversation from the other families within the room fluttered into their cluster like zephyrs at a picnic.

Marie had a logical and practical sense of the situation. She spoke, not to demean or scold her father, but merely to give his hospitalization a neighborhood perspective. "You have to realize, Dad, that the people here want you, Mom, and our neighbors to be safe."

Tim slowly rotated his head from its fixed position, staring at Mame, to a new target. "Marie, I'll behave." The words were delivered with a docile, childlike energy. "Nobody's going to be hurt. Honest!" The twins shared some unspoken word or idea. Their annoyance, their anger, and the physical nature of their restraining Black Dad during his frequent episodes prompted a wave of pity, melancholy, and sorrow for their grandfather.

His tears were foreign to them; his humble manner disconcerted them; and his woeful appeals to return home saddened them. For two months, the 631 West Lafayette Street residence was quiet and tranquil, but joy failed to accompany the peace. When the patriarch finally returned, he did so as a butterfly, a physically and mentally relaxed man. Gone, though, were his fiery passion, his tense arms, and his rigid posturing in defiance of the world outside. He retired to daily multiple scoops of ice cream, cards with the twins, his favorite television variety shows, his Phillies, and a growing admiration of John F. Kennedy.

Chapter Thirteen

"The Road to Rhawnhurst"

In 1957, Bessie and Franny tried to work the annulment process for his marriage with Florrie, but it was denied by the Catholic Church. Franny and Bessie had taken up residence in the apartment above the luncheonette in the Rhawnhurst section of Northeast Philadelphia, but the two boys shared a bedroom on Grove Street with their grandparents in Bridgeport. The step-father's concern for the fifteen and ten year old boys prompted him to seek out Albert and assure him that the marriage and the family relationships would work out. One evening, Franny interrupted Albert's study time, pulled up a kitchen chair, and slid himself next to the young man. Albert carried an air of maturity in his short, stocky frame. His heavy growth of black beard covered the lower portion of his round face and added to the perception that he was older than his years. The short cropped black hair added to the clean lines of his carriage.

"What's up, Franny?" quizzed the youth.

"I wanted to let you know how I feel about our situation here," he posed.

"Sure, but I'm okay with it. As long as Mom's happy, so are we – Georgie and me," summarized Albert. He had pushed the chair backward and swung to face his step-father.

"The twins, Fran and Bernie, are going to be around a lot more, and your Mom and I will probably spend more time visiting them in Norristown." This report had come as a directive from Bessie to Franny as she insisted on closer ties with his sons.

"Georgie and I kinda expected that," he offered with a touch of adult bravado.

"Al, I can never be your father," he spoke with sincerity. "But I'll be here for you."

"Thanks. I appreciate that, Franny." A slight grimace twitched into his face. "Ah, you know I haven't figured out what to call you."

"Well, you've stuck with 'Franny' so far, Albert. Why, what are you thinking?" The older man grinned with the prospect of being renamed by his oldest step-son.

"I think I like 'Frank' instead of 'Franny'," he evaluated.

"That will take some time for me to get used to, but I'll try to answer to 'Frank'." A smile and a handshake sealed the deal.

Albert had been concerned about his mother's health and her future. This single exchange with his new step-father brought him much peace. He remembered it always as a "saving" moment. In a few months Franny was "Frank" to Albert and "Dad" to Georgie.

With the new start to his life, Franny purchased a brand new 1957 blue and white De Soto with a hemi. He took Al and Georgie with him for a spin into Norristown to show the twins, Mame, and Tim his pride and joy. Mame and Tim had a Buick sedan, and they played at being impressed by the bigger and faster car. Fran and Bernie jumped into the back seat behind their father and Albert. Their adventure smelled of fresh leather seats and a hint of cigarette smoke. Franny kept his window rolled down as it was a warm sultry day.

"Where're we goin'?" chimed Bernie into the back of his father's head. He sat to one side of Georgie with his brother at the other window in the back seat. The twins were lean like their father and had his and their mother's black hair. Their "Peter Gunn" haircuts failed to give them the television character's debonair maturity. The adjective "cute" annoyed them and tested the politeness that they had been taught.

George took up his share of the rear seat. He was big boned and moved with athleticism. His shifts of position were quick and deft. The bookends hardly sensed his shuffling. His oval face lit up with anticipation.

"Guys, there's a new road that just opened up, and we're going to take a spin on the Schuylkill Expressway." His voice spilled out with a light trill.

"Are we gonna go fast?" spurted young Fran from the back seat.

"This thing can fly," added Albert.

Talk of baseball, sports, and Bridgeport lightened the trip to the expressway. The father confessed to liking Stan Musial over the local celebrities from the Phillies. He received a litany of "Boos" from the back seat. Bernie touted the batting average of Richie Ashburn, but Fran liked the power hitters and the pitching staff, Roberts and Simmons. Albert brought them back to Bridgeport with his sand lot baseball activities. "Frank and I are both left-handed," he blurted at the conclusion of his stories.

The twins did not respond to the name "Frank" because it seemed rude to bring up. The name sounded awkward to them. Albert had gained special status to call "White Dad" by the moniker "Frank" and not "Franny". There was the hint that Albert's prestige had bumped them farther back in the pecking order. It stung like an insect bite.

The issue was lost as the car sped up the on-ramp at Gulph Mills and headed west to King of Prussia. Franny rolled his window up under the pretext of gaining more speed. The passengers had no sense of the velocity of the auto, for its weight and construction sealed them in comfort and safety.

"How fast we goin?" yelled Fran over the purr of the motor. Bernie could see the speedometer needle touching one hundred.

"Not as fast as this guy!" shouted their father, jerking his head backward to indicate an on-coming car. Before the lads could jump up and twist their heads to the rear, the roar of an engine stormed passed the De Soto. "That's a '57 Chevy!" concluded Franny, "and he must be doing one fifteen, at least!" The numbers were irrelevant to the three youngsters, but the event would soon take on the power of science fiction. Schoolmates would learn that they had travelled at rocket speed up the newly opened expressway.

***

Bessie and Franny picked the last Saturday in December to show the family the sights of New York City. Franny had visited the metropolis many times as a bus driver, but now he wanted to share his favorite stops with the family. It was a blustery winter day when they picked up Bessie's niece, Connie, and headed to Norristown for the twins. Fran and Bernie appeared at the door in dapper dress. Their newest Christmas wardrobe of tan, camel hair knee length overcoats made the young teens awkward gentlemen. The youthful faces seemed out of place wearing a mature man's outerwear. The four boys pressed into the back seat. The new taut fabric bunched up when the twins sat in the De Soto, and Bernie spent considerable time pressing the waves of material down onto his chest throughout most of the two hour trip to New York.

From the parking garage, the first site of interest came into view. Rockefeller Center suddenly appeared as a Christmas post card in a cut of space amid the skyscrapers along the street. People darted into the void carrying ice skates and wrapped snugly with scarves and wool hats. The family Brownie camera recorded the delight of the New Yorkers gliding beneath the enormous Christmas tree along the rink surface.

Franny placed St. Patrick's Cathedral high on his list of favorite places. He knew the building well, for he spent long hours in its pews waiting for the time to pick up his fares on their tour of New York City. This became his chosen lay-over hostel.

Once inside, the troupe saw penitents waiting in the side aisles of the cathedral near the confessionals. Franny moved the tour rapidly through the church using finger gestures. When young Fran took out the Brownie from its case, he saw the waving finger of Bessie followed by its placement over her lips. With the boy's attention, she then motioned for him and the others to go outside for the picture. The height of the buildings surrounding the cathedral and the use of Eastern Standard Time prompted the camera to flash. Later the darkened photo would show Fran and Albert in the back row behind Bernie, Connie, and Georgie. They posed on the steps before the grand front door of the church.

During previous solitary visits, Franny's offered prayers centered on returning to the church and courage to again see Dennis. His search for a priest who would grant him absolution met with denials, even in this vast Archdiocese of New York. Loneliness accompanied him during his church visits, but his visits buoyed him with the sense that he still was connected to that Biblical vine, the house with many rooms.

Dinner brought the travelers to Franny's treasured Italian restaurant. The owners greeted him by name and asked the names of the family members once they had been seated. The children were dutifully polite and mannerly. The twins were amazed that White Dad had friends in this big city. Georgie and Albert enjoyed the familiarity of the cuisine and the Italian accents that filled the conversations with the wait staff and the owners.

The return trip to Pennsylvania began with boisterous reminisces of the day's activities. Slowly, the chatter and rustlings ebbed into a hushed silence as the weary teenagers nodded to sleep. The city had worn them out.

***

By now the twins were entering high school. Marie was working in Germantown in a prestigious real estate business, and Eleanor was engaged to a chemist, Joseph Schaffer. The couple would soon move to East Norriton. Pat was dating a young executive, Larry Hennessy, at Lee's Carpet in Swedeland. The twins had yet to have any long term relationship with their father.

Bessie and Franny breached the question with Mame and Tim of the twins coming to live with the couple and the two Pastino boys.

"The two of them would probably stop going to church," Mame theorized. It was still a sore point for her.

"Bessie, George, and Al go regularly, Mom," her son countered.

"The church is…"

"Is unreasonable!" thrust Franny into her sentence. "You know what the priest asked me to do to return to the church?"

She swept her head left to right, "No."

"They want me to agree to live in celibacy with Bessie, to treat her like a sister – no sexual contact. Now, Mom, that's unreasonable and unnatural."

"But they'd let you attend the sacraments?" She had not heard his argument.

"Yes. But..." he conceded and then ended the conversation as he swept his head left to right, "But it's not going to happen."

Tim never voiced his position on the subject. His medication put him in neutral. Marie and Pat were in favor of the twins moving in with their natural father, but Mame presented the counter-point. Franny had no place large enough for six people, the twins had just settled into high school, and all of their social friends were neighbors. She elaborated that, with Bessie and Franny both working, there would be little supervision. Mame kept the twins.

So, Franny had left the bus company with the dream to make his own way in the restaurant business. The Pastino boys were excited about their new schools and their parents' new plans. Franny loved being with people, and his new wife was an excellent cook. After securing a loan of $ 10,000.00 from Breyers Ice Cream Company, adding funds from savings, and taking personal loans from family and friends, Franny and Bessie settled in Northeast Philadelphia.

They rented an establishment in the Rhawnhurst section. They named it the Rhawnhurst Luncheonette, and it sat at 7735 Castor Avenue at Hartell Street. It was closer to a restaurant than a diner, for they served breakfast, lunch, and dinner. The luncheonette flourished with its Italian menu topped off with Breyers Ice Cream. Locals made the eatery a daily stop for coffee in the morning, business lunches, and tasty home cooked dinners.

Albert was registered as a sophomore at Father Judge Roman Catholic High School, and George was matriculated at Resurrection Parish Elementary School. Everything had its place in the perfect puzzle.

A few summer weeks brought the twins to Rhawnhurst. The business did best during the summers, so Bernie and Fran found little time to spend with their busy Dad. Al and George both worked at the luncheonette and ice cream business. The four step-brothers enjoyed stick ball or "half-ball" as the Rhawnhurst locals called it. The rest of the day was spent watching Bessie and the staff serving up wonderful meals for friendly patrons. The bonus was always an Italian Hoagie or a big dish of fresh scooped ice cream.

Albert Pastino thrived at Father Judge RC High School. His independence endeared him to Franny, who saw the fifteen year old as responsible and respectful. If he needed advice, Franny would offer it, but Albert generally knew the sensible thing to do. It was the younger Georgie who Franny took to fathering. By age eleven, Georgie needed transport to sporting events, assistance with homework, and nurturing by both parents. His athleticism brought Franny to him as a needed second for the baseball catches, basketball games of "Horse", and some stick ball afternoons.

The family team of Franny, Albert, and Georgie took on a teenage contingent in the local schoolyard in a pick-me-up basketball game. The Pastino/Blanche squad held its own until the Blanche member crumpled to the ground with a bad sprain while attempting to block a jump shot from the thirteen year old neighborhood hotshot. The boys carried, lifted, and sometimes dragged Franny back to the restaurant. His recuperation on crutches kept him behind the counter for the next few days. Albert and Georgie were proud of his efforts, but soon found the incident to be a source of instant laughter.

***

Up in Norristown, Timothy retired on March 3, 1958, and the additional time at home proved restful for him and peaceful for the family. The twins sought out a myriad of role models as pseudo-fathers. Grandpop, White dad, Ralph McLaughlin, Martin Bernot, their aunts' beaus, and teachers were targeted. Joe Shaffer, who worked for Allentown-Portland Cement Company, and Sister Mary Sarah, SSJ, who taught chemistry at Bishop Kenrick High School, aimed the twins toward a career in science.

***

The Rhawnhurst Luncheonette became the biggest seller of Breyers' ice cream in the Philadelphia area. By 1959, they were able to move the business to a mid-block property at 7729 Castor Avenue. The couple purchased this store with an apartment on the second floor. It was just two doors south of the original restaurant. This time Franny and Bessie had a true retirement investment.

Franny preferred to slip into the background of the business and even parenting at times. Bessie motivated him to become more of the front man. The role grew on him and he began to enjoy the responsibility. Franny assisted with Albert's decision to enter St. Joseph's College and pursue a course in business. Bessie initiated many discussions about the twins and how they might fit into the new family arrangement. She was also very much concerned about Dennis. The dutiful wife wanted her husband to have the opportunity to participate in as much of his sons' lives as possible.

When Bobbie Mc Arthur's union went on strike, Franny found out that he was having difficulties financially. He called him down to the Rhawnhurst Luncheonette, gave him a place to sleep, and put him to work bussing and waiting tables. Franny enjoyed being one of the Carfagnos. Their warmth embraced him and he felt secure and welcomed. His life had a normalcy to it: he had the Blanches and he had the Carfagnos.

Georgie grew into an agile, athletic young man. His prowess took Franny to various ball games at recreation centers all over the Northeast of Philadelphia. Georgie would drag him down to the local "Rec" Center for some hoops or a catch. The conversations on the trips covered sports, the family, school, friends, and sometimes business. Without realizing the themes of his talks with the two boys, he was gearing them into careers in business.

Franny and Bessie managed to take trips to New York City with neighborhood friends or Bill Geppert and Marie. He could even schedule an occasional round of golf with one of his customers. Playing Pine Valley with Jim O Brien, one of the Carfagno in-laws, was his favorite venue, but he only played two rounds there.

The twins had also taken an interest in golf. Through the tutelage of Marie, who was a Ben Hogan fan, they graduated from miniature golf, to driving range, to chip-n-putt, and finally to the actual eighteen hole courses around Norristown. Ralph and Margaret became members of George Washington Country Club in Audubon. They placed the twins on the family membership. Courses like Westover and Valley Forge would send coupons out to golfers to encourage play at their sites. Fran and Bernie received a coupon for a foursome of golf at Jeffersonville Golf Course. For Father's Day, 1960, they decided to invite Dad to play with them. He cordially accepted and made arrangements to pick the pair up for the Father's Day round.

"It's our treat, Dad," promised Fran as the trio strode toward the club house toting their bags. The parking lot indicated that a hoard of golfers was on the course, but the boys hoped that their later arrival might get them a slot on the first tee.

"Well, I don't mind kicking in my fair share," offered Dad to the boys as they dropped their bags and entered the pro shop.

Bernie was busy pulling the coupon from his pocket as Fran announced to the head professional, who was standing near the door, "We're a threesome, but we have a coupon to play a free round."

"We can fit you on the course," stammered the clerk from behind the counter who heard the comment, "but this is a holiday weekend."

"Yeah…?" The boy mused with the confused question. In an attempt to clarify the clerk's statement, Bernie offered, "Here's the coupon." He placed the billet on the counter with certainty, but felt his father nudge alongside of him.

"I'm sorry, but Jeffersonville doesn't take coupons on weekends, Son," explained the professional as he walked toward the trio.

"You'll have to pay for the round," added the clerk who was now joined by the golf professional behind the counter.

The two sons were glaring up at the price lists for the various days' rounds. Their faces reddened as the dire nature of the situation hit them. They had no means of paying for the three rounds – especially the round that they had promised their father. "What d'ya mean? This is good for a foursome," bellowed Bernie as he sought to gain a foothold with the clerk.

Fran had moved toward his father. "Dad, sorry. I guess this isn't going to work out."

"We'll square this up," assured the father. He moved toward the head professional and gestured for him to speak with him at a location in the shop away from the counter. Bernie was pointing out the coupon to the clerk, but Fran indicated the sign behind the register on the wall to his brother. "No Coupons on Holidays or Weekends!"

"We're good to go, Guys!" invited Franny as his returned to the counter. "Let's get to the first tee!"

"Okay…" began Bernie, but his comment was cut short as he noted his father placing his wallet in his back pocket.

The boys carried a numbing disappointment along with their golf bags during the first few holes with their father. The game gradually absorbed their interests as the sons began to enjoy the skill of the "Lefty" on the links. Bernie was impressed by his Dad's two iron shot to the two hundred and ten yard par three ninth hole. Franny would remember Dad's high fade, moving left; but Bernie would recall a mid-range draw, left to right. The time spent together, not the misplayed coupon or shots, made this Father's Day special to them.

A great convergence occurred in June of 1961 on the high school graduation day of Bernie and Fran. Martin Bernot and Lydie Van Sant came to Norristown from Bustleton, Francis Blanche and Bessie arrived from the greater northeast of Philadelphia, and Timothy and Mary Blanche were the host and hostess for the day's celebrations.

At the school, the Blanches kept company while Martin and Lydie generally stood a few paces from the center of attention. Lydie had Martin well-dressed in a coordinated tan sport coat and light brown trousers. In polite company, in difference to Lydie, he wore a wedding band on his left hand ring finger. His carriage was strong and confident. Martin took matches from his trouser pocket and lit a Lucky Strike. The matches were returned and a watch was pulled from the right side pant pocket. The chain glistened in the sun and the gold face burst with reflected sunlight as he flipped it open. At times the celebrants meandered around the flagpole in front of Bishop Kenrick High School for pictures or found themselves being introduced to classmates and their parents and some teachers. Martin donned a soft amicable smile as he enjoyed his time with the boys. When Franny passed by his father-in-law, a mere nod of Franny's head or a slight tip of Martin's hat became the social exchange. All that needed to be said transpired seventeen years ago.

Timothy wandered feebly amid the strangers and his family without initiating any conversation on his own. His black suit was ill-fitted since his recent weight loss. His pure white hair was neatly parted down the center. Gusts of wind taunted the light and now thinning tresses. His black bow tie signaled the significance of the day along with Mame's large corsage pinned to her left shoulder. Tim addressed people cordially when they approached the couple, but his emotions were muted and muffled.

Franny always dressed well. He had a keen sense of fashion and appreciated the finer clothing lines. His dark suit was tailored and the pocket kerchief finished the dashing look. Bessie and Franny savored the events of the day with energy and delight.

The reception for all the relatives was held at the Lafayette Street home. The full accompaniment of aunts, uncles, cousins, friends, and neighbors filled the dining room and parlor, forcing many small pockets onto the back and front porches. Except for Mary Mack's funeral many years ago, this was the first time that the twins had seen Grand Pop Bernot, Black Dad and White Dad all together at the same time and place. The boys dutifully spent equal time with each couple. Martin and Lydie were presented to the guests, and Pat and Eleanor made attempts to sit and chat with them for an extended period of time. The Bustleton couple sat under the side window on the loveseat observing the festivities and appreciated being served with food and appetizers from the kitchen. Timothy took his patriarchal seat at the front windows with his view facing into the room.

It appeared at times that he would have preferred to have the television tuned to a favorite program. The family waited on him, but there was minimal social exchange. His family honored his comfort zone.

Bessie settled into the kitchen, helping out with vigor and good natured banter. She touted the merits of Albert and Georgie with pride and details that made everyone feel that they knew the boys intimately. Franny shuffled from one of his siblings to another, catching up on the newest facts and rumors concerning their children and old friends from Bridgeport and Norristown. In passing, he always cordially acknowledged Martin on the loveseat. Martin managed a wink in return, but the brief and simple communication lost any meaning after Franny's third pass by the loveseat.

For the graduates, the day at home ended without any catharsis, or conversations about their history or their future. The twins heard, "Your mother would be so proud of you two," on occasion, but no additional details followed. The comment always arose from one of the ladies or aunts present. The trio of men never mentioned Camille. When everything that was going to be said had been spoken, the twins were dismissed or, rather, excused themselves to attend various classmates' parties all over the area. They had Mame's car keys, bid their farewells, and swept themselves through the house, across the porch, and down the steps to the Volkswagen. From the porch, Aunt Marie yelled, "Be careful!"

After their 1961 graduation from Bishop Kenrick High School, the twins went to Villanova University as chemistry majors. Al focused on his business studies at St. Joseph's College, and George attended Father Judge Roman Catholic High School as a freshman. The long weekend trips to the Bustleton house or the summer weeks in the Northeast ended. The Atlantic &

Pacific Tea Company took the twin's time as they earned money to support their college education at Villanova University. Marie and Ralph knew Al Bissey, the manager of one of the local groceries, and he gave them work. Their earnings as part time employees never amounted to the required tuition. They had no idea that their father and Marie were supporting their higher education.

After a long courtship with William Geppert, a friend of her employer, Marie married and moved to his family estate in Germantown. They had a modern, beautifully accented ranch-style home built on a lot adjacent to his mother's home. Their marriage brought them into a triad of fun-loving, gregarious couples: Margaret and Ralph Mc Laughlin, Bessie and Franny Blanche, Helen and Larry Blanche. Marie and Bill Geppert visited each others' homes, attending parties, and sometimes traveled together.

The twins had watched the transition of Uncle Franny through his White Dad phase. The somber flat-lipped visage that they had known in Uncle Franny had evolved into a softer face with fewer edges as White Dad emerged from his cocoon. The curious wry smile, an interested raised eyebrow, and a spontaneous laugh mixed into his newly found broad emotional response. At Rhawnhurst, their father carried a broad, beaming smile in all his social and family encounters. He laughed uproariously, played practical jokes on friends, and rarely said "No" to any request. He learned to enjoy the life into which he had been led. He blossomed as Al's mentor and Georgie's Dad. He reflected on his earlier choices; like a pool ball struck by directed cue balls, his decisions had sent him ricocheting across life's playing surface. He learned to control the loose elements and accept some of the settled aspects of his life. Bessie encouraged him and watched him grow into a man of broad interests. He cherished with deep personal feelings the twins and those in his various circles. Franny now made choices, defined his own limits, and seasoned the moments in his life with emotional spices from his own recipes.

Albert passed his driver's test four years earlier; and, in 1962, Franny purchased a brand new Oldsmobile Rocket 88. It was in pristine condition. By that summer, Al was dating Mim McNally and had enough courage to ask Frank if he could use the car. Albert had saved enough for gas and date money, for Frank had permitted Al and sometimes Georgie to take the change from the register as their pay for the hours that they worked. The car remained the last piece of the puzzle. His date, Mim, was a bubbly girl whom he had been dating for nearly six months. Bessie did not mind that she was a "Public" because she knew her parents from the restaurant. As Albert pled his case, Franny realized that he was cutting two sets of apron strings: one for Albert and one for himself if he left the Rocket 88 in Albert's hands.

"We're just going down to Castor and Cottman to the movie theater, Frank. I won't drive more than about five or six miles. I'll be real careful. Mim's dad said he's okay with us goin' out. I have gas money and enough for the tickets and, maybe, a burger after the movie." His monologue rambled on without a pause as if to assure that all of his arguments were heard before Franny could interrupt him with a refusal. His excitement eroded his hard earned maturity. If he entered a bar under the legal age, he would most likely not have been asked for identification, but now he stammered like a young teenager.

"That sounds fine to me, Al. What time are you picking Mim up?" He was enjoying his own nonchalance. The surprised look on the boy's face brought a smile to Franny.

"You mean I can…thanks, Frank! This is great. I'll call Mim. Oh, I guess I'll pick her up by seven. You think that'll work?"

"Yep! It sounds like you have it all figured out. Be home by eleven. Okay?"

"No problem, Frank! Thanks again," he intoned as he headed for the phone.

The date followed Al's plans with the exception of the length of the featured film. It ran for almost three hours; and, after a stop at the local diner on Cottman Street, Al found himself pulling the Oldsmobile into the neighborhood around midnight. His lateness caused him to ignore Frank's ultimatum to park the car at the rear of the building and never on Castor Street. A two car parking space loomed into sight in front of the restaurant. Albert swung the big sedan into the gap, touched the curbing with the front right tire, stopped and snuggled the auto into the space. He took a deep breath, pleased with his efforts and hopeful that he could sneak into the apartment.

When he exited his room the next morning, Bessie called to him, "Albert…Albert!"

The teen knew instantly that he was in trouble with his mother, for she rarely called him "Albert". He approached her believing that he had been caught after his eleven o'clock curfew. "I can explain, Mom," he started.

"No, Albert, I don't think you can." The words were accompanied by a right hand swat to the back of his head.

"Mom, I was only a little late!" he confessed.

"That's not why you're going to be grounded!" Another right hand swatted his left shoulder.

The boy recognized the seriousness of his misbehavior through the impact of the slaps which Bessie was delivering. "You can't be this mad over a half an hour, Mom?"

"Look out the front window!" she ordered.

Bright sunlight forced him to shade his eyes momentarily, but he began to focus on the police car and neighbors milling about the front of the establishment. "What? We get robbed?" The thought left him wondering why he was responsible for the break in.

"No! The Oldsmobile got run into early this morning. Some guy must've fallen asleep at the wheel." Anger and disappointment etched the words. At least she had stopped hitting him.

"Oh, man! That's terrible, but how's it my fault?" His mind raced, trying to figure his connection to this obvious accident.

"Franny never, I mean, never parks the car on the street. Why didn't you put it in the back?" The truth filled his stomach with a sickening weight.

Albert could see Franny standing with the officer and neighbors, examining the entire left side of the prized sedan. The rear bumper of the Olds was crushed into the trunk space.

"Mom, I'm sorry." His contrition painted the apology, and his head bowed in his own disappointment.

"You are going to Aunt Rita today. They're picking you up at noon. That was too irresponsible for me to take. You go stay with Aunt Rita." Bessie was livid.

"Oh, gees! Aw, Mom, come on. This is nuts. Just ground me at home," he negotiated.

"No! And that's final."

Al wended his way downstairs to offer his apology to Frank. He read the disappointment in Frank's eyes. A brief explanation ensued, and the mentor, although upset, never railed against the young man for his mistake. Always in check, Franny handled this first and only time of frustration with Albert with quiet surrender to the fates.

So the delinquent trudged off to Bridgeport under the guard of Aunt Rita. His confinement would last three days, for Franny refused to allow Bessie to enforce the punishment any longer. He brought the prodigal son home in a borrowed vehicle. The two males shared the ride without amusement, polite and respectful. A bit of comic relief, directed at Bessie's over-reaction, eased the reunion of Father and Son.

Chapter Fourteen

"Games of Mirrors"

Out of this warm and supportive environment, Franny was convinced by Bessie and the group to try to locate Dennis. By the late spring of 1963, after a number of inquiries in New Jersey, Franny learned that Florence had married after their divorce in 1955. With her new husband, she moved to Tennessee with Dennis, and the marriage bore four more children. Her husband, Corporal Douglas Crane, died of a heart attack at thirty-nine years of age in Tennessee. Florie, as a single parent, chose to return to New Jersey to rear the five children.

Everyone gave advice, and the plan became a simple one. Franny and Bessie would drive to New Jersey unannounced on a Friday afternoon. Since Dennis would be in school at the time, it gave Franny a chance to speak with Florence alone. If a problem occurred, they could stay overnight at a nearby motel and work out any difficulties over the weekend.

The morning mellowed into a warm sun-drenched day. As Franny drove north and the rising sun swung overhead, he rolled down the driver's side window to savor the fresh spring air. Near Princeton, they stopped for a coffee, and Franny submitted to the urge to have a smoke. The strong aroma of the Chesterfield and the bite of the coffee were agreeable to him. A coughing spell irritated his restful moment. They were soon on the road and headed to Spotswood, New Jersey.

The stone front on the façade of the Cape Cod gave a sense of strength to the home. A tan colored addition, sided with aluminum, stretched the original building into comfortable quarters for the family of five. He pulled up in a parallel slot across the street from the residence. Instinctively, he reached in his shirt pocket to pull out a Chesterfield cigarette. Bessie saw his maneuver and he smiled at her. He declined the cigarette smoke that would have relaxed him but relished the deep breath of spring air that he took into his lungs. The engine continued to idle with the Lennon Sisters crooning on the am dial. Franny mumbled to himself, "What am I doing here?" He was poised to stir up a maelstrom, and the chaos to come worried him. Bessie sat quietly beside him, patient so as not to prod him. He finished the reflection before he opened the car door. His body was heavy, "Old," he thought as he shook the two hour voyage from his limbs. The leather soles beneath him scraped the gravel and squealed in annoyance at his steps. Distracted by the sound, by the green of the fresh spring growth, and by the smell of lilac in a neighbor's lawn, he found himself at the front door – almost too soon. "Not ready!" raced through his head. "Never be ready!" was the debate rebut. Bessie stood by his side.

Before cowardice, doubt, or futility moved him from the door, he heard a rustling from within. The curtain of the front window was pulled back and an inquisitive face appraised him. He froze without a decision to stand or flee. The female was familiar, yet different. The woman had moved ahead in years without his daily scrutiny. He had missed her youth, aged now by her own weary life and joyful times.

A hint of recognition lit her eyes. The features of the questioning face contorted with the fear of possibility. Providence moved her to the door. The reaction/stimuli of the moment pulled her to the man on the front stoop. She never considered a retreat to the protection of her home. Instead, she gently pulled open the wooden door. "So, you've come!"

The room lay heavy with the three adults waiting in awkward silence, broken with occasional staccato whiffs of mundane conversation. "Yes," Florence had other children. There were Colleen, Diane, Bryan, and Janice. And "Yes," their father, Doug Crane, died in Tennessee. Franny passively took in the information, but Bessie sensed the need for social decorum. She voiced the responses petitioned of Florence of her husband, giving the necessary exchange of histories. The conversation shifted away from Franny onto her own past.

"So, Bessie, you have two boys of your own." Florence seemed relieved to have another topic to explore.

"Albert and George. Their father, George Pastino, passed away before Georgie was even born. Franny's been a great father for them. They are wonderful young men."

The facts matched some memory for the woman. There was a searching pause and the simple question to Franny, "The twins?"

Bluntly, came the response, "They're with their grandmother still." Every word had an almost lethal emotional edge. The danger of retracing those bitter roads lurked like a ghost in the room. Franny wanted no part of those avenues. He scanned the room and noted a doorway to the kitchen on his left that led from a neatly furnished dining room. Six chairs encircled the rectangular table that was sparsely set for a future meal.

"So, when do you expect Dennis?" Bessie asked when she felt the edge in his voice – its somber treble.

The question forced Florence to be satisfied with the brevity of details from Franny. "He's a sophomore at South River High School."

Three sets of eyes wandered to the floor. For Franny and Bessie, there seemed to be no further place to explore; and there was the lurking fear that any word might unleash a torrent of buried animosity.

Florence's hands began a ritual. They played at washing and rubbing as she shifted her weight beneath her. Seated as in church before the confessional, Florence examined her conscience. A deep breath summoned her courage and brought Franny and Bessie's attention to her. "All of my children are 'Cranes,'" she blurted quickly. It rather erupted as if to prevent it from never being spoken. "Dennis believes Doug was his father." The delivery came without eye contact, dry and factual. "He probably doesn't remember…" unfinished as an act of kindness, it still felt like a crucifixion.

"What? You mean I'm…," Franny had no ability at that moment to express the myriad of explosions racing through his mind.

"How are we going to bring this up to Dennis?" directed Bessie to Florence. While her husband took a seat, imprisoned between rage and chaos, Bessie faced the distraught woman across the room from her.

"I knew if this day ever came, I would have to deal with the consequence," she admitted with head and eyes bowed as if accepting forgiveness and a penance. "Dennis will be angry and upset, but he's a good boy. I'll have to live with it." Her words of submission allowed her eyes to search upward toward the couple.

"I didn't come here to be a villain." Franny reflected; and then, to the women, he added, "But we're all going to be and very soon."

A doorknob turned, a gust of spring air and warm afternoon sunlight dashed into the room, introducing a slender, energetic teen. His blond hair chased the current of spring breeze that played about him. Tall and beaming with youth, he greeted his mother, "Hi, Mom!" He completed one stride toward her, and then realized that others were present. Nodding toward the interlopers, he crossed in front of them to give Florence a warm, yet subdued embrace. "D'ya have a good day, Mom?" he quizzed, glancing at the couple with friendly eyes.

"It's been …" she could not find the answer.

Franny began to rise, and Bessie now took a seat.

"Why don't you put your things away? I want you to meet these people." Dennis sensed the quiet nervousness in her request, and he left the room with a quizzical purse on his lips. "Please let me tell him, first," she begged as she retired to the nearby sofa.

Franny nodded his approval and began to pace the room with short, delicate strides. He jammed his hands into his pockets. Bessie realized that she had never seen him do that. She knew how difficult the next few moments were going to be.

Dennis made a polite entrance to the living room from the kitchen. Standing respectfully in the entranceway, he waited for his mother to begin.

"Dennis, this is Franny Blanche and his wife Bessie." She delivered the information from her seat. Dennis remained fixed a few feet from the couple. Franny had turned to face the young man and managed to nod in Dennis' direction. "They have come from Philadelphia to meet you." Florence looked from Dennis to Franny and back. Dennis was familiar with social graces, and with comfort he walked briskly toward Franny and reached to shake his hand.

Both of the older man's hands came from his pockets as if expecting an embrace. A split second delay and Franny's right hand reached up to grasp Dennis' outstretched palm. Before Franny could speak, Dennis turned and extended his hand toward the seated figure of Bessie. She presented the youth with a warm smile.

Dennis turned to his mother. "So, what's up, Mom?" he offered.

"Dennis, this is so very difficult," she began, "but you have a different history than your sisters and brother." She paused as Franny moved to stand next to Bessie across the room from the mother and son. "I was married before I met your father. This man, Francis, is my first husband."

The young man before her stood with his mind racing. Awestruck he managed to whisper, "What are you telling me, Mom? …What?" A fight had begun within him: for the teenager, inside passion and rage wrestled with calmness and maturity.

"Doug Crane was not your father, Dennis." Tears reddened her eyes and regret choked her delivery. "Franny, here, is your real father."

The young man's head recoiled, driving his body backward a few steps. "What are you telling me? No way, this is happening!" His singular focus remained on Florence. "Why wouldn't you tell me something like this, Mom?" Anger sought a vent, but Dennis felt the presence of the two strangers near him. Raging, he swung away from his seated mother, but managed the semblance of calm to face Franny. "Why now?" he uttered with a touch of contempt. "Where have you been?" he shot with a sense of manliness. "What do I do now?" he supplicated humbly with both arms draped at his sides.

"I'm sorry you had to find out this way. I had no idea that you never knew." The father stood relaxed and made no attempt to approach the young man. "Could we talk in private somewhere?" Franny petitioned; and, as his face sought a refuge within the home, his glance settled on the nearby dining room.

"Mom, can we use the dinner table?" responded the lad interpreting the older man's signal.

Florence looked up dejectedly and motioned the pair into the adjacent room. From her perch on the sofa, she watched the pair shuffle toward the chairs in the dining room. Left alone with Bessie, the women found the quiet disconcerting.

The father and son took seats across the table from one another. Florence rose, spoke briefly to Bessie, and went into the kitchen. She busied herself preparing coffee and light refreshments as Bessie sat alone in the parlor.

"There's no good place to begin, Dennis," stammered Franny, "but I think you should know that I've always wanted to find you."

"How long has it been? I mean since you last saw me?" countered the young man.

"After your mother and I split up... I guess it's nearly twelve years." The words were soft, and the ease of them surprised Franny. The worse was behind him, and he decided that the conversation should not be all about him. "You seem to be doing very well, and I don't wish that you should be unhappy about all of this, Dennis."

"I can't believe that my life was such a secret. Do my brother and sisters know?" He looked squarely into Franny's eyes. Dennis studied the man across the table from him.

"I don't believe they do. But I can tell that you are loved and are a very important part of this family."

"Where have you been all these years?" Dennis leaned forward, placing his elbows on the table top.

Franny marveled at the young boy's poise. "I've been trying to bring my crazy life together."

"So, it's taken you twelve years to come to me." The tone of the statement was cold and deliberate. His youthful blond hair and blue eyes did not overcome the weariness of his expression.

"My first wife died in childbirth. I've been able to get closer to my twin sons from that marriage. You only met them a few times. They spent a week in Jersey with you, your mother, and me."

"I don't remember any of this," he said in quiet acceptance. "I remember Florida and the farm in Tennessee with my family. When we lost Dad down there, it was a terrible time."

"You must have many great memories, too, Dennis." Franny began to reach across the table to touch him, but stopped and folded his hands on the surface instead.

"I'm doing well in school, and I plan to go into the service when I graduate," he ventured. The information seemed trivial to him at that moment; and he added, "So why now?"

"Well, after my marriage to your mother broke up, I met Bessie. She has two boys of her own. She's given me the push to see you. I lost touch with you after I signed your adoption papers over to your mother. I didn't know where you were. I just found out that Florence had moved back into the area." The words rushed passed him like the fleeting years that had separated them.

"What happens now?" requested Dennis as if searching for some direction amid the confusion and mystery of the visit.

"You'll need some time to take all this in. Why don't you wait awhile, think it through, and decide what you'd like to do about our relationship." He knew the risk of placing the next move with Dennis, but this reunion might be more disruptive than Franny could imagine. Franny did not wish to tear Dennis's life apart. If he and his son could manage a broader relationship, then Franny would welcome that decision. On the other hand, Dennis may find his contentment in New Jersey as something which he did not want to lose.

"Okay, that's a start," he agreed.

The conversation shifted to mundane interests and references to friends, family, likes and dislikes. The banter remained friendly, easy, and polite. An hour passed, coffee was served, and the other children arrived. Florence ushered them into the kitchen for snacks, homework and play out-of-doors. The four strangers parted with a semblance of hospitality and decorum.

The door closed behind Franny and Bessie, and the flood gates opened upon Florence. His siblings heard the shouting and anger from their brother directed toward their mother. It was the first time Dennis had spoken to her in that fashion. Florence explained some of her frustration to her son. Later she pled for his forgiveness as the argument waned. Over the ensuing days and weeks, Dennis slowly returned to the routine of his life. He became tentative in his desire to explore the relationship with his newfound father.

The ride home for Franny and Bessie provided time for thoughts of moments and time lost. The conversation never filled with sorrow, for Franny sensed release and euphoria. He had longed to be free of this task which haunted his days. The confessional had been approached, the forgiveness attempted, and the atonement was left for a later date. The rueful day had passed, and Dennis was left to act on the truth of his past. A chasm separated him from his father, and the construction of the bridge across, begun by the father, had to be completed by the young man. Franny decided not to interfere with Dennis' plans. The father had made the first gesture; the son had the next move.

Chapter Fifteen

"The Kennedy Assassination"

Since Black Dad retired from the Alan Wood Steel Company, he spent his time recuperating from his mental issues. The medication quieted him, and he was able to have a semblance of normalcy. His days were spent with Mame and the twins, and his routine became sedentary. A hearty breakfast prepared him to ride with Mame on daily trips to stores, church, or doctors' offices. The water chore of collecting twenty-two gallons of fresh spring water went by the wayside when Mame purchased the small, compact Volkswagen. After lunch on weekdays, Tim settled into his favorite lounge chair in the front parlor and watched – he watched television, he watched the twins study, he watched them play board games when they were not in school, he watched Mame with little concern for any stalkers, and he watched his life pass by. The medication produced a stoic gentleman, seemingly reflective and unemotional.

In the summertime on a warm afternoon, he would shuffle a deck of cards and join the twins playing poker for toothpicks or jellybeans. His slow, methodical play tried the patience of the boys. The games usually ended with no clear winner. It was a practice that seemed foreign to his manner. Before his hospitalization, the boys had never seen him participate in any game, let alone a game of chance.

For the family, the prescriptions made the home livable, and Grandpop Tim took his place in the family with some calm, some joy and some peacefulness. Eleanor and Pat still lacked his attention; and, in return, the girls granted the same level of recognition to him. The feminine side of the family made few attempts to blend with the masculine. The family held their battle lines like a voyage along the boundary of a Ying-Yang symbol. It avoided mixing unlike the soda and ice cream in a malted fountain drink. The parties were present but they rarely mingled.

The evenings brought a nightly bowl of his favorite Breyers ice cream, heaped high to the brim. His nights passed with quality sleep and physical rest. His strength waned from inactivity, and he began to shuffle from place to place.

One errand to the basement brought him a terrible fall. The twins heard his body strike several of the steps followed by a heavy thud as he slammed onto the concrete floor. Mame and the boys rushed toward the kitchen door that led to the basement. There was silence. Scurrying down the flight, the trio picked up a low moaning sound, but still Black Dad was not visible to them. Half way down the staircase, they saw his strewn body moving slowly, attempting to raise himself from the cold floor. The twins reached him before Mame, and their first directive was to prevent him from moving. He struggled, dazed, to right himself, and he fought their attempts to keep him still and quite. His left eye had taken the brunt of the direct contact with the solid floor. He bled profusely from a head wound just above the eye. His speech was incoherent, and his body lay limp like a rolled rag tossed onto the floor. Mame dispatched herself to get wet towels. The decision was made to take him to the emergency room at Sacred Heart Hospital.

The immediate difficulty that concerned everyone was moving the injured parent. Once Mame and the twins realized that he had feeling in all off his extremities, they supported him and brought him to a standing position. Bernie grabbed him firmly by his belt: Fran took the weight of his body in an embrace just under his right arm. Mame hurried to the landing and rushed in her waddling fashion to collect her car keys. Fran and Mame seated him in the passenger seat. Bernie and his twin slithered behind the driver's seat into the back of the little car before Mame took position as the driver.

The hospital staff ran all the necessary checks for broken bones and a possible concussion. The family received instructions to keep him awake and monitor his sleeping hours. Tim's mind cleared and he became coherent while at the hospital. The end result for Tim focused on keeping him from any stairs unless he was accompanied by some family member. The family took measures to assist him when sitting or rising. He took the loss of this independence in stride, seemingly pleased to have more attention than normal.

***

The family lived vicariously in Daley Plaza, Texas, and Washington, DC, for those horrendous days in November, 1963. Black Dad participated in the national mourning as a Kennedy family member. The television gave him access to the Kennedy family, and he participated in their sorrow as if it were a traditional Irish night watch. He walked symbolically beside Jacqueline during the funeral procession. Thanksgiving was the following Thursday, but no one in the house had thoughts of preparing for the feast. Tim had a scheduled doctor's appointment scheduled for the Tuesday following President Kennedy's burial. He followed his daily routine that morning and shuffled from the house into the little off-white Volkswagen that Mame had grown to enjoy as "her" car. The twins were home from Villanova early that afternoon. When the phone rang Bernie answered the call.

Mame was on the other line and spoke in distraught garbled sentences. "Grandpop," she managed to say but hesitated with some difficulty. After several attempts to continue, she voiced the words, "Just died."

"Oh, Mame, no!" sprang almost reflexively from the twin. "How did this happen? Weren't you going to the doctor's?" The words tumbled from his disbelieving thoughts.

"Bernie, Dad was just sitting there in the doctor's office. Oh, my God – I can't believe this has happened!" she cried.

"Don't drive home, Mom. I'll call Margaret to come and get you." His concern shifted to the lonely Grandmother at the hospital.

"No, I won't, Bernie," she promised. "No, Margaret's here." There was a slight pause as she retrained her thought. "We had an appointment at the State Hospital. This was Dad's psychologist appointment." Then, almost as a sensed requirement, she added, "Margaret was at work in her building." The pain and loss etched her words, "The doctor called her. She came right over."

"Is there anything you want me to do, Mom?" volunteered the young man.

"No, Bernie, just stay home. Everyone's going to be calling," she suggested. Then, almost as an afterthought, Mame shared her last personal moment with her husband, "Dad just fell asleep waiting for the nurse to call him in to see the doctor. I thought I'd let him doze a bit. You know how exhausted he seemed watching all the Kennedy stuff on television? When the nurse came to get him, he was already gone. So quiet, so peaceful after all his troubles."

"God's gift, Mom," consoled Bernie in reaction to her musing. He felt useless to her in this moment.

The phone call continued with consolation and mourning, but gradually Bernie began to sense an epiphany of sorts. Remorse worked its way into the dialogue, for he tried to control the things he knew he should say against the relief that sifted into his being. A long and painful journey had ended, and peace would have its day. Black Dad, Grandpop, and Tim had the blessing of a peaceful death.

After the internment, the family surmised that the trauma of the Kennedy assassination and the long hours of public mourning had taken the vitality from Timothy. Thanksgiving Day had a new significance carved into its tradition. The children urged Mame not to fret with the preparation for the meal, but she found surcease in the kitchen. The pumpkin and apple pies that she baked were therapeutic. Her normal production of minced meat, lemon meringue, pumpkin, covered apple, and something she called milk pie usually resulted in eight or nine pies. The two desserts, however, gave her joy and satisfaction as if she had presented herself with a small gift, a luxury. President Kennedy and Timothy Blanche were forever joined in the remembrances and thankfulness of the day.

Bernard Blanche had struggled with sophomore chemistry along with Fran and the rest of the forty students. Cut in half, twenty chemistry majors remained in the curriculum. Oddly, one-half of the biology, mathematics, and engineering students succumbed to the same fate in the same course. Quantitative chemistry had been blended with analytic chemistry for all sophomore science students. By second semester at the start of 1963, Bernie enrolled in the College of Education with an American Literature major and Fran was now a biology student. The twins discussed this move with Aunt Marie who was their primary mentored. White Dad visited the boys and made his suggestions known to both of them.

"You're not going to be able to raise a family on a teacher's salary," he advised Bernie. The parent considered the science choice of Fran with biology to be a little more productive as a career.

Bernie's response centered on his self-evaluation and the academics where he had the most success. He explained that an English professor, Mr. James J. Mitchell, M.A., had counseled him and encouraged him as a writer. "I just think I could be a really good high school English teacher, Dad"

"Like I told Albert and Georgie, the most profitable careers are in business, Bernie."

"I've never had an interest in business, and Mr. George Harris in the Education department has been very helpful saving me credits that I can switch." Marie and Franny both knew George from their own school days in Bridgeport. His name and the family's familiarity with him eased the acceptance of Bernie's choice of career with Franny.

Martin Bernot learned of Timothy's passing, but the young college students did not report to him of their academic setback. He still lived with Lydie Van Sant in the Bustleton section of Northeast Philadelphia and frequented Florida for winter trips. The twins saw him infrequently and usually around the holidays. They remained a part of his extended family with Lydie, her daughter and her family. The tether and restrictions had long gone, and Martin and his grandsons enjoyed an adult relationship.

Franny and Bessie relished the success of their thriving business at the newer location. The fatigue brought on by long hours gave them a sense of satisfaction. One lingering issue in Franny's life continued to surface, and it put a biting edge on his contentment. Franny always had a nagging question darken the good times, "Will Dennis call?" His wife comforted him through his concerns. She drew him to focus on the vitality of

Al, Georgie, and the twins. Bessie worked tirelessly with him to make the business and their marriage succeed.

Albert surprised everyone by announcing that he was named the St. Joseph's Hawk – the college's mascot. Since the major sport at St. Joseph's was basketball, he would need to attend all the home and away games. His schedule included those played at the University of Pennsylvania's Palestra, the local Big Five games. Al initiated the tradition of the "Hawk Soaring". Throughout an entire game, Al, as The Hawk, flapped his mascot wings rhythmically, never ceasing, urging fans to sustain the team's momentum. Bernie and Fran's friends at Villanova were brutally frank about their dislike of this ritual. Once, a whole, de-feathered chicken was hurled upon the Palestra court during a cheerleading intermission. The Villanova twins reminded their raucous fans, "Hey! That's my step-brother out there!" A tremendous intra-family rivalry was spawned as Bernie and Fran had become friends with the Villanova Wildcat mascot, Andy Smith.

The line from Kennedy's inaugural address, "Ask not what your country can do for you, but what you can do for your country," put Bernie on a track to enter the Peace Corps. He reminisced about a particular lesson in grade school. A fifth grade Sister of St. Joseph taught him about the dream of a country to build its new federal capital out of the wild brush of its interior. That needle of curiosity placed wonderment into his psyche. The enticement to watch Brazil accomplish this daunting feat fed his desire to witness the possible construction and outcome. During his junior year at Villanova he submitted the preliminary application needed to apply for the corps.

Fran and he had begun to sever their strong ties. The biology and the education studies diverted their paths. They found different companions, sought new horizons, and stopped dressing alike as had been their custom. Fran began dating Iris Young from Worcester, a nearby township to Norristown, but Bernie had left a long time relationship and now "played the field."

Albert married immediately after graduation to Mim McNally, his constant companion for his entire senior year. They had a small wedding and a frugal reception at a local firehouse. All of the wedding gift money paid the cost of the celebration, and none went into savings or a honeymoon. He took a position with Haskin & Sells Accounting firm in Philadelphia. His employment with this firm proved very beneficial. The couple was soon expecting their first child. Al appreciated the firm's "family" orientation, but the company also wanted long term commitments from their employees.

When 1964 began, Franny hoped with renewed expectations that Dennis might resolve to make contact and perhaps open up a relationship. The absentee father chose to patiently wait on his son's decision. Stirring up a personal or family situation was never a part of Franny's make-up. He prayed about it, but the church's doors remained closed to him. His only visits to Resurrection Parish Church were to pick up Bessie and the boys. Bessie attended church only on special occasions, for her annoyance with the hierarchy festered. "How could the church keep a good man who was willing to marry a widow and raise her two boys from the sacraments and marriage?" she echoed frequently to any would-be listeners.

There were visits to chapels during the afternoon lulls at the business. The formal ties to his church may have been severed, but Franny made short ventures into the solitude of these often vacant, small side chapels and shrines. His conscience was eased and his focus restored by his one-on-one relationship with his God.

Bessie had on-going issues with the results of her traumatic recovery from her childhood cancer which left her with unrelenting pain in her extremities. She had always worked through this, but now Franny noticed her pain brought an increased burden on her physically.

Bessie and her husband took time from the restaurant to do more healing: visits to chapels and to people who made their life more abundant with meaning. They tested newer interests. Travel and part time excursions into other divergent fields became part of their agenda.

A part time job opportunity served as a distraction for Franny. A patron of the eatery, who befriended the couple, had a love of horse racing and the tracks. He convinced Franny to work the betting kiosks at several local racetracks. Freehold in New Jersey and Philadelphia Park in the Northeast were his usual haunts. Along with the job, Franny continued to evolve as an elegant dresser and grew to appreciate the finer trappings of the gentleman. Bessie presented him with a simple and tasteful pinky ring. The gold setting held a three-quarter carat diamond, and he wore it every time he put on a suit. His younger hair style ran vertical, up and down, from his right-sided part. The racetrack version introduced a sweptback combing from front to back above and below the part. Bessie loved that he appeared to have walked straight out of a men's fashion magazine.

Franny had re-evaluated the course of his life. He was willing to rent out the business space and the apartment. The motivation to move back to Bridgeport was prompted by Jimmy O'Brien, Bessie's doctor, and the proximity to their cherished family members. Ralph had hinted at the possibility of working with his company which distributed supplies to various grocery chains. The hours would be better, and Franny would not be on his feet all day behind the counter. The months wore on without any immediate solution, but soon Bessie's condition necessitated a change.

Once the restaurant and the apartment were leased, Franny and Bessie took Georgie out of Father Judge and enrolled him in his senior year in Bishop Kenrick Catholic High School.

Al and Mim's first child, Lisa, was born. Georgie, Bernie, and Fran were all graduating from their respective schools. Georgie was enlisting in the army. Bernie was headed to Brazil in the Peace Corps for two years. Fran and Iris became engaged and set their wedding date for September of 1965. He had some summer credits to take to complete his degree requirements. When Bernie left for Milwaukee, Wisconsin, to train for the work in Brazil, he knew he would probably miss his own twin brother's wedding.

For Bessie and Franny, there were graduation parties, farewell events, bridal showers and countless visits with family and friends. The couple was always a gracious host or a grateful guest.

Ralph and Margaret gave them great support, both emotionally and mentally, for his old Coast Guard friend made every room he entered lighter and happier. To further the dynamic, Gregory McLaughlin, Margaret and Ralph's son, had matriculated at LaSalle College, also a member of the Big Five. Family reunions continued to sparkle with the talk of Philadelphia collegiate sports.

Bill Geppert and Marie added elegance to the mix. The gourmet meals that Marie prepared at the Germantown home magnified their warmth. Marie, at age forty-one, was also expecting her first child. That forthcoming birth moved some of the focus of the family to her. Franny and Bessie foisted much attention on Marie and Bill, and the friendship added to the familial normalcy of their lives.

Franny's visits to his mother were much quieter. One of the twins, all her children, and Tim, of course, were gone from the home. Sometimes she spoke of this with him; but, when Bessie was present, the matriarch was dutifully pleasant and managed to portray an aura of cheerfulness. She was growing to tolerate her daughter-in-law, and a certain comradeship took seed as the mother witnessed Bessie as wife. Mame watched her give joy to her son, and she even complimented Bessie to Margaret. During the daily discussions they had during lunches, Margaret found amusement in her mother's charitable comments about Bessie. The praise did not get voiced directly to Bessie, but a common understanding drew them closer.

Chapter Sixteen

"Comings, Goings, and Births"

The Viet Nam draft numbers were picked in July of 1965. Bernie watched the lotto drawing of the draft birthdays with his Peace Corps trainee companions in Milwaukee at Marquette University. Fran had classes at Villanova to complete his degree and moved his wedding date to November 6, 1965. Albert was married with a one year old daughter, Lisa. Georgie, as a recent high school graduate, faced the numbers while his brother and step-brothers lived under deferments. Bessie worried for him, and the concern added to the burden of her health issues. The high school graduate chose to enlist in the army with options for the type of work he would have in the service. He chose Computer School for his option, and he entered boot camp with his hopes set on continuing schooling in that field.

In mid August, Bernie called home to notify everyone that he had passed the selection process and would return to Norristown for a brief visit before leaving for Brazil.

The Peace Corps Volunteer had begun regular correspondence with Dorothy Madden whom he had met at the Trooper A&P store where he worked. Dottie, family and friends had time to prepare a large send-off party. All the aunts and uncles, Franny and Bessie, Fran and Iris, and neighborhood friends filled the residence with food, stories, and well-wishes.

As a gesture of sincerity to Dottie, Bernie passed his treasured "Little Black Book" to his Villanova friend, John De Marco. The friend promised to put the date book to good use because he intended to live with Mame and Fran until his courses were completed at the university.

Bernie and Dottie found some quiet time together on the front porch, and the uncertainty of the next two years occupied most of the conversation. "I'd like to keep in contact with you, Dottie," he posed to her.

"We can write as much as possible," voiced Dottie with a soft and beguiling tone.

"You shouldn't be tied to me, though, as far as dating goes," he suggested. This young lady meant the world to him, but he realistically could not ask her to wait for him. "You should date other guys. See if you want to keep committed to our relationship."

"That's not something I've thought about, Bernie," she offered with a taste of sadness in her voice.

"I'm going to become part of an entirely different culture, and there's no telling where it will take me. It wouldn't be fair to you if I was going out with Brazilians and you were stuck home for two years."

"So, you want me to date?" she asked. The subject was not a comfortable one for the couple.

"Yes, let's date, and if it is meant to be, we'll be back together again in two years."

"Okay, but you better be ready for my letters because I am going to write to you as often as I can. You'd better answer them, too," she demanded with a coy sensitivity.

Bernie had some cash from his three month service in Milwaukee which he placed in an envelope and gave to Dottie. She was to present it to Fran and Iris on their wedding day.

His father spent a few moments with him and expressed his concern for the young man's safety. Bernie explained the Peace Corps policies, and added that he probably would share a work site with another volunteer. The host country sponsors were checked out and the sites were carefully chosen.

"Well, I envy you in a way because you're headed to a great adventure," assured Franny.

"I'll be fine, Dad. Don't you fret!" He delivered the words with confidence, hoping to allay his father's fears. Bernie and his twin had ceased referring to their father as "White Dad". The title "Dad" rang comfortable to them as young men.

The parting with Fran and Iris filled him with other emotions, for the thought of their up-coming wedding left him feeling alone and empty. The twins felt the conversation rather than spoke it. Words had little importance when the two knew each other so well.

The international flight left from La Guardia Airport in New York City, and an entourage of Dottie and seven family members saw Bernie onto his flight to Rio de Janeiro. They had the opportunity to meet briefly a few of Bernie's fellow volunteers that travelled with him.

His first letters from Brazil arrived at home four weeks later with his new address, his assignment, and the fact that he would be working with two other volunteers. He mentioned in passing in Dottie's letter his "good fortune" to have broken his foot in the surf on Copacabana beach on his first full day in Rio de Janeiro. It was fortuitous for him because it forced him to spend free time with Brazilians in a park in front of his hotel. He improved his Portuguese with all the extra practice. He could put away his cane in four more weeks. The letters to Mame and Dottie were shared with any ready listeners. When Franny received the news from Dottie, he was relieved that Bernie had found something positive from the accident. Dottie had begun her ritual of two to three letters a week to his town: Ipu, Ceara, Brasil.

Fran and Iris's honeymoon to New York City mingled with one of the biggest news stories of the year. In November, the entire northeast corridor suffered a major electrical blackout. The couple found the adventure of living in the dark in a strange environment a worthwhile challenge. Nine months later they would be parents to Fran, their first child. All the news captivated Bernie in his outpost in Brazil. Dottie and other family members kept him updated on all the recent happenings. Plans were in the works to visit him during his second vacation in Brazil. Aunt Marie, Uncle Bill Geppert, Franny and Bessie, and Dottie planned a tourist visit to South America. Later his father and stepmother decided not to make the trip. Bessie health and finances were the main considerations for remaining in the states. Franny continued to work with Ralph Mc Laughlin at the food distribution company. It was a tenuous period with three of the boys scattered around the globe, and uncertainty marked most of the couple's decisions.

When baby Fran was born, the new grandfather began a deep involvement in the lives of his grandchildren. He doted on the child and spoiled his son and Iris. Bessie and he frequented the Norristown apartment on West Airy Street. They made a deliberate effort to immerse themselves in the lives of their families.

Albert, Mim, and Lisa benefited from the same grandparent over-indulgence. Weekends meant travel to either Philadelphia or Norristown to share time with the babies. In the presence of an infant or toddler, the grandfather erupted spontaneously with joy and warmth. His reputation grew as an affectionate holder and a gentle hugger of children. Bessie consumed the babies. Her approach to them beamed with a broad smile as she buried her head in their abdomens, snuggling and caressing them with muffled sounds of delight. Both grandparents reveled in children's messes, their impishness, and their vitality. Franny was prone to offer advice, both directly and sometimes indirectly. Bessie sometimes served as his conduit to either of the young couples. The message was always sprinkled with down-home common sense mixed with a cautious protection of the rights of the littlest family members. The grandparent wished them to be coddled and encouraged and to enjoy life to the fullest. There were times, however, when correction was suggested. Both sets of parents heard his warm and caring quips and sensible directions for learning life's rules.

The young married children led divergent lives and had divergent paths of careers, schools, and residences. Al and Fran rarely socialized together. The babies shared only the vigilant grandparents: they shared the same bedtime stories, the same measured gestures, and the same beneficence of Franny and Bessie. The youthful parents never thought about the connection.

Bernie thrived and grew in Brazil; his struggles with language, illness, and the constant demands on him honed his self-confidence. Georgie found a computer career in Viet Nam. His assignment at control stations buffered the dangers around him. Their father watched the processes from afar, but both young men sensed his faith in them and his respect of them.

With a full commitment to his children's families and the exploits of Georgie and Bernie, the relationship with Dennis took a back seat. Then, he received a surprising phone call from Spotswood, New Jersey.

"Fran, it's me, Florie," echoed through the receiver.

"Yes, I'm here…," replied Franny with an effort to gather his wits about himself. "Ah, you kinda caught me off guard. What's up, Florie?" he ventured.

181

"My brother said I should give you a call," she related with some hesitancy.

"Is everything okay?" rushed from him with unrestrained urgency.

"Oh, yeah, Franny," she comforted. "Dennis enlisted in the Marine Corps and is home from boot camp."

"That's quite a serious decision he made," he shared with pride in his voice.

"We're having a send-off party for him here in Spotswood, and we thought you might like to attend." A sense of relief colored the invitation. She seemed glad to have accomplished her main goal.

"Well, thank you, Florie. That would be nice. I'd love to see him."

She gave him the details of the event and concluded, "We'll see you then?"

"Sure, but it will only be me. Bessie's been a little under the weather. By the way, my youngest stepson is in Viet Nam with an Army computer company." Giving his news to her, Franny felt like he had evened the experiences with her.

"Yeah, I'm not looking forward to this choice that Dennis made." Then, abruptly, she closed, "Bye!"

Francis, the Marine's father, found a parking spot three blocks from Dennis's home. It was obvious that a large contingent of high school friends had arrived much earlier. He swung through the front door unannounced with a group of local well-wishers. Neither the host nor Florie were visible in the crowded front rooms. Music played loudly enough to be heard throughout the house and even into the back yard. Some traffic moved to and from the basement. Others wandered into the kitchen from the back yard. Still Franny had not spotted his son. Awkwardly milling through the guests, Franny sensed the distance that time and circumstance had given to this day. He recognized no one in his son's life. Alone and an outsider, the visit suddenly took on the aspects of a chore. He put the thought aside, but the discomfort lingered. Someone had noticed him as he approached the back door.

"Hello!" bubbled from a young preteen girl who sauntered into his space.

"Hi! And who might you be, Young Lady?" managed Franny with a smile of relief to have someone with whom to speak .

"I'm Colleen. You looking for my Mommy or my brother, Dennis?" she cordially asked.

"Well, yes, I'm looking for both of them," confirmed the visitor.

The lass had no interest, it seemed, in whom the man before her might be, but she was determined to be a good hostess. "I'll take you to Mom, Okay?"

"That would be fine," agreed Franny. "You're being very helpful."

Florie was busy sorting foodstuffs on the array of picnic tables in the yard. Colleen raced ahead of her gentleman companion, pulled at the woman's apron, and turned her into the approaching guest. The exchange was polite, friendly, and difficult for both of them. "What was she to do with Franny with so much to do?" He read the implied concern in her voice, her nervous motions, and her flitting eyes. The hostess was keenly aware of the goings-on at the house, and Franny alleviated most of her concerns.

"Look, Florie, you've got your hands full. Don't worry about me. I'll do my best to mingle." He forced a smile and light laugh into the last phrase.

"Let's find Dennis," she invited. Florie led the father to the son. Dennis was standing among classmates beneath the biggest tree in the yard. He wore jeans, sneakers, and a rock band's tee shirt. The blond hair was Marine Corps cropped, and he possessed a strength and confidence in his demeanor. The pair interrupted laughter and broad smiles. Dennis excused himself from his friends and ushered his father to a quieter corner of the lawn.

"Thanks for coming!" began Dennis. "Mom said she and my uncle invited you."

The father now realized that Dennis had not prompted his uncle or mother to initiate the phone call. "No matter how I got here, I'm very proud of your decision to serve in the Marines, Dennis." Very few common threads of experience were available for a continuing, longer conversation. They touched upon a few topics that focused on careers, expectations, and the things they most cherished, but the words could not hold them together. Sensing a decline in the dialogue, Franny offered, "Looks like you have plenty of people here who want to have some of your time."

Dennis nodded but stood politely awaiting a directive.

"I'll make my way around, meet some people, and maybe we'll get together a little later. Okay?" The words held promise and a sense of renewal, but the over-riding tone was finality.

The Crane children would remember Dennis's father standing along a fence, a wall, or at a table alone, observing the well-wishers that had come to support his son on the first rung of his voyage into adulthood. Dennis made no overt attempt to rejoin his father at the send-off. Francis had little to do with the past, present or future life of his son.

Once in his car, the windshield blurred with moisture as Franny headed west. A handkerchief, not the windshield wipers, helped to clear his vision enough to traverse the New Jersey and Pennsylvania countrysides.

***

Beth Pastino was born in 1966, another wonderful granddaughter to cherish and bedazzle. Her father was still with Haskins & Sells, and Mim appreciated being a stay-at-home mother.

Fran worked on a Masters in Social Work at the University of Pennsylvania and accepted a post at St. Gabriel's Hall in Phoenixville, Pennsylvania. His case work duties kept the family in the Norristown area.

With Franny and Bessie living in Bridgeport, many family ties tightened. His brother Larry and his wife Helen shared more and more time with the Mc Laughlins and the Gepperts. Larry had left the bus line for health reasons after an episode with a collapsed lung. He now worked as an electrician, which afforded him free time on weekends and holidays. New Year's Day at Larry's became the subject of folk lore and tradition. Now an electrician, and rarely a cook, Larry hosted a feast on New Year's Day. The uniqueness of the event focused on his preparing the entire meal. The sauerkraut and "pigs-in-the-blanket" drew his adult peers, family members, and some of the children into his culinary world. The magic lasted only this one day each year, and Franny and Bessie savored every moment of the camaraderie. Franny seemed to relish the simplicity of the arrangement; for serious conversations never materialized. Bessie and Mame shared very little kitchen time together, for Larry shoed them from his domain. The children had permission to serve the adults and attend to napkins, beverages, and the like. Fran and Iris garnered an invitation and were honored to be numbered among the privileged attendees.

Al and Mim were overlooked on the haphazard invitation list. The oversight to Bessie tasted like a salad dressing where one of the condiments, oil or vinegar, is forgotten. It was not a deliberate act on anyone's part, and the situation was tolerated by

Bessie. Explanations were not expected or offered, and the issue buried its head in the sand.

The New Year's festivities with family and the required attendance at church prompted the rising of two old scars: the relationship with Dennis and the issue of re-entering the church. One resolution focused on the on-going search for a parish or priest that might alleviate Franny's excommunication for marrying Bessie. Concerning the second decision about Dennis, Franny resolved to await a message from his son rather than impose himself on the young man. None came.

Each Lent or Advent, Franny continued to seek chapels for prayer. Earlier, the Catholic Church refused to consider an annulment from his second marriage. Those months of waiting had given him no reward, and his spiritual condition remained the same. Physically, he did not want this to break or defeat him. The children and grandchildren buoyed him and prevented the pain from depressing him, but he sorely wished for closure and comfort. Mame continued praying a novena for the return of her son to the church.

Franny and Bessie found the Shrine of St. Jude, "The Patron Saint of Impossible Causes." It was located in Chalfont, just south of Doylestown on route 202. The pair found themselves visiting the chapel on quiet afternoons when the silence of their apartment spoke to them in somber thoughts.

Work at the grocery stores brought stability, and he still traveled to the tracks when he felt up to the extra hours. Ralph Mc Laughlin and he had their own districts and visited the Acmes, A&P's, and privately owned stores in their areas. The regular hours meant more time with the growing families.

Al and Mim had their third daughter Gina in 1967. Bernie had returned from Brazil in August, began dating Dorothy again, and was preparing to teach with his twin brother at St. Gabriel's

Hall. Villanova University had accepted him for a Master of Arts program in English. His busy itinerary kept him from participating in many of the weekend gatherings. Georgie had another year in the service, but his safety and his future traveled an optimistic course. The twin, Fran Blanche, had mutated into Frank Blanche at St. Gabriel's Hall. The new moniker suited his role as a caseworker. It took months for Bernie to adjust to the new title for his twin, and some of the aunts and uncles refused to use the "Frank" alias. The issue ruffled his self-image at times, but the newer "nom de guerre" fit his practice with the sound of authority. Frank needed a strong first impression and a lasting vote of confidence from his clients, adults and juveniles.

Bernie asked Dorothy to marry him on her twenty-first birthday, November 17, 1967. The preparations for their June wedding mingled with the excitement of Al and Mim setting up house in New Jersey. There was a sense of letting go of the adult sons and taking in of two married couples. The transition was remarkably easy.

Through all of the family decisions and changes, Franny emerged as a sage. His passionless directions had clear value, for they grew from his fair and just view of his own circumstances. The earlier detachment that dominated his actions eroded under the warmth and openness of his present marriage. Bessie brought gifts of commitment, family history, and a sense of obligation to the table, and Franny learned by her example. He had never been happier.

Al took a position with a new company, Deloitte, in late 1968. It had an office in San Juan, Puerto Rico, and his boss advised him to transfer there. The move signified a personal commitment to the company and the beginning of a long term relationship with promotions and bonuses attached. The entire family, as company policy dictated, generally travelled with the employee, set up residence, and stayed for a two or three year period. The Pastinos had concerns about taking three toddlers to San Juan.

The weekend that Albert was asked to take the position, he arranged to have Bessie and Franny for a late night dinner. After Mim put the girls to bed, they sat with Franny and sought his guidance about the move.

"I'm not sure that I want the girls in Puerto Rico," aired the young father of three.

"Why not?" voiced Franny with a nonchalance that contradicted the seriousness of the topic.

"Well, they're so young. The diet and housing will be so different," he attempted as a response.

Bessie nodded affirmation and Franny pivoted his head side to side in denial. "Kids are resilient, Al. Besides this will be a great learning experience for them…and for you." He took a sip of the dry martini that Mim had placed in front of him. Bessie sipped an Italian red from a wide mouthed stemware glass.

"Traveling with three little ones, new summer wardrobes, a foreign language, finding a place to live… It's a lot on top of all my other odds and ends, Frank." summed Albert.

"First of all, Al and Mim, your company does this kind of thing all the time. They'll take care of those nagging little arrangements for you. Secondly, what're the 'other odds and ends'?" He glanced at Bessie who dutifully gave him the lead. It was not in her nature to interrupt these conversations. Bessie usually waited until they were home to air her thoughts on issues so serious and business related.

Al's beer was untouched on the table in front of him. "Mom's gonna miss the girls so much. Georgie's away. You know I feel I should be here," he stammered.

Before he spoke, Franny turned and faced Bessie. He wished to present a united front to Al. Bessie's consent to continue was a shrug and a mild grimace. "You, George, and Mom have always been together; but, now, George is on the other side of the world. Mom and I are getting used to these changes. It's your turn, Al. We aren't about to hold you back." Franny spoke the summary with a heartfelt wisdom.

"You think we should do this?" appraised Al.

"You've got to do it. It will change your life," he voiced to both Al and Mim.

Al held to his concerns, "But, Frank, there are still too many loose ends here at home."

"I'll take care of your mother," assured Franny who sensed that the "loose ends" were Bessie and Georgie. "Besides, George is his own man now, Al."

"Are you okay with this, Mom," Al questioned his mother.

Her teary eyes seemed to contradict the concession of her nod. "Sure, Al," forced itself into the open air.

Albert remembered that Frank had once told him, "I'll always be there for you," and the young business man and father of three placed his faith in that decision.

Chapter Seventeen

"Home, Home, and Away!"

The weddings of Frank, Al, and finally Bernie in June commenced a litany of many wonderful and new experiences. Franny shared them jovially with Bernie, Frank, Al, and his siblings. The celebrations brought contentment and pleasure into life. Images of Bessie and him radiated with his broad, unrestrained smile. Loud laughter burst into conversations after meals with his adult children and their families. Finally, the twins learned that their father loved Italian food, especially spaghetti with clams in white sauce, dry gin martinis, crab cakes, the Mets baseball team, golf, and travel. New York City still topped his list. He and Bessie never turned down a dinner invitation to any of his sisters, brother, or boys' homes.

They discovered that he played pool with a passionate stroke and a flair for the classic. Once he pulled off a perfect masse shot in a game of eight ball with Bernie in the Goodwill Firehouse hall. The lefty could deftly produce a carom shot off any side rail or ball. No one ever learned if the Coast Guard, the pickle business, or the bus lines had been the site of his pool hall experiences. Mame and Tim never had a pool table in any of their homes. The skill at billiards fell onto the list of mysteries associated with the private life of Francis J. Blanche.

Franny continued to spoil the grandchildren, to elate their parents with his sheer joy of being with them, and finally to create a family despite the distance that had earlier separated them.

Three personal crosses pushed him to find solace in the church. Firstly, the lingering void left by Dennis gnawed at him with the guilt of his youthful decisions, but still he left the next move to his son. It would be Dennis's choice. Secondly, Bessie and he agonized over Gina's on-going need for surgeries. The spirited, optimistic child took on her illness with a warm heart and playful attitude. Her demeanor drew everyone to her side. Bessie had the privilege,when she wished, of attending mass, receiving communion, and praying with a congregation. Franny, without dispensation or annulment, searched for the child's healing through quiet, personal prayer. Lastly, Bessie's health had deteriorated during the luncheonette years. The excitement of the recent plethora of marriages, the boy's careers, and grandchildren expended much of her energy. The cancelled trip to Brazil to visit Bernie was the couple's only act of submission to her disease. Franny did, however, let the subjects enter into his prayers. The triumvirate in his lonely moments became Dennis, Gina, and Bessie.

Bessie had taken a chef position at the Norristown Sate Hospital and her lunch and dinner preparations there kept her from home until early evening. When Franny finished early in the afternoon, he found time to rummage through local open churches seeking respite from his three pronged nightmare. After some earlier reluctance to visit Mount Carmel Church in Bridgeport, he ventured into its quiet sanctuary. After a particular visit, he also discovered the social club and bar on the premises. Sometimes both prayer and martinis filled the time waiting to meet Bessie after work. St. Jude, Patron of Impossible Causes, remained on his list. Franny did not mind the drive to the shrine in Chalfont, for he could clear his secular concerns en route before he challenged the spiritual. He had numerous locations across the breath of his distribution area. Sometimes the martini came from the bartender at Goodwill Fire Station, where he would meet Larry after his shift. Larry only drank beer; Franny always drank Beefeaters Gin. The give-and-take of martinis and meditation or of Bessie and his boys blended into a palatable recipe that fed his moods.

In mid September of 1968, Franny received an unexpected phone call. He had just returned home from Our Lady of Mount Carmel, had showered, and had picked up his keys to drive to Norristown to bring Bessie home after her shift. The ring stopped him at the front door. He ignored it for a moment; but, with a check of his watch, he realized that he had a few minutes to spare. The phone was in hand by the third ring.

"Hello! This is Franny." He waited for a familiar voice to greet his answer. The dead silence unnerved him, but he waited a few seconds before adding, "I'm on my way out the door, so what's up?"

"Ah..." broke through the receiver. "Franny, this Florie." The words crackled through the receiver with a nervous uncertainty. The softness of her voice belied any calculated precision.

Franny looked to the ceiling with questioning brows. "Huh!" he managed. A short staccato of phrases and utterances followed which betrayed Franny's shock and confusion. "Ah...how, I mean, why? I'm a...," he mumbled. Then with a better footing he refocused, "You caught me by surprise, Florie."

"I figured this call would come out of the blue, Franny," she apologized with more resolve in her delivery.

Franny sensed that some serious reason necessitated the call. With some enlightenment edging into his mind, he managed, "Is everything okay?"

"I've tried to get my brother to make this call, but I just didn't think it right to put this on his shoulders." The voice took on a semblance of quiet concern mixed with regret. The comment salted her tone with a hint of sorrow.

"I have no idea where this is going, Florie, but I figure it's not pleasant," posited Franny with a heaviness that sank deeply into his being.

"In July this year," she began, "we got a call from one of Dennis's Marine Corps buddies."

"Yes, the Marine Corps." He slipped his words over her narrative.

Florie did not react to his reflection. "He wanted to know how Dennis was comin' along after his injury."

"What injury?" Franny let free the frantic thought which scurried through his mind. "Florie, I haven't heard from Dennis since his going-away party." The possibility that Florie might want information about Dennis led Franny along a completely different track.

"No, Franny, I know he hasn't written to you. But let me get through this. Okay?"

"Sure, Florie, go ahead," conceded Franny who now took a seat, placed the keys on the phone table, and unbuttoned his jacket.

"I know you're in the dark about all of this, Franny." She now realized that Franny had been misled. The sound of her deep breath followed. "Well, I knew nothing about what the young caller had said. Apparently, there had been an incident at a forward scouting post, and Dennis's squad had suffered some injuries and fatalities." Florence Crane read from her memory of that phone call. The factual data came through the wires as reportage.

"I figured Dennis was deployed to Viet Nam," contributed Franny; and, then as an innocent second thought, he added, "my step-son, George is over there too."

Florie heard none of the father's words running through her receiver. She plowed onward. "We called the Marine Corps to obtain some information because we hadn't heard from Dennis in a while. They promised to get back to us within the week." She stopped her narrative. The silence on the other end conveyed the woman's discomfort.

The abrupt cessation of the narration prompted Franny to intervene. "So…, Dennis is alright?" Franny waited politely several seconds for Florie to come back to the conversation. Then, he posed, "What did the Marines tell you?"

"They never called us back, but two weeks later we received a letter from Dennis's commander. This is so hard…" At this point, she only wished to share the details and not the anguish of her last few months.

The hints and subtleties were gone. Franny surmised the worst, "Oh my God! What happened?"

"The letter didn't tell us that Dennis had died." Tears were in her voice. "It notified us that his body…" she paused with a gasp of freshly sensed agony. Each subsequent word struggled for life through the strength that she possessed, "It… Dennis was already in New Jersey awaiting the family to claim his remains." The mother's words ceased, but the inner pain echoed through the phone lines in woeful spasms.

"No! No, no!" plead the father from his sitting room. Alone with his stifled tears, his soul sought comfort from words that human language cannot speak. The finality ripped his inner being.

"We buried Dennis in August in the local cemetery. I'm so sorry, Franny, I could not make this call to you then. I so wanted to call you sooner, but I wasn't thinking." She caught her breath and forged ahead with the details.

"I understand," he offered with a hint of forgiveness, tempered by his emotional exhaustion.

"Everything had already been done without our knowledge. The delays from the Corps were caused by their investigation into his death. Franny, they initially thought he died under friendly fire. But witnesses finally told how he was carrying a wounded buddy to a helicopter when he was shot by the Viet Cong. It's such a terrible thing! Terrible! We only had to lay him to rest."

"God,"sifted into the phone, and a half beat later, "What… Where can I…"? The questions were left unfinished, for the father sensed that no information could fill the void within him.

"I know you made an attempt to re-enter his life. He was a great kid. Everything you'd ever want in a son." The couple shared muffled breaths, riddled with paroxysms of pain and anguish. The two, now almost strangers, made vain attempts to comfort each other from the privacy of their own homes. At the close of the conversation, only the duties awaiting Francis moved him beyond his front door in Bridgeport. He had to pick up his wife at work.

Later, back home, the sunny fall weather mocked the turmoil of the day's events. Bessie was distraught, angry, but sage enough to leave Franny to quiet time on the front porch. When Al arrived early that evening with his family for a quick visit, he read his step-father's demeanor from afar. The smile of joy in anticipation of shared family time faded from his face like a message in the tidal sand. His step father sat on the porch hunched over with fisted hands jammed between his folded legs. Liquid furrows ran down his cheeks; eyes scanned the painted wooden floor. The portrait of Frank did not resemble the face of his mentor. The figure before him was alien, a person that Albert had never seen. Franny did not burden the young father with his onerous news; but, rather, he waved the father and his family into the house. Honoring his silent remorse, the parents ushered the children to Bessie who related the details.

Albert Pastino left that night with a goodly dose of added respect. As he took his somber leave from Frank, a man he already held in high regard, Albert felt the inner strength of the man. He also recognized the depth of his pain.

That weekend, Bessie and Franny made a respectful visit to the local cemetery in Spotswood, New Jersey. The tombstone read the following:

Dennis Crane
Corporal, United States Marine Corps
F BTRY, 2ND BN, 11TH Marines, 1ST MARDIV
b. September 20, 1947
d. June 15, 1968

The twins learned of the tragic event from Mame. Franny never approached them with his sorrow. Their father's entire emotional life remained personal to him. So, it remained that no one breached his solitude or discussed the events with him. Mame relinquished bits and pieces of Franny's history to them, but it was never an open book. To a fault, she had bared the twins' lives to everyone except them. No one detailed their past to them. Their father, who now participated in their adult lives, still held a firm line against any incursion by them into his. Somehow he felt his silence offered protection to them. They need not incur the wrath of the gods or of the furies that had bedeviled him.

Francis J. Blanche spent this time of mourning awaiting the arrival of some joy in his life. A shadow,however, began to stretch itself into his days. A winter cold turned into a nagging cough which persisted long enough to give him chest pain. Bessie's nephew and her doctor, Jimmy O'Brien, had his office nearby.Franny took a day off to see him in Norristown. He had waited until after the holidays. The New Year might be kinder to him. Bessie came along although Franny urged her to stay home and rest. She insisted, and that was enough to put her in the passenger's seat on the trip to Doctor Jimmy. Bessie had good and bad days filled with wrenching pain or given to milder spasms calmed by heavy medication.

The youthful physician noted that Franny had lost some weight since the holidays, went through the regular check up procedures, and sat with the couple for his evaluation.

"Well, you definitely have some fluid in your left lung, Franny," related the young physician in a matter-of-fact delivery.

"Jimmy, what's that mean?" shot Bessie with some concerned reaction.

"Probably nothing because I didn't pick up a fever," assured the doctor to his Aunt Bessie. "It could be a touch of pneumonia, so I'd like you to get an x-ray today before you go back to Bridgeport."

"Sure, we have time for that. Are you going to give me a prescription?" questioned Franny with a little uncertainty about his diagnosis.

"No, Franny, I'd like to wait on the results of the x-ray. I can call something in for you afterwards." The doctor visit then turned to a reunion of rumor, gossip, and recent information on the children and adults in the family. Jimmy had more news on the younger crowd, and Bessie contributed the tidbits about the aunts, uncles, and grandparents.

After a brief stop at the Friendship Grill to see Bessie's mother, the couple headed home. Almost two hours had passed since they left Dr. O'Brien's office, but neither one expected to hear from the physician until the morning. Franny parked the car as Bessie made her way inside. He heard her greet Georgie. Hearing the young man's deep voice, he knew it must be near dinner time. When Franny entered the door, the computer businessman had the television tuned to the evening news.

"Hey, Dad, Uncle Jimmy called," blurted the young man with a slight Philly accent that he had absorbed over his years in the Northeast. "He wants you to give him a call."

"It's late. I'll reach him tomorrow. Thanks, Georgie." Franny busied himself depositing his keys in the usual counter spot and putting his jacket in the hall closet. Georgie interrupted his routine before he went into the kitchen to mix his martini.

"No, Dad. Uncle Jimmy said to call him tonight – even if it's late. He'll wait up for your call."

"I guess he wants to get me my medication right away," mumbled the patient to himself with Georgie privy to the thought.

Franny dialed the young doctor at his home. Bessie scurried about the kitchen putting a quick meal together. Georgie had announced he had a movie date, but wanted to eat before he left. Franny intended to make the conversation as short as possible. He was tired and knew that the alarm would not be welcomed tomorrow morning.

"Hello? This is Jimmy." His family would have tormented him if he used "Doctor O'Brien" as a greeting over the home phone.

"Yeah, Jimmy, it's Franny. I got your message from Georgie," he spoke his introduction quickly.

"Glad you got back to me, Franny," issued from the speaker.

"What's up? You have some medicine for me to pick up?"

"Actually," there was a pause, ever so slight, "no, I wanted to bring you back up here for another test," relayed the physician.

Franny sensed that the relative on the line had now become the professional. "What test? How come, Jimmy?" The words stumbled from his thoughts. He felt well enough in his own mind not to need another examination.

"The x-ray showed some fluid, but there was also a blemish, a dark spot, just outside your lung. It's located in the lining of your left lung." He waited, but his words were met with silence. So he continued, "Franny, I'd like to do a biopsy on that tissue."

"Can't we just treat this with some medication? I mean I don't feel all that bad," defended the patient.

"You are a smoker. You have no bacterial infection. And I don't believe this is viral in nature. I need more information, Franny, and that's my next logical step." His words were definitive, calm and certain.

Two days later the biopsy was performed at Sacred Heart Hospital in Norristown. Bessie displayed agitation with the people she encountered that day but managed a cooler demeanor during light conversation. The subject of her spouse's health pulled her into ponderings on her medical history and the loss of her first husband. Worry and concern for Franny and the boys made her withdrawn.

The tissue sample had to be sent out to a laboratory, so the patient and his wife returned to their home to await the results of the test. Franny told Bessie that he did not want to share any of this with the boys or either of the families. Bessie agreed because, as Franny put it, "This is probably nothing to worry about. Why get everyone upset?"

The pair was back in Norristown on the following Monday to see Jimmy with the results. They sat in comfortable leather chairs in Jimmy's warmly furnished upscale office. He stood and approached Franny who remained seated.

"There's no easy way to tell someone this, Franny," a right hand moved softly onto Franny's right shoulder, "but the biopsy showed that you have a spot of cancer on that lung." Being a heavy smoker, the concern was real, but the villain became asbestos, inhaled doing brake work on the pickle trucks in New Jersey or during his service with the Coast Guard.

Bessie's gasp was the first audible signal of concern from the couple. Franny had simply looked up toward his doctor and shared a glance that read, "I had that feeling!"

Jimmy knew he was dealing with a realist, and Franny could be treated with more openness than a stranger who might have come to him. The plan was outlined: surgery to remove the area of the cancer, an injection of mustard-based chemo-therapy, medications, and radiation treatment. The steps would be taken and on-going evaluations would alter the plan as necessary. Now, the situation forced them to tell the boys.

By 1969, Al learned that the company did have an existing residence rented for Mim and the family. Al took the initial trip on his own. Later with Mim, the couple planned to purchase the necessary wares for the children and set up service help for Mim.

The young businessman found himself sitting in a strange hotel in a new environment preparing for his first true work for Deloitte. The ring of the phone did not startle him, for he suspected that his mother or Mim would be keeping in touch with him. It was his mother who greeted him.

"Hi, Mom! I figured you'd check up on me. How's everything?" uttered Al with his usual nasalized light air.

"Well, I know you're busy, so I won't keep you too long," began Bessie with a hint of nervousness in her offering. "You know Dad had some tests done with Jimmy. Right?"

She quizzed.

"Yeah, I know. Why?" he ventured with added concern.

"The rest of the boys know, and I didn't want them telling you about it." The slow, soft calm in her voice held him at bay. "Jimmy says Dad has lung cancer, Al. But he's going to get the best treatment." The strength with which she began the phone call left her. A sob broke the short silence.

"Oh my God!" he pled in prayer and shock. The dutiful son switched his concern, "Mom, you gonna be okay?"

"Sure. You know me – tough old Italian lady," she attempted to lighten the news. "Dad feels pretty good, but he'll be having a lot of procedures over the next few weeks. Keep him in your prayers. Okay?"

"Sure, Mom." Then, as a side thought, he managed, "This is a lot to take in. I'm on my way out of the hotel to meet with clients."

"Dad and I are sorry to give you this news on your first day down there, but we wanted to be sure no one else told you first." The apology had not to be spoken, for Al understood her dilemma.

"It's fine. Don't worry. You two take care of yourselves." He rushed the sentences into the speaker. A glance at his watch precipitated, "I'll call you later tonight for the details. Okay?"

"Yes, you'll do great today, I know," she felt his urgency. "Bye, Al. We love you!"

When the receiver clicked in his ear, he took on solitude. Sitting on the hotel bed, he wrestled with the many stimuli begging for his time. He sorted and filed them, preparing himself for his first day of work in San Juan. A second, invisible, briefcase went with him that day. Although it remained unopened until that evening, its contents occupied his quiet and restful moments.

Into the first month of treatment following surgery, Franny's physical endurance suffered. The couple began to discuss the possibility of selling, instead of renting, the business and the apartment if the treatments continued to drain his energy. The healing process swept through a wider path, however, for the rehabilitation provided additional time with the boys and their families.

When the Albert Pastino family's flights to San Juan were actually planned, Al initiated a family custom. He decided to travel with two of the girls while Mim scheduled the next possible flight with the remaining child. Gina usually flew with her mother, and they were met at the airport by the already deplaned part of the family. The rationale for this unusual tradition came from Al and Mim's infrequent travels. The fear of an air disaster that would decimate the entire family weighed heavily upon him. The company had no problem supporting this request as his success in the field painted him as a valued employee.

The Pastinos had initial concerns over the language barrier that they faced. The children led the way, picking up the necessary skills and giving added confidence to the parents. Spanish had to be earned the hard way – practice on the go.

Franny and Bessie never hesitated when asked to visit the relocated family. They rested and healed in the southern island climate, and the energy of the three little ones was captivating. Franny loved Porto Rico.

Some physical concerns about Gina, the youngest girl, brought caution into the situation. She began to necessitate frequent trips to specialists in the states. When she and her father or mother returned for a doctor's appointment, they stayed in Bridgeport or with Mim's family, the Mc Nallys.

Throughout 1969, the father's illness had acted as a catalyst to the relationship of the two sets of step-brothers. With George home from the service and into stable employment, he found himself in a wonderful relationship. When he decided to get engaged to Shirley Lukens, he summoned the three brothers. He chose a weekend when Albert was in town. The youngest of the group invited the trio to "Jewelry Row" in Philadelphia along North Fifth Street. He figured the three older siblings had already done the groundwork and could provide invaluable advice regarding "The Ring". George drove and knew his way around the city. It was a windy day with enough chilliness in the air to prompt a shopper to stay indoors a little while. It became evident in the first jewelry store that three different minds were at work on the type, size, cost, and flawlessness of the diamond-to-be.

"I like the traditional rounded shape," offered Bernie as he overlooked the tray of white diamonds on the tray before the four lads.

"George, you need a statement piece," advised Frank before adding, "you know, something pear shaped or oval." He nodded his head in approval of his own suggestion.

"Come on you guys," interrupted Al, "George, you can't go spending too much money on fancy."

"Great!" resolved George, "We're going to be here on this street all day." George had no knowledge of what Bernie and Frank had done when they purchased their fiancés' rings, but he knew Albert had married under near-poverty conditions. "Al, you probably want me to look at a pin head sized stone placed in a narrow, fourteen carat setting. Right?"

"Well, that makes sense, George. You're just getting started and you've got no capital…"

"Listen to you, the bank president," snipped George, knowing that he had figured Al's tastes perfectly. The unknown quotient was the sentiment of the twins. "So, Frank, what d'ya get for Iris?"

"She's a farm girl with simpler taste, but I went around a carat, traditional. She seems to like it," bemused the taller of the twins showing his satisfaction in the memory that he had just evoked.

Bernie did not await an invitation to offer his appraisal of any purchase. "George, stick to perfect. You can't go wrong with a perfect stone. That's my take on it." He spoke as he perused the stones before them. "When I bought Dottie's diamond, I went with cousin Greg to one of his in-law's places in Bridgeport. After he showed me the perfect ones, I couldn't consider a flawed stone. Now, the one I got was smaller, but it is absolutely perfect." The tone of his voice echoed his pleasure in making that choice a few years ago.

"Let's shop around a little bit...- to, kinda, let this settle in my head," reflected George. So they were off to several establishments. It became evident after the third shop that George had begun to refine his selection. At first, the process pitted "As fancy as possible with the least amount of flaws" up against "Small and perfect" or "Huge and imperfect." The final outcome landed Shirley a fairly large, barely flawed, non-traditional shaped beauty. The four young men left pleased with Shirley Lukens' engagement ring.

***

Uncle Bill Geppert had been born into a Philadelphian family with deep ties to sports' teams. His father's demolition company, Geppert Brothers, had dismantled numerous venues including Connie Mack Stadium at Twenty-second and Allegheny. He developed from his childhood a loyalty to local teams. Athletic in his youth, World War II had left him crippled, but the fire of competition still invigorated him. Both Bill and Marie enjoyed the friendly sports' banter that took place at meals and family parties with Bessie and Franny. This rivalry intensified because Franny supported many New York athletic teams. The 1969 New York Mets won the division and were headed to the World Series. The only rabid Mets fan that Bill knew was his own brother-in-law.

The Francis Blanches relished the bragging rights that the playoffs gave them with the siblings. Franny anticipated each televised game with the avid enthusiasm of a teenage fan. Bill had teased Franny with false information that there was a possibility that games would be "Blacked Out." After all, Philadelphia was within ninety miles of the game site. Since the Philadelphia Phillies were not participating, it was a moot point; but Bill insisted on tormenting his brother-in-law with the rumor.

When the certainty of a final seventh game arose, Franny invited the Gepperts, the Mc Laughlins, and Larry and Helen to his place to enjoy the assured victory. Disappointment rippled through his veins as each one turned down the offer to watch the game with him. Bill was the last one to undermine the festivities.

"Why can't you make it, Bill? You and Marie don't have anything planned, do you?" he cajoled.

"Well, actually, yes, I do have plans. I'm going to be out of town. Sorry."

"You and the rest must be poor sports. I've put up with all of your Phillie's hoopla, and you won't sit through this game with me. Wow! Some friends!" Anger was absent from his tone, but Bill knew the disappointment that prompted his words.

"Well, I hear that *you're* going to be out of town, too," prodded Bill as he fingered his moustache, pondering his next move.

"What do you mean, Bill?" he flung back with some impatience. "I'm not goin' anywhere during the final game." Finality marked his words like the orders from a five star general.

"That's a shame because I checked with Bessie and the rest of the group and none of them want to go either." He rocked slightly on his easy chair pleased that the prey had taken the bait.

"Go? Go where? Hey, Bill, what are you driving at?" Uncertainty riveted itself to the questions.

"A buddy of mine in the demolition business in New York wanted to know if I'd want two tickets to game seven." Bill only heard breathing through the earphone, so he continued, "Yeah, I don't want to drive up there by myself, so I guess I'll turn the tickets back."

"Tickets! Bill, you have game seven tickets?" Franny could not restrain himself. "I know my way around there like I wrote the map. Bill, don't you dare give those tickets up!" Somewhere in the middle of his last demand to Bill, he realized the joke being played on him.

"Franny, you'd better go because I just spent the better part of my day calling all of your invited guests to tell them to turn you down." His laughter formed into a prankish giggle as he awaited Franny's response.

"Man, we are going to have one great time! This is just super, Bill. Thank you! Thank you for thinking of me." He was turning forty-nine and this would be his first World Series game. Nothing could be better.

The "Miracle Mets" made it even better by winning the game amid a crowd of fanatical, disbelieving patrons. The hoards could be seen laying siege to the playing surface after the final out. The police had long ago lost control of the ecstasy of the supporters. The television showed the extent of the revelry. Mobs of people pillaged the playing field stealing bases, home plate, the pitcher's rubber and any possible souvenir that they could grasp and run away with.

Franny's sons had watched the game within their respective homes, and each felt a true sense of Franny's elation. Calculating the time of Bill and Franny's return to Germantown, the step-sons and twins called to ascertain the details of the day. Each received the same message related to them by Franny and then repeated by Bill as confirmation.

Franny's report ran like ticker-tape through the phone. "We ran down onto the field with the whole mob. It was pandemonium down there. I looked over at Bill and we were both watching everybody grabbing stuff. So I asked him, 'Bill, you need any sod down there in Germantown?' And he says, 'Yeah, I have a few bare spots.' Well, then we both get on our knees and yanked up a good two square feet of Shea Stadium sod. Bill had a square foot of it stuffed in his jacket, and mine was jammed into an empty peanut bag. We took off lookin' over our shoulders to see if the cops were after us. Bill's not too quick with his war injury, but he impressed me with how fast we got out of there."

Everyone wished to know where the turf ended up. Bill related that the ceremony had already taken place. He proudly stated, "The two foot square of 'Amazing Mets' memorabilia was place right off of the front step, and it's been watered and protected by a vast network of sturdy fencing." Laughter filled the pause. "Franny put up some poles and ropes after he had his second martini, so I'm sure it's a permanent fixture in my yard," he said with obvious sarcasm.

The sea has its troughs and valleys. Dennis' loss weighed heavily on Franny, but he found distractions in the families, in Bessie, and with his four boys. The couple visited and dined with the children, with the in-laws, or with his siblings on frequent occasions. This was a deliberate plot on Bessie's part: to keep Franny as involved in good emotional experiences as possible.

She became his shield, his emissary, and his buffer. She held her own with Mame and worked at her relationships with the twins. All of this commitment began to increase the level of her stress. She had more physical pain from the nerve damage of her childhood radiation. Her emotional concern for Gina escalated. Bessie took on the persona of a woman fixated on her husband, her two sons, and the grandchildren. Conversations began with give and take, but quickly turned to issues she needed to air.

A call from Bernie or Frank to share their most recent news of children or trivia eased into an update of Al and George's lives. The twins fought the temptation to feel that her mannerisms ignored their families, but each recognized her monopoly of the conversations as the pride of a mother. She always spoke her mind, and people knew exactly what mattered most to her. Bessie projected a confidence, an inner worth, and strength, though her body was frail and pained. Franny rarely saw any inner weakness in her armor, but her physical needs always concerned him.

Then there was Franny and his penchant for emotional privacy: still no cathartic conversation with the twins about his history with them; still no confrontations with Mame over her obstinate choices; and still no reconciliation with his church.

The myriad vignettes in life continued with stop-ins, visits, and Italian cooking. Days passed with crossword puzzles done in pen, telephone calls, chapel visits, martinis, and sports on the television. Franny blamed his run-down malaise on the social schedule that he and Bessie were keeping, but the fear that his body held a secret from him rested in the back of his mind.

Chapter Eighteen

"Father Peter Krebs, Shepherd in New Jersey."

George's preoccupation with his pending marriage made him the most frequent visitor. Albert had become mired in his necessary move from Philadelphia to New Providence, New Jersey. He decided to take another position at Deloitte and to return to the States. This enabled the family to better address the issues with Gina's surgeries. Beth and Lisa were fine.

Frank B. Blanche focused on completing his Master's in Social Work at the University of Pennsylvania and raising Fran and Camille. His visits occurred on a spontaneous basis. Bernie found himself entrenched in teaching the court adjudicated youth at St. Gabriels while taking his Master's of Arts classes at Villanova University. He and Dottie lived in an apartment off Arch Street in Norristown, adjacent to Bishop Kenrick High School.

One particular Saturday morning, Albert and Mim scheduled a tour of northern New Jersey on a house hunting mission. They drove to Bridgeport first for a courtesy visit. When the family arrived, the girls and Mim greeted Franny in the living room with all the pomp and circumstance due a king in his castle, but Mim soon prodded them into the kitchen to see Grandmother. They may have been lured by the aroma of her "gravy", the red sauce, simmering on the stove top. After embraces, Mim immediately expressed her concern that Franny looked tired. Bessie waved off her concerns with the spoon, like a wand in her right hand.

Albert strolled through the front door after parking the car. "I hope the girls behaved themselves," he greeted.

"They are always polite and wonderful young ladies," replied Franny, putting aside his puzzle book. It was lunchtime, but Franny still had an early morning edge to his voice. "Mim has set good example for them."

"Well, that's who I meant when I said, 'Girls,'" retorted Al. "Mim's the ringleader of misbehavior!" He approached Franny in his lounge chair and placed a firm left hand on Franny's right shoulder. "So, how are you doing, Frank?"

"Aaah, '*mens a mens*'!" Frank liked to throw in an occasional bit of Bessie's Italian.

"Well, you look a little worn out. Did ya' stay up late last night?" inquired Al.

"Actually, I went to bed early, thank you." Franny attempted to alleviate Al's concerns with some mild sarcasm.

"Seriously, Frank! You all right?" The young man bowed toward his step-father seated before him.

The seated man looked up with heavy eyes and shook his head from side to side. Submission masked his face; fatigue haunted his actions.

"Wanna' talk about it?" He took a seat next to Frank. Noises of glee and cheer fluttered into the living room from the kitchen.

"Bessie doesn't know, but I saw Jimmy yesterday." The speaker checked the face of his listener to read its interpretation of his message before he continued. Al waited during the pause. "Al, this time is it. It feels different."

Albert had met Jesuit priests through his association with St. Joseph's University; but, in New Providence, Father Peter Krebs, a Trinitarian, shepherded himself into their lives. His youth gave him a dynamic energy, and the spiritual life he led prompted him to a more liberal bent regarding church affectations. The rites and sacraments were followed as per dogma, but the service to his flock at the shrine of St. Joseph in Sterling, New Jersey, took on a more humane and merciful aspect. The lay persons appreciated his manner so much so that they took him into their lives as family. Albert and Father Pete, as he became affectionately known, liked each other from the first meeting. The young man sought every opportunity to bring Frank and the priest together.

George and Shirley were married on May 30, 1970. All the boys and their families gathered to celebrate his step into adulthood as a wedded man. As the youngest son, George set a new optimistic course for Bessie and Franny, for his wedding also ended their concern and doubt as to his future choices. The mother and step-father would always be parents, especially to George who had spent more time with Franny as a son than any of the other boys. One outcome of the event for the boys was their celebration of Franny in their lives. Each young man viewed his relationship with Franny differently: to Albert he was Frank; to Bernie he was a father; to Fran he was an enigma; but to George he was Dad.

When the Chemotherapy began, hope spread its wing far into the family. Everyone remained positive, but Franny's emotional state concerned the medical staff much more than his physical strength. He had weathered his first bout with cancer and had come out quite strong, gaining weight and energy. Those were plusses for him, but the lingering concern over what precipitated the return of his illness remained a mystery. Bessie confided to Dr. Jimmy O'Brien that Franny had never been the same since he had learned of Dennis' death. She thought that much of his hard earned joy over his recent years escaped him that day. At times, his steps slowed and the smile slipped from his voice. Energy ebbed from him and his daily encounters with the community left him fatigued. His visits to the chapels and shrines lasted longer, and interests in the martinis and fine Italian food he so savored diminished. With the boys and their families, however, he always managed to muster the strength and energy to be sociable and gracious.

Bernie had left St. Gabriel's Hall school in June of 1970 and took a position in public education in the Wissahickon School District in Ambler. After spending the summer with Dottie's parents in Worcester, the couple moved into their first home with their first son Bernard James in toe.

Despite the increase in salary that he was receiving, the house made extra cash a rarity. Gifts put on lists for various occasions were crossed off without their purchase, and the baby's first Christmas looked bleak. The new home had to serve as everyone's Christmas present; even the child would make the sacrifice. The new father refused to deny the baby and his wife of the trappings of Christmas – a tree. Bernie scoured every pocket, sofa, and drawer, counter top and the car in search of any cash that he could find. He had one dollar and eight-three cents.

After the last day of school, he drove past the shopping center at Swede Street and Germantown Pikes on his way home from Shady Grove Junior High School. He noticed that the Christmas tree venders were busily grinding and shredding the unsold trees on the lot. He pulled up to the shredder, rolled down his window, and hoped for a miracle.

"Any chance you might give one of those trees away before you shred it?" he requested of the operator.

The man beaded with sweat, his face steamed from the cold air, but his answer was frigid, "No way, Man. I got a count, and the boss wants it right."

"I don't suppose any are for sale, then?" he continued in his pursuit. The 1969 Cougar's engine idled smoothly under the conversation.

"Yeah! I could do that." The man turned now and faced Bernie, seated behind the wheel.

"Well, I'll give you all the cash I have for one of those little trees - one that will fit in my trunk." The driver swung the door open, stood, and rummaged into his left hand trouser pocket for his cash.

"How much you got to offer?" countered the worker.

"Actually, I have one dollar and eight-three cents," he stammered meekly and added, "Honestly."

"You're kiddin' me, right?" came from the seller. "Let me see the cash?" he added as if to check the truth of Bernie's count.

In his bared right hand, lay the coinage. The act of showing it to the man seemed to put the seller in an awkward dilemma.

"Okay, take any one out of that pile over there," he directed with the sound of his embarrassment touching his words.

The man made no sign to accept the money for which he had bargained, but Bernie thrust the change into his hand. Elated that he had managed to buy a tree at such a late hour and with his remaining cash, he rushed to the pile, selected a tree, opened the trunk, and delicately placed the small spruce into the space. "Merry Christmas!" he wished to the attendant as he pulled away.

"You, too!" followed after the departing car.

The little spruce occupied the table top in the front window. The couple shared the happiness and aroma that it brought to their new home. The Yule tree made its feeble attempt to alleviate the lingering tinge of sadness that the evening held. The pair accepted the reality of a Spartan Christmas for their child. They rationalized that, being so young, he would not remember this night; but they had it indelibly imprinted in their shared experience. Resigned to the course of events, the couple sat on the green faux leather sofa satisfied with the view of their first Christmas tree. The doorbell rang.

"Merry Christmas!" rang from the outdoor air as Franny and Bessie appeared, standing on the shallow stoop. "Bernie, get out to the car and get the rest of the stuff," ordered Franny as he wedged Bessie and himself past Bernie in the doorway.

"What did you guys do?" wondered Bernie as he descended the three steps toward the parked car. No response came to his inquiry.

Tonka dump truck and mobile crane truck, clothes, puzzles, books, and other toys suddenly filled the room. "Dad, Bessie, this is so appreciated," thanked Dottie with a warm embrace. "We're a little lean this year."

"We remember how it was," Franny reminisced. "We already made a trip to Fran and Iris."

"Tomorrow, we want to be at Al's as early as possible to see the girls. We're going to meet George and Shirley there," added Bessie.

They stayed for cookies and drinks. The conversation warmed the home, and Franny and Bessie entered the lore of Christmas for Bernie and Dottie. In the child rearing years to come, the question, "Is there a Santa Claus?", always would have an immediate, positive response. "Yes, Children, there is a Santa Claus. We ate cookies with him and Mrs. Claus one Christmas Eve when they came to our home."

So Christmas Eve traditions began with present-laden visits to the homes of the twins and their families. The morning of each Christmas found Bessie and Franny at Albert and Mim's home in New Jersey and at George and Shirley's by the afternoon.

The recovery process for which everyone hoped and prayed did not materialize into a return to health for Franny. The deterioration of his affected body moved onward with unrelenting and uncharitable pace. The excursions to St. Jude's chapel became less frequent, and transportation was burdensome. Alone or with Bessie in the pews of the chapel, his silent prayer remained fixated on the issues of his excommunication and his past decisions. The realization of the seriousness of his condition evoked a wish, "Please, Lord, don't let me die with all this baggage!" Father Peter made the trek to Bridgeport as often as possible. The patient was thankful for the time that the young priest managed to give him, for Franny understood the myriad of duties that the young priest performed at the shrine. Their friendship grew, and hope sputtered to life like the birth of a flame.

Confined to long periods in his apartment and then to the single bedroom, he insisted that Bessie continue to work at the state hospital. Whenever possible in her absence, the boys, other family members or friends visited. His deterioration weighed heavily upon the caregivers. Franny remained cordial and appeared buoyed by the attention and distractions.

Bessie bore the illness personally, but stood firm in his presence. When guests arrived, her hostess duties availed her time in the kitchen where she was refreshed. Their presence alleviated her of the responsibility to attend to Franny's on-going needs. Each arrival voluntarily took a chore or task unto themselves. Errands were run, household duties were completed, and the chats alleviated the monotony and routine of the days.

On one visit after teaching school, Bernie found his father in bed with his bedside light lit. A crossword puzzle book lay open under the beam of light on the side table. He had abandoned the words and the grids and seemed to have a more pressing issue on his mind. Bernie moved the book slightly and pulled a glass from his coat pocket. He placed the stemware in the space adjacent to the puzzle book. Next, like a stage magician, he displayed a tightly lidded jar. From the vessel, he presented a martini and poured it into the glass. Franny's eyes widened.

"I'm supposed to be off those right now. My meds, you know, but I'll manage to sip that one down. Thanks!"

"You done with the puzzle for a while or do you want me to help you with it?" suggested Bernie.

Franny paid heed to the book only with a cursory glance. "No, I've done as much as I want to right now," he mulled over in his mind as his left hand rose to stroke his face. In the action, Bernie noticed the scattering of bristled growth on his face. The beard was spotty and colored in splotches of white, gray, and a trace of black hairs.

What's on your mind, Dad?" quizzed the young visitor.

"Ahm…well, this face of mine's getting a bit itchy, and I'm sure I look a mess," he confessed. The elegant, dapper dresser with the slicked hair style no longer resided in Franny's apartment, but still his sense of refinement motivated his sensibilities.

"You still shave," wondered the son almost as an aside to himself. Then he added, "or does Bessie do it for you?"

"Nah, that's still my job when I have the time to get around to it." A smile traced across his gaunt face. He searched his son's eyes and found a reward in his son's amusement at his lighthearted humor.

"I'm still using a safety razor, you know," volunteered the visitor. "I could give it a try if you want?"

"Barber school…when did you go?" he quipped. He appeared to be considering the shave, but turning over his personal care felt awkward to him. "Maybe, I'll get around to it tomorrow," he decided.

"Seriously, Dad, I'll get your stuff, and you'll be clean shaven by the time Bessie gets home. What'd ya' think?" They faced each other like boxers preparing to spar.

216

The lack of historic physical contact between the two made this an issue of courage for Franny and one of confidence for Bernie. Beyond embraces and handshakes, Bernie had little tactile experience with his father. The man opened his eyes widely and tightened his lips across his mouth. The younger man rose to attempt to gather the needed supplies from the bathroom. As long as Franny left the last question unanswered, Bernie continued to diligently search for the lather mug, the brush, and his father's razor in the adjacent room. He returned in a matter of moments with a lather mug, moistened with warm water, a towel, and the needed supplies.

The first part of the procedure went without incident. The barber lathered his father's face with the agility of a classical painter. The beard was neatly blanketed with a smooth snowy coating of rich fragrant lather. The aroma of Old Spice filled the bedroom. Franny seemed hypnotically pleased with the effort, and the second phase began at the left sideburn down toward the chin. The first stroke wiped the lather from the skin, but the pressure on the blade was too light to remove all of the bristles beneath. When the apprentice re-lathered the section, Franny let his eyes speak for him.

"I just have to figure the right touch. It's easy on my own face, but you're a different story," confessed the rookie barber.

"It's okay. I don't mind if you miss a few spots," he said with some tact, and added, "I'm not going anywhere." The joke succeeded in producing a second stroke down the already cleaved area. The result met with some minimal approval from the barber. With confidence building, Bernie ventured onto the other smooth and flat surfaces of his father's face. To the young novice, the moustache and chin appeared like a volcano rising from a sea of foam. The prospect of running the razor over the contours of this terrain momentarily froze the caregiver.

What's the problem?" interjected the client with renewed concern.

"I wanna make sure I don't nick your pretty face," he retorted in defense of his momentary lapse of action.

Franny reached up and surveyed the surface of the completed work. "My life's in your hands – but, only when you get to my throat, Bernie," confided Franny lightheartedly. The words missed the comic relief intended, for Bernie's expression froze.

"I'll be very careful, Dad," assured the young man. The first pass above the upper lip necessitated a second lathering again. He began to start and stop the effort to shave under the lower lip. Bernie had difficulty initiating any stokes on this undulating surface.

Franny began to shift his weight in bed under the pressure of his son's dilemma. His patience waned, his confidence sagged, and his eyes peered widely down at his son's right hand and the razor it held.

"I can do it myself, Bernie. Don't worry about it, I'll finish from here. You got me motivated. I've enough energy to finish up," he rambled, stopping Bernie amid his faltering indecision.

With the task finally completed, the two men conversed quietly about inane subjects and never breeched any meaningful topics. "Camille" remained unspoken, the El Estera stayed under lock and key, and Dennis existed in their silent prayers. Neither of the twins ever pressed their father about these weighty matters for fear of fracturing the shield that protected the man from his darkest memories. If Franny did not bring up the matter, neither would anyone else.

Bessie arrived as Bernie was leaving. She left him at the door after a cordial and polite greeting and hurried to check on her husband in the bedroom. As Bernie stepped into the hallway he heard Bessie's surprise, "Oh my God! Franny you shaved!"

The family crowded the waiting room, and people continued to arrive and leave during the two days since Franny was admitted to Sacred Heart Hospital. Mame held a private vigil in the lounge chair in the corner of the large sitting area. She did not mingle nor did she seek out those in the room. She pondered the loss of a second son and petitioned God for the answer to her frequent prayer.

Bessie moved flittingly from person to person and waiting room to private hospital room. Every ounce of her frail body was taxed to its extreme. Albert and George supported her weaker moments and lauded her stronger ones.

Exiting the patient's room, Dr. Jimmy stopped at Albert and Frank who were stationed outside the door guarding the privacy of the doctor visit. "You know I'm amazed that Franny is still with us. There's nothing to explain this 'holding on' of his." The doctor checked with Bessie before excusing himself to run some short errands. "I'll be back as soon as I possibly can, Aunt Bessie. You take care of yourself," he added with sincere concern.

In the room Bessie pulled the armchair up to the left side head of the bed. Albert generally stood by her side. Frank and Bernie made occasional bedside visits to touch and speak to their father, but George seemed to be held on a strong tether. He paced from window to door, occasionally looking over at Franny as he passed the foot of the bed.

Franny communicated with his eyes during these hours. The fear and uncertainty present within him leapt from those glistening eyes. As if seeking some specific person or object, he looked frantically about the room. He did not answer Albert's entreaty, "What do you need, Frank?" What he wanted, he did not find in the room. The patient would slip into brief stages of unconsciousness, but his body heaved and rattled with raspy breathing and pain. At one conscious moment he pulled Albert close to him and in the quiet of the room, the five witnesses heard him make a request.

"I don't want any of you to see me after I'm gone. Don't remember me that way, okay?" That was not a momentary whim that had suddenly drifted into his mind; the thought had roots in his own pain and how he had so long carried those memories with him.

There was a rustle at the door, and Mim poked her head into the room. "Father Pete's here, Al."

The room vacated immediately to allow the priest to administer to Franny. As people left his presence, Franny forced a smile, and one could read the relief in his being. In the waiting area, the family also sensed a relaxation of their tenseness. Several of Mame's daughters and Larry clustered about her corner of the lounge. Bessie stood trembling with Al and George supporting her efforts to endure the moment. She had no tears to give, but her eyes displayed the ache and pain of the long months of Franny's fall from health.

"You know, Al, he's been waiting all along for Father Pete," managed Bessie.

"We've all kinda suspected that, Mom," surmised George as he reached to embrace her.

"I'm relieved for Dad," began Bernie, "Father finally made it." The twin strode to the side of his brother who had taken a position in the chorus surrounding Mame.

"This is the way it has to be," Frank said as his brother reached him. "I can't imagine what all this church nonsense has put him through." There was no bitterness in the statement. It fell on the listeners as a simple summation of Franny's journey.

Only mere seconds seemed to pass since Father Peter Krebs had arrived and entered Franny's room. An attending nurse suddenly and unexpectedly walked into the waiting room. "You can go in now," she invited.

The twins and the step-sons moved quickly to join Father Pete and their father. The communication from the nurse had been too abrupt, too incomplete, for it was misunderstood. Their entrance and first glance toward the bed found their father lying across his pillow in the arms of the young priest. "He's gone. It's over," softly and delicately conveyed the priest. The four young men were left with his death image, imbedded irrevocably in their memory of the day. They had entered the room with the hope of seeing Franny without worry or concern. They found him, contrary to his wishes, still and in a pose of utter exhaustion. Reverting from the image, Albert moved to console his mother at the lounge chair, and the twins with George drifted to the lone window of the room. Transfixed, the trio hovered there looking from the window toward the street scene beyond the hospital. None of the three saw the movement of life below. Frank stood to one side of George and Bernie at his other, and the three wept.

Across the hall, Mame asked the nurse to draw close to her. "Did he receive the Last Rites and Holy Communion?"

Her reply was a slow bow in affirmation, and with it the mother could endure the days ahead.

No one else had been privy to the man's request to his children, and they stoically moved into the room, paid their final respects, and exited.

In passing, Franny died at a very old fifty-one years of age. The casket was closed for the viewing, and the funeral was well attended by most standards. Emotional closure began with the ceremony that day. For Bessie, however, it commenced an endless state of mourning. She longed for more time with the man she had grown to adore and cherish.

Albert did the eulogy for Frank, the man he sought for counsel, the man who gave happiness to his mother, the man who reared and fathered his brother, and the man who brought the twins into his and his families' lives.

There was another eulogy that went undelivered. Bernie could not read his tribute to his father. The words from his soul went unspoken into an envelope which sealed his heartfelt thoughts about the mysterious man who was his father. The tribute was titled, "In Recognition of My Father." It had no voice save the written word.

"Many of us sensed that these last few weeks would be difficult ones. In reality, they were not. My father made them beautiful for those whom he loved. He overcame his knowledge of his pain with smiles, courage, and honor. We felt a sense of sharing a unique adventure with this great man. We felt we were preparing him to meet Jesus. No, he prepared us: prepared us to meet ourselves, prepared us to depend on one another, prepared us to find a way through life, and prepared us for the reality of his own death.'

"Dad was a man – a man in the truest sense of the word - full of patience, goodwill, and respect for others. But, perhaps more importantly, he was patient with and respectful of himself and his own certain knowledge of right and wrong.'

"We have all grown mature and courageous by having spoken quietly with him. We have become wise by observing his incomparable patience with others. We have become a family because he has loved us.'

"Long ago, we did not know him, but he knew us. Many years ago, he spoke softly, stepped into our lives, and we began to recognize the warmth and understanding which he offered to us. His character demanded respect, not out of fear, but rather in his sense of fairness and the strength of his own convictions. He never willingly hurt another person, but rather made known his views and quietly stepped aside to allow time to prove his point.'

"We are here today recognizing another point. He was a very special man: a husband, a father, and a true friend of Jesus and Saint Jude."

Martin Bernot offered the family a cemetery plot alongside his wife Camille at St. Matthew's Cemetery in Conshohocken. Bessie had a parcel in St. Augustine's Cemetery where George Pastino was interred. Mame owned the gravesite of Timothy L. Blanche where baby Joseph was also buried. The Pastinos expressed their wish to permit his burial at any site as long as provisions were made for Bessie. In the end Mame agreed to the Pastino's wish and she prevailed. Francis Joseph Blanche, her oldest son, was interred with his father and his brother Joseph.

The four boys met at Bessie's apartment to clear out various items of clothing and memorabilia for her; and, in a Biblical sense, a ritualistic "Casting of Lots" took place. George and Albert graciously offered the twins their choice of relic from their father's life store. From the closets and chests of drawers, pieces were selected by each son and removed to their separate homes.

Al, Bernie, and George stayed the course with the Catholic Church, but Frank felt disenfranchised by it. His disappointment with the rites and rituals resolved itself with his commitment to disavow formal religion. The influence of Francis J. Blanche would ever be with each of them.

Chapter Nineteen

"Martin's Gift"

For most of the parties, life settled in like a bear preparing for hibernation. Two people, however, remained restless. Bessie continued to mourn with deep sorrow the absence of Franny. Her caregivers chauffeured, nursed, and supported their relative and friend. As the families grew and prospered, she found herself firmly entrenched in their activities.

Martin Bernot had surgery done and his recovery tested the relationship he had with Lydie. Her daughter's family, the Daltons, began to take a major role in his care. Betty would travel to Bustleton to help with his daily needs, and the boys, Bobby and Billy, assisted on weekends.

Lydie began to struggle with a personality disorder, and a belligerent side emerged. Betty suspected that the exchanges between Martin and Lydie had evolved into battles of self-defense and obstinacy. She telephoned his grandson Frank with the recent details. Because of his background in social work, she felt that he could suggest some organizations or individuals that might alleviate the stress in the household. They outlined some strategies over the phone; but, before any such plans bore fruit, Lydie slammed the opening shut.

She displayed one flaw. This fastidious "Gold Star Mother" disliked all things dirty and unkempt. Unpleasant odors, impolite noises, filth, and messiness triggered first annoyance, then agitation, and finally rage. Lydie confronted her daughter in such a mood one morning when Betty arrived to do the couple's laundry.

"I don't care what it takes," stormed Lydie before the front door had even closed behind Betty, "but I want him out of this house!" Her head shook, her weak right eyelid pulsed like a shutter on a yoyo string, and her voice gurgled and rattled with the energy of her rant.

"Mother, Mother, calm down!" directed the shocked daughter. "I'm here. It'll be alright," insisted Betty.

"No it won't!" stammered the distraught mother. Betty directed her mother toward the kitchen and then sat her at the table under the center window. The elderly woman's passage occurred without her knowledge, for the rage had numbed her external senses. She fixated on her inner emotions.

"What's wrong, Mother?" asked Betty now seated with her mother.

"He's soiled the bed. The room's a disaster. It smells in there. He's still trying to smoke in the house. He won't lift a finger to help himself." Betty placed a gentle finger on Lydie's lips and forestalled the litany of grievances.

"Martin's not able to do a lot of that, Mother," confided Betty. Lydie let her head drop onto her hands which rested on the table surface. "I'll make us some tea, Mother," she suggested. The chore accomplished, she left the kitchen to visit with Martin.

Betty found the rogue sitting on the edge of his bed. His hands worked feverishly to take a cigarette from his shirt pocket. When he espied her at the door, he ceased his rummaging. Caught in the act, like a dog over his puddle of urine, he feigned a cough. "Hi, Betty! Good to see you," he invited.

Her head swayed to and fro to admonish his effort to smoke as she approached his bedside.

225

"Mother's having a tough time. How about you?" she probed.

"That woman wants me dressed in coat and tails, clean shaven, and ready to walk the boardwalk," he reported. The wry smirk on his face told of his attempt to downplay the comment.

"You still have your sense of humor." Her pleasant delivery and the embrace she offered him pulled his momentary tension from him. "Is there anything you can do to make things easier on the both of you?"

"Nah! Canasta's out, and I can't sit long enough to do those blamed thousand piece puzzles she keeps setting up on the card table." Martin fumbled to straighten out the bed sheets.

"Do you get out at all?"

"Hell, no! She might shoot me if she caught me out in the back yard," he laughed.

"Oh, Martin, you're a rascal," she countered. "I think a visiting nurse could be of some help." She sat next to him.

"Lydie won't want someone coming in here and seeing the mess I've made of the place. She'd been embarrassed to death, Betty," apprised Martin with a finger pointed menacingly toward the kitchen.

"Yes, she can be a handful, I know, but we have to figure something out."

"I'm really not up to such duties. I haven't the energy. The pain pills get me drowsy, and she needs a song and dance man." He did not like the critical sound of the statement, and he added, "Wanna see me strut my stuff?"

Betty laughed and patted his shoulder. "I hope you can do that soon." The bedroom reeked of soiled garments, and his clothes lay in rumpled piles at various locations throughout the room. She excused herself and returned to her Mother.

Lydie had her cup to her mouth sipping the warm tea as her daughter entered. "Martin seems like his old self. Ornery as ever," reported the young woman.

"He's an old, dirty fool," fell bitterly from her mouth. The firm, unflinching stance that Lydie took worried the daughter more for her mother than for Martin.

"Maybe, you're right. It's time for him to find more appropriate quarters."

"I've made up my mind, and that's final. I don't want him here anymore." No annulment, no divorce, but the friendship was thoroughly dispatched all at once. Amid her aging bitterness, Lydie rejected him.

Martin came to belong to his grandchildren. Bernie and Dottie considered giving Martin a room in their small townhouse; but, with two little children under wing, the care of an adult with his physical needs would overextend the household. The brunt of the nursing care would fall on Dottie who was a "stay-at-home" mother.

Frank and Iris had two school aged children at home, but Iris was a working mother. Within the network of connections that Frank had for the juveniles with which he worked, he also called upon agencies that supported some of the older members of these families. He was able to set Martin into the veterans' programs in the area.

All of Martin's earthly possessions fit loosely into the two family sedans. Bernie and Frank moved their Grandfather to the Artman Home on Penllyn Pike in Blue Bell. The government supported his placement and paid the monthly fees. Extra items fell to the grandsons' families to pay out-of-pocket. The first few months of adapting and familiarizing himself to the home's procedures went very well. Having spent time in the Merchant Marines, Martin accustomed himself easily to the communal routine. On visits, the twins often found his room empty and him sitting in the smoking room. His pain revealed itself in his constant rubbing of his abdomen. The constant physical discomfort led to increased emotional distress.

"Damn people here steal my clothes. The attendants give some of it to guys down the hall. I see 'em walking around with my shirts and pants on," he complained.

At first there was a mellow resolution to his annoyances, but over the next month a deeper anger welled up. When he chased a fellow patient down the hallway yelling and demanding his sweater, the staff asked for a meeting with the twins. The home agreed to monitor his compliance with the rules for a few weeks. Their concern centered on Martin's growing frustration and inability to handle the unintentional intrusions into his personal space by some of the Alzheimer's and other senile patients.

The system worked slowly, grinding out any progress at first gear speed. His time spent in the Merchant Marines and his draft status during World War I had to be confirmed and documented. Little help came financially from the young families, and the vast majority of Martin's care came from Social Security and the Veterans' Administration. The Artman home wanted more funds to care for Martin, and the twins had little recourse to assist with his needs.

Martin had stumbled and cut himself on a cabinet in his room. That became the focal point for the home to make an effort to reassign him. Martin's grace period with the Artman Home ended that day. The phone call to Frank and Bernie came as an emergency and brought them from work to resolve Martin's transfer. The process took a few days, but Frank found a possible temporary location for his Grandfather. He hoped to eventually place him under the exclusive care of the Veterans' Administration. The government money available for Martin eventually forced placement in a more unfavorable location with less comfortable conditions.

Driven to a second home in Spring Mount, near Schwenksville, Pennsylvania, Martin accepted the transfer, but it was a less favorable habitat. The residence, a vacation hotel built in the 1800's to house the Philadelphia wealthy on their summer weekends, provided succor for the elite from the steamy city heat. Now, disrepair was evident, and the Spartan accommodations bothered the twins. Martin, however, did not indicate to them that he noticed the inadequacy of his situation. He continued to have the same complaints, though. People roamed about other patients' rooms with little awareness of their intrusions into someone's private space. His health deteriorated such that he spent more time napping than rousting his fellow residents.

Hints of the feisty Martin erupted on occasion. Martin awoke from an afternoon nap to find a man standing at his chest of drawers with his back to Martin's bed. The man was unsteady and held onto the top of the cabinet with his trembling left hand.

"Hey, there! What the hell are ya' doing in my stuff!" screamed Martin in a volume that echoed down the hallway.

The man slowly reacted to Martin, making a turn toward him. "Huh!" he mumbled.

"What did ya' take? That's my stuff in there," bellowed Martin rising from his bed and honing in on his target. Once he had his balance set, Martin charged the "would be" thief with enough speed and force to knock both combatants onto the cold, linoleum floor. The assault that ensued looked more like a childhood wrestling match. The dispute took on the air of a cinematic silent movie farce. In slow motion, as if under strobe lights, the two elderly men rolled and twisted in an eerie dance. One might have suspected that the brawl might escalate into a fist fight by the time the orderlies arrived. The skirmish caused the intruder to bite his tongue while Martin had attempted to pummel the man's face.

"Hey? What are you doin' in my room?" wailed the intruder from underneath Martin, surprised that he had been attacked.

"Your room – you old Coot! This is my room," bellowed Martin, claiming his rightful territory.

The orderly came between the men at that point yelling to both men, "Hey! We don't do things this way, Gentlemen!" He had the visitor under the arm. "Martin, you sit there in that chair while I take Sam, here, to the nurse's for his bloody mouth."

Martin obeyed, sure that the interloper had been arrested. "I'll press charges if I have to," he shouted into the backs of the two men exiting his quarters. The moment was his and he relished the victory.

Betty and Fran Dalton visited with her boys. Her phone call to Bernie afterwards reported their disappointment at Martin's situation. "He's aged in that place, Bernie, - really slowed down."

Bernie mentioned in self-defense, "This old hotel was the only place that would take Martin on such short notice, but Frank still hopes to find a better fit within the veteran's system."

"I hope you are successful in doing that," she wished, and then to set a different tone, she posed jokingly, "Martin does appear less cantankerous." Her description of Lydie came as a pragmatic evaluation, "You know, Mother is just turning into a cranky old woman. She was mad at me the other day for 'taking' Martin from her."

"We have our hands full, Betty," he shared.

"We do. I'll try to keep in touch. Let me know when Martin is moved, okay?"

"Sure. Give my regards to the family."

Martin usually sauntered or sometimes shuffled into the solarium for his quiet time. On visits, guests found him in a corner chair facing the broad picture window. In those days, he could smoke his Camels or Chesterfields there or on a patio just outside the sitting room. A faraway stare into the lawn and forest beyond the property pulled him to the farm, the sea, the open road. The sky and land always drew him into their midst. He was in the throes of a memory of the Atlantic City Boardwalk when Bernie entered the sun room.

The young man approached the lone resident without startling the older man. Adjacent to Martin's chair, Bernie made an introductory cough and greeted, "How are you doin' today, Grandpop?"

Martin stirred with the words, turned, and smiled at his grandson. He moved in his seat, straightening his posture, and responded, "I'm having a good day. Good to see you."

"You have the place to yourself. You king of the hill or something?"

"No, but they give me my space. How're the kids and Dottie?" he inquired.

The request surprised Bernie, for Martin did not generally check up on people and things. He tended to leave them to their own devices and happenings. Bernie found the question a bit unusual. "Everyone's doing well." He recalled the times that Frank and he had brought their children and wives to see their great grandfather. "You enjoyed seeing the kids, Grandpop?"

"They make for a busy day around here," he bemused. "That little Rene'…that daughter of yours is a pistol. She's got too much energy for one person."

"Bernie and her, they keep us hustling all right," contributed the visitor. "I couldn't bring them today. I thought we'd just chat a bit."

The elderly man made a clicking sound within his mouth, letting his upper denture drop onto one of his permanent teeth.

The twins had heard this ritualistic "click" everyday they spent with Martin. His eyes rose and aimed upward at Bernie who remained standing by the chair. "Sure. What's up?" Patting the arm of the nearby chair he invited, "Here. Sit!"

"Nothing in particular. We're still working on a more permanent residence for you," informed Bernie.

"Your wife still baking those cookies of hers?" reflected Martin, eyeing the brown paper bag that was placed on an adjacent seat.

"Yeah, she sent some along for you."

Martin smudged the remnants of his cigarette in a handy ashtray, and the treasured bag was brought onto his lap. "Make sure you tell her I said 'Thanks.'" His right hand blindly searched the contents of the bag, and he pulled two pastries from the sack. "Oatmeal and chocolate chip!" he declared and, then, bit into the chocolate chip cookie.

"So, this view here. Does it remind you of Bustleton?" offered Bernie reflexively.

Martin ceased chewing and let his eyes fall on his grandson. "No. It reminds me of today. Something new and different."

Bernie pondered that the question may have offended his grandfather. "I just thought you might have been doing some thinking about the past," he defended.

"I don't have much use for the past, Bernie," he theorized.

"You've been a lot of places and seen so many things," tempted Bernie, hoping to receive some insight into the life of the man.

"It's the present moment where you do your best work – set example and all that, you know," he said coyly with a nonchalance that tasted of conviction.

"You and my Dad always did that for sure," mused the interviewer.

"You know how your meal arrives on the table, nice and hot?" He watched Bernie nod in acceptance of the image. "Well, you have to eat it while it's hot. The taste is better. You don't want it to get cold."

The writer in Bernie enjoyed the metaphor. "You sound like a painter. That's a pretty good visual picture you drew, Grandpop."

"The days gone by are cold, and they don't have any taste for me." An oatmeal raisin cookie now occupied his present moment.

"Dottie do a good job on the oatmeals?" quizzed the visitor.

"Oh my, yes!" rated Martin as he took a second bite of the pastry.

"I'm surprised you had room after the chocolate chip?" teased Bernie.

"Oh! I sure did," he volunteered, and, pointing a teaching finger toward the young man, added, "Remember, take only what..."

"You can eat," finished Bernie, and then he dutifully completed the adage, "you can always take seconds." He laughed with Martin who popped the last chunk of oatmeal raisin cookie into his mouth.

Then the sage within Martin voiced another application of his wisdom, "Take only from today what you can handle. If that sits well, you can always take the next step."

He only ate two cookies; it was a fair sample as far as he was concerned of Dottie's baking skills. He kept the bag of delights nearby, saved for another moment. They sat together through a Chesterfield, talking about the mundane, but Martin made the topics colorful, aromatic, and alive. Bernie felt the exercise to be meditative. Stress was absent, and calmness managed to exist in his spontaneous approach to life.

The drive home gave time to reflect about Martin's comments. The twins and everyone around Timothy, Franny, and Martin had to take what was offered. Sometimes this "Nowness" translated incorrectly: "Nothing in their lives seemed important enough to share with anyone else. The past was there, but dormant and unused." Rather, Bernie realized that to Martin the nuts and bolts of whom we present to people rest between the bookends of each fleeting moment. Good example stood foremost.

Subsequent visits found Martin using a wheel chair to make his runs to the solarium. He smoked less, slept more under medication, and also fought the pain that came with the reoccurrence of his colon cancer.

Within the second year away from Lydie and the Bustleton Pike residence, Martin needed a full-care facility. Frank managed to contact the appropriate bureaucrats and have Martin assigned a room at the Johnson Home in Royersford off of route 113. The hospital was located just a short distance from Frank's home, and the twins met in Martin's room frequently. The grandfather's presence held the twins together, for their divergent interests, families, and mind sets nudged them apart.

The pair agreed that in self-defense their grandfathers and their father had relied heavily on the present moment. It was their veil, their shield, their padlock, but never their stepping stone. They had no intention of retracing their steps. Life sprang from the seeds of the moment, bound like a flower in a pot in a smaller world with limited horizons. Frank and Bernie hoped to believed that, if the earlier experiences of their male parents had been joyous and pleasant, then the men would have given more credence to the value of sharing their pasts. As it was, the twins had very little knowledge of their parents' experiences. Only fresh clay molded the present day. The shards of the past went undiscovered and unread.

At the Johnson Home, Martin slipped from frequent wheelchair treks on the grounds to occasional short amblings within the floors of the hospital. Eventually, he became isolated in his room, sometimes seated in the soft chair by the window of his room. As the disease wore on, it confined him to his bed.

Bernie and Dottie celebrated the birth of their third child, a boy whom they named Jeremy Martin. At four months of age, Bernie brought the lad to the Johnson Home to present the child to his great grandfather.

Wearied by his illness, Bernie had to awaken Martin from a fretful sleep that afternoon. Too weak to sit up or take the infant in his arms, the proud father placed Jeremy Martin on the chest of his great grandfather. At first disoriented by the interruption to his nap, Martin struggled to understand the presentation. He made no attempt to reach up to the child, but lay in quiet reflection.

"Grandpop, this is Martin, your great grandson. He's four months old. I wanted him to meet you." The young father found it difficult to say the first name of the child, for he wanted the honorarium to be more complete, more significant to the sickly grandparent abed in his solitary room.

A smile grew from the awakening elder. He said nothing, but pondered the gift upon his breast. Slowly, he pushed one arm from his coverlet and reached for the infant's shoulder. Then the second hand appeared as he folded his arms about the swaddled youngster atop his heaving chest. "Gee, how about that. Another Martin," he celebrated.

"Yeah, I wanted you to see him now that we're taking him out of the house once in a while," proudly related Bernie.

"That's great – wonderful." came from him with great effort. "I'm pleased to meet you, Martin," he managed in feeble voice. His spirits seemed elevated and his head propped upward to get a more advantageous view of the lad. The child lay longwise upon Martin; and, when the older man shuffled to see the baby,

Bernie moved the child to facilitate Martin's scrutiny. "He's a good looker, alright," chimed Martin.

"We can't stay too long this time, Grandpop, so this is just a short visit." A nurse entered the room, and the social nature of the visit took on a festive air. Several other attendants were summoned to meet the child.

"His name is Martin," announced the grandfather in a forced whisper to those arriving. The effort to entertain and socialize with the people within the room quickly sapped his energy.

His attending nurse noticed the difficulty in Martin. "Maybe, we should let him rest. This has been a lot of excitement for one day," she evaluated. She ushered the extraneous guests from the room. "You and your grandson can have a few more minutes together." She excused herself. Martin drifted into a peaceful and deep sleep.

Bernie left a handwritten note on the bedside table when he left. He asked the nurse to read it to Martin when he awoke. The message was a prayer, one Bernie composed and used regularly in response to his concerns and tribulations. He had no idea of the effect it might have on his grandfather. Martin had never been a "Church-goer", but Bernie thought he remained a Catholic by preference. It was titled "Good Start, a Meditation." It read:

"Dear Lord, I offer all my thoughts, words, and deeds on this day for your honor and glory. My prayers this day are for the spiritual, physical, emotional, and psychological well-being of all my loved ones and those special intentions which I have this day. Protect us in our travels, Lord, and grant the intersession of St. Joseph as our protector and companion. Help us to grow closer to you and to each other. Grant the intersession of the Blessed Mother, St. Monica, St. Anthony, your Holy Spirit, and you, Dear Jesus, to help us to find the path that you have chosen for us. May we know and recognize your presence in our lives."

Easter week approached, and both Frank and Bernie planned to spend additional time with Martin at the home. A phone call alerted them to some concern for Martin as he seemed to have developed a case of pneumonia. Bernie reminded the caller that Martin was Roman Catholic, and requested that a priest see him. The plan was for Bernie to meet Frank on Good Friday afternoon in Martin's room.

That morning Bernie received a telephone call from Frank. The Johnson Home had reached him that morning.

"Martin passed away this morning, Bernie," he informed his brother in a quiet and solemn monotone. He waited during a short pause for Bernie to speak.

Bernie finally pondered, "I had a sense that we'd see him today for the last time. Darn. We weren't there for him."

"He was alone when he died," reflected Frank, "but that's the kind of life he led, very much his own man – independent to the last."

"Well, I hope the priest saw him this week," fell from Bernie's thoughts.

Frank chose not to respond to Bernie's expressed wish. "I had a dream about him last night, and he told me everything was all right."

"Did you call the Daltons?" asked Bernie.

"No, but I'll take care of that. Do you want to come up here or meet me at the home?"

Despite the finality of the news, they both realized that there were duties to handle. "I'll see you at the Johnson Home, Frank."

"The nurse said that we could see Martin anytime today. They'll give us time with him, and we can begin to make the necessary arrangements," directed his sibling.

Martin died in 1974 on Good Friday morning at The Johnson Home for Veterans.

The funeral evolved into a simple, tasteful gathering of family and the Daltons. Martin was buried in the Catholic Church with which he had had little to do. He was interred in St. Matthew's Cemetery in the plot with his first wife and daughter Camille. It was a site he had pledged to avoid since the death of Camille. Only once did he approach that gravesite: the day Mary Mack, his first wife, was buried.

Martin left a legacy of questions unanswered, conversations never held, and mysteries about the myriad lives and adventures that he had experienced. The twins were his last and only heirs; inheritors of only their experiences with him. The painter, the canasta coach, the hobo, the cigarette smoker, the charming older man escorted the pair through a maze of the gifts of his life, but only his present life. The father of the mother that they had never known buried his trials. What could have been a treasure for the twins became an enigma, a series of unsolved puzzles. As observers of Timothy, Martin, and Franny, the boys had reconciled the silence, the secrets, and the pain underlying the family's history with the reality given to them in the present moments. Nurtured in love and caring, they grew secure within the world that was bestowed upon them. This schooling and the frenzied stage around them allowed them to adapt and learn from Mame, Timothy, Martin, Franny, and their aunts and uncles. In particular, the brief, but often intense, moments with the men of the family honed their character as well as any boot camp could. Like many children and families of post World War II, they evolved and survived.

Who among you has not thrown the first stone? To judge the actions or non-actions of the three men whose lives opened before you, one must focus on the results of their total experiences.

Parenting by example works. It may appear negative at times, but the long range outcomes will be positive. The growth in adults is closely monitored by children. Civility at meals soon reflects a demeanor that promotes respect. Martin, Timothy, and Francis all held the table and social gatherings as integral aspects of good parenting, and the time spent together in civility reaped much rewards.

Anger is not necessarily a negative emotion. Timothy's deeply rooted frustrations boiled into visible tirades of anger. The children in his household watched his inner pain and became familiar with it. By dealing with his illness, the family still took positive traits from him into adulthood. He had little or no control over what he presented to his family during the times of psychosis, but it became a shared element of family life, producing a more sensitive awareness of troubled people. The old adage of "Walk a mile in someone else's shoes" presents a textbook of wisdom.

Change can reap countless rewards for those screening the process in another. Martin's emergence from hobo to gentleman garnered much insight for the families. People granted him the time and the opportunity to initiate his own personal reforms, conquer his demon of alcoholism, and find a gentler self within his on-going development. Martin bore his inner addiction without knowing the full portrait which he presented to the family. Still, his personal growth into a refined gentleman before the eyes of others provided a positive example of an individual's will to be a better person. The children were tutored to tolerate the underdogs in life because the pain of ostracism was familiar to them.

Sacrifice can instruct everyone who is willing to value its merits. Francis in his stoic acceptance of inner pain never displayed any outward anger. A peaceable, retiring man, he refused to air the troubles through which he had lived. This protection of the people whom he met from his past agonies slowly endeared him to others. The model of his long-suffering taught his family about true strength and caring.

Albert, Frank, Bernie, and George took possession of the vision of Franny's emotional hardships, of his enduring pain, and of his unhealed wounds. The courage, strength, and humanity within him strove equally to be heard, seen, tasted, and felt. Life has facets that permit endurance to exist with finality, rawness to partner with delicacy, and remorse to bed with satisfaction. The sons confirmed the worth of their upbringing by growing into successful citizens, competent providers, and honored fathers.

Chapter Twenty

Epilogue

"And There Are Miracles"

How often do we pass over the incidentals of life without realizing the implications of their origin? Even more seductive is our penchant for looking to luck, happenstance, or alien encounters to explain the greater mysteries of our lives. Despite our free will and the choices that others make around our lives, events do occur which should play a more prominent role in our thanksgivings. We are all susceptible to miracles; some of us just never perceive them that way.

On a lonely stretch of Lancaster Pike outside of Villanova University in 1964, I was wending my way home after a late date. It was well passed one o'clock in the morning, and the pike was void of traffic. Finally, the headlights of an approaching vehicle shot over the rise of highway before me. The roadbed had a yellow tint caused by the street lamps that dotted the neighborhood. I recall being extremely alert, perked perhaps by the success of the evenings events, but also conscious of the one hour drive to reach Norristown.

The on-coming car must have been passing another vehicle because, as he reached the summit of the highway, the automobile was on my side of the road. No panic; it was a quarter mile away and approaching at a moderate speed. Seconds later, no passed vehicle crested the hill behind him, but the lights of the approaching car still held fast to my lane. It swerved as if to return to its side of the roadway, but then quickly shot back in front of me. The quarter mile of separation had turned to a hundred yards. Another sharp cut back to his lane was followed abruptly by a more severe swerve toward my Volkswagen, my grandmother's favorite little car.

It was not an instinctive thing to do, but something possessed me calmly, prodding me to park my car along the curb. "Give the guy as much room as you can!" raced through my mind. Two headlights became one large ball of glaring light in an instant. Seat belted, I could not leap to the passenger side seat. I found myself pressing my body over the gear shift knob and lying flat across the two front seats. A horrendous roar of mechanical noise, movement initiated by head-on impact, and a sense of weightlessness occurred in a fraction of a second.

Suddenly, I was conscious of absolute stillness and quiet. A breeze wafted gently over my left ear, and I became aware of my position traversing both front Volkswagen seats. I struggled to sit upright and discovered the pain in my left elbow and the numb fingers of my left hand. The fabric of my tan raincoat was pinned between the passenger seat and the right door. I could not sit upright. Finally, I squirmed enough to become somewhat elevated. I could barely see over the dashboard. Startled, I was sitting in a convertible – no windows, no door jambs, no supports, and no roof were overhead or surrounding me. My vista was not the Lancaster Pike ahead of me, but the sidewalk and an empty street. "You're on someone's lawn, facing down onto the pike," I garnered.

Perhaps twenty seconds had flown by as near as I could recollect, and suddenly the blue-red staccato of emergency lights approached from the right. The wail and scream of the patrol car's alarm pierced the evening silence. I never saw the policeman until he stopped his patrol car in the middle of the pike which was strewn with debris. There lay the roof of the Volkswagen in front of the patrolman as he exited the auto.

Still trying to sit up, I attempted to sound the auto's horn. It did not function. It was then that I realized that the officer had spotted my car on the lawn above him. He began a dance of repulsion and hesitation. I was privy to his steps toward my car and his retreat. The policeman's head shook back and forth condemning himself for his faltering gait, but signaling his fear of seeing carnage within the Volkswagen. He made three unsuccessful attempts to reach my car. His last forward movement placed him twenty-five feet from me.

I had to help him. "I'm okay, Officer!" I stammered from my prone position. The dashboard muffled my attempt. I sensed that he had heard a voice, but he did not understand the words. Again, I announced, "I'm okay, Officer!"

His hat shot upward with the jerk; he had finally understood my second effort.

It took him several minutes to extricate me from the vehicle because my clothes were literally stapled to the body of the car. Gingerly protecting my left side, the Policeman ushered me onto the lawn. I had not noticed the arrival of an ambulance on the other side of the pike. The two of us paused momentarily to watch another officer escort a single male across the street toward the emergency vehicle. The passenger of the other car was also ambulatory but was placed in the confines of the medical unit and ushered away.

My Good Samaritan drove me personally to the same hospital as my accident companion. In the Emergency Room, I was aware of the other driver's groans and cries of pain behind the curtain in his cell where the technicians had placed him.

My attending nurse arrived. When I attempted to scratch a spot on my head, she lit up like a road flare, "No, no, no!" she flew at me, "don't touch your hair!"

"I must have a head injury," I surmised and thought it curious that I felt no pain, no pain anywhere on my body. With that appraisal, I then asked aloud, "Am I bleeding?"

"No, I'm sorry to have startled you, but you have a head full of glass shards," she reported.

She administered a very relaxing head shampoo, tended to my sprained elbow, and proceeded to discharge me. During the time at the hospital my twin brother was called and was en-route to pick me up. Awaiting his arrival, I learned that the dentist driving the other car had fallen asleep at the wheel. The impact flipped my car over, and it landed upright on the lawn. His vehicle crossed the corner behind my auto, and stopped head-long into a tree on another front lawn. The babysitter there, although shocked, managed to call the police almost immediately.

Aunt Marie and Frank told me, after seeing the remains of the Volkswagen, that I was certainly lucky to be alive. Luck had absolutely nothing to do with it! What about Guardian Angels? What about my spiritual connection? "Thank you, Camille, for taking care of your son on that lonely road."

***

My Brazilian friends had loaned me a rifle for the duck hunt. I carried the small bore, single shot, muzzle loading, and percussion cap firearm all morning through the flooded acreage of a landowner's property. My party and I had awakened before dawn in Ipu, Ceara, Brazil, mounted horses, forged a stream, and arrived at the farm for breakfast. The cold desert air of the morning had quickly turned sweltering. At mid day, shouts across the shallow lake summoned the hunters to lunch.

I remember being dehydrated, very tired, and also quite hungry. So, I exited the sandy lake and headed onto the beach at the base of a small rise. I stood to get my bearings, realized that I was barefoot, and tried to pick a civilized path back to the farmhouse. A flat line of land approached me from my left, and I knew it was the head of the dam that held back the seasonal rain that formed this lake. If I could work my way up the sandy slope in front of me, I could easily follow the dam to my lunch. I took one step....

There was nothingness! No desert rose before me. No heat burnt my arms and head. No sounds warbled on the currents of air. There was no air, and the whole world had turned into a white sheet without texture of any kind.

"What the hell is going on?" jumped into my thoughts. It was then that I sensed my lack of breathing and tenseness in my chest. I had once experienced a heat stroke, and that event was full of confetti color and chills. This was definitely different.

Fear surged within me as I realized that I had no sensory perception of my surroundings. "What could be out there?" My body told me to try to inhale. Focusing on my initial breath and drawing air into my mouth, I experienced the sensations of warmth and calmness. The white sheet that blanketed my vision began to display red splotches. Exhaling the red marks formed letters: "E K A N S". They were backward and inverted, but I managed to decode, "S N A K E".

Suddenly, I was free! All was normal again, except the wonderment over what had just happened to me. Immediately, I checked my bare toes thinking, "Coral Snake!" No animal was below me, and I scanned the beach and terrain ahead of me. I picked up nothing to alarm me. Satisfied that the heat and sun had played a nasty trick on me, I took another step.

There was nothingness! No desert rose before me. No heat burnt my arms and head. No sounds warbled on the currents of air. There was no air, and the whole world had turned into a white sheet without texture of any kind. I was entrapped again. My limited experience with this event instructed me to try to breathe again.

Successfully dispatching the vision for a second time, I was determined to scour the countryside looking for the snake in my message. Without moving any part of my lower body, I absorbed the Brazilian desert before me. The monsoons which brought this lake into life also released the insects and animals of the marsh and water. Above me toward the dam face was a patch of thin reedy grass, waving from side to side with the wind. I had not noticed it before, but the hypnotic swaying drew my closer attention. There, at the head of the seed ears moving to and fro was a green, diamond shaped coloration foreign to the grass. "Snake!" I read, "green…must be nine or ten foot long." The mimicry of the wind-blown grass put the head of the snake three feet off the ground.

I had only one shot that would clear my way toward my friends and the farmhouse. I lowered the barrel, letting the rifle and my eye measure the oscillation of the grass and the snake. "Bam!" or rather, "Swoosh!" sounded the discharge. The lack of a sharp snap of explosion from the flintlock did not make it any less lethal. The grasses in front and around the snake bent backward toward the target as the pellets arrived with their impact. Some struck the grass, but the main fusillade drove the head of the animal backward.

"Wounded?" was my next fear. Rushing back into the lake, I hurried along a wide arc which looped to the base of the dam wall. At lunch the hunt and my snake occupied the conversations. A group of curious hunters set out to the location of my snake sighting. They returned later with a green tree viper approximately nine foot long. It had been shot in the head. The Brazilian's related that these snakes only come out of the trees when they hunt. If I had startled it, the snake would have struck. I was, "Really fortunate!" they told me. Fortune had nothing to do with it! Visions do not arise from hunger pangs in the desert. Spiritually, I have to thank my family members and Camille for their prayers and protection.

As an added note on this mysterious event, it happened twice to me. About four years later while fishing along Lake Nockamixon in Pennsylvania, I went to cross through a hedgerow at the edge of the water. When I touched the bush with my left hand in which I held my fishing rod and reel, the white sheet appeared again. After the prescribed recovery process, I peered over the hedge to spot an eight foot Timber Rattlesnake sunning itself on a log right in my path. The ranger at the park captured the snake and transported it to the Pocono Mountains farther north. No, that's not fortune. I have been around non-venomous snakes all my life, handled them, and never had this happen. These were my only two encounters with venomous snakes.

***

Lying on the parlor floor watching television can sometimes be a dangerous thing. With three teenage boys and a daughter rousting about, one never knows what to expect. A particular summer evening in 1990 certainly comes to mind.

It was quiet enough until Jeremy, my sixteen year old, bounded into the room from the kitchen. With too much energy to expend, the youth pounced upon me without warning. One of our wrestling matches ensued.

My son had the upper hand quickly, and I soon found myself locked in a vice grip. His attack focused on my midsection, and he had my torso and head clinched in his lanky arms. My struggle rolled us about the floor, pushing aside some nearby furniture. I managed to pivot from his embrace, and latched onto his legs. I gained some leverage, and he shifted into a headlock of sorts. It was not strong enough to contain me, and I spun free releasing his legs. At that point, I was kneeling beside him. He looked up, thought a second about his next maneuver, and sprung into my chest. His right elbow caught me solidly in my right breast.

"Ouch!" I screamed in reaction.

Startled by my painful yelp, Jeremy fell to the side. His glance was full of surprise and worry. "Geez, Dad, sorry!" he blurted.

I knelt by him, rubbing my nipple and breast. The pain was sharp and did not wane. "That's okay, Jer!" I managed, but I could see the concern in his face.

"You alright?" he questioned. He waited for my reaction.

It took a few seconds before I affirmed, "Yeah. No broken bones, but you caught me in an awkward spot." The television occupied us until we were summoned to dinner.

The next few days the pain subsided but a dull soreness remained. I waited until I thought any bruise had dissipated, but a week later the discomfort and soreness remained. After three weeks, the thought of seeing my doctor entered my mind, but I put it off. My schedule was full of coaching and refereeing soccer games.

The following week we had a cold spell come through the region, and I decided to wear a sweater. My attempts to pull the garment over my head and over my torso produced sharp pain from the breast area. Now, the doctor's visit was finally scheduled.

I remember going on a Tuesday afternoon for the check up. Doctor Steven Bimson found a swelling under the nipple. He set up an x-ray for Wednesday morning at Grandview Hospital. It seemed like a normal procedure, and I left feeling confident that all was well.

On Thursday, I was called to Dr. Bimson's office to get the results, and I looked forward to getting medication to alleviate the swelling and soreness.

"We're going to need another test to conclude my diagnosis," the young physician informed me.

"Sure, Doctor, I just want things to get back to normal," I replied. The nagging feeling that I had somehow been through this before unnerved me. "I can come back next week some time," was my offering.

"No, Bernie," began Dr. Bimson, "You need this done as soon as possible. I have already contacted Dr. Finklestein at Grandview, and you are set up for a biopsy. You'll see him tomorrow." He was firm, direct, and serious.

"Biopsy?" I muttered. I could not find anything else to say.

The doctor took the lead and assured me that this was only something he wanted to check off of his list.

The day of the surgery forced me to rearrange my schedule and my wife's, for she had to be my transportation. I accepted the pre-op and biopsy as a necessary inconvenience, but my rationalization did not remove my lingering fears and doubts.

In recovery, the surgeon, Dr. Finklestein, approached my bed side. He stood next to my seated wife, Dorothy. The surgical mask dangled under his chin, and one could see he was a handsome man.

"How'd I do?" I requested.

"The procedure went without a hitch, Bernie," he reported.

I felt some relief, but did not know what the process might entail. "Are you sending the results to Dr. Bimson?"

"Actually, we usually send the specimen to a lab, and then they send the results to your doctor." He stood poised and confident; and, as his patient, I was at ease with his manner. "I'm going to do that, but I need you to know that I have done many of these preliminary biopsies, and yours is pretty obvious."

"Where's this going?" I wondered.

"Doctor," my wife ventured, "what did you find?"

"No one likes to hear this, and I hate to be the person with the news," he delivered with calm, concern, and compassion.

I knew now that the next few words were going to change my life.

"Bernie, in all likelihood, your tumor is malignant."

"Cancer," I uttered before he could continue.

"Yes, you have breast cancer, probably stage two." He reached down to me and placed a gentle hand on my shoulder.

The remaining conversation spoken in the recovery room never entered my head. I was in turmoil, but my wife recorded the details and schedule that the surgeon planned. I could have a second opinion, the biopsy would soon arrive at Dr. Bimson's office, and I should act quickly to resolve the situation.

I had a keen sense of the seriousness of the matter, for no free moment was afforded me. I was in the midst of a whirlwind of activity. My surgery two days later involved a right side radical mastectomy with the removal of the lymph nodes under my right arm. I remember keeping my emotions in check until the day an aide came to take me to have my hair shampooed. She was a wonderful middle aged woman who confessed to having breast cancer herself. Our time together left the floodgates open, and I found myself crying during the therapeutic washing. I could not have managed the next days, weeks, or months without the women who intervened on my behalf. My cancer was foreign to men, but the women were counselors, therapists, and comrades for me.

I returned to teaching seventeen days after my surgery, and I now know that was a mistake. The regiment took a toll on my recovery, and the medication, a form of estrogen, seemed harmless enough. Later on, it shoved me into moods of depression and flighty emotions. During recovery and recuperation, I learned how rare breast cancer is among men and how deadly. I became a spokesman of sorts, speaking to groups about preventative measures and my own journey. Many of my audience talked to me about how fate has a way of working in one's favor, but I know better. Fate had nothing to do with my survival.

Dr. Finklestein shared a thought with me about my son's role in all of this. From that insight, I discovered my mantra for my audiences. "Wrestle with your kids!" In all probability, Jeremy saved my life that day in the parlor. For without his intervention and his striking the exact tumor site, I would never have known the dark secret that lurked within me. He was an instrument of some guiding force. Chances are I would have died that following year. My oncologist set me free as a cure seven years later. So, who do I thank for this miracle? Well, spiritually, there's my father, my mother, my deceased relatives, and perhaps Dennis. Never to be forgotten are the countless family members, friends, and fellow breast cancer patients who offered me their prayers and good will.

***

My twin brother Frank and I had an agreement that whoever had the first daughters would name one Camille after our mother. His second daughter was born in 1968.

Rene', my daughter, was born in 1971, and I chose the masculine form rather than Renee. I did not want Rene' to grow up and feel any bias from personnel directors at schools or workplaces because she was a woman. In my translation, Rene' means "Re-birth" and that's how I will always see my daughter – the new Camille.

The birth of our first grandchild, Grace, necessitated a road trip to visit our daughter. Rene' and her husband Phillip lived in Rochester, New York. He was studying organ and harpsichord for a Master's Degree at Eastman School of Music. My wife and I drove to Rochester to see Grace and her parents after the birth and again for the formal baptism. We spoke about the rest of the family meeting the child, but Phillip could not get away from his studies.

When Grace reached six months of age, Rene' booked airfare and flew to Pennsylvania to introduce Grace to the clan. One evening we sent Rene' out with some of her friends and took a turn at babysitting. Grace finished the breast milk that Rene' had left with us, but continued to demonstrate that she was hungry. My wife prepared a little oatmeal with corn syrup to placate the baby. We understood that Grace had yet to be introduced to solid foods, and the remedy for her appetite seemed harmless enough. They flew home on a Sunday morning.

When Rene' called that evening, we thought she was being a dutiful daughter by confirming their safe travel and arrival. The conversation, however, focused on Grace's listlessness during the journey. Mom and I put Rene' at ease, relating that the travel, the unfamiliar schedule, and new sleeping quarters probably, "Tired little Gracie out".

Monday began normally in Pennsylvania, but not so in Rochester. Rene' took Grace to her pediatrician, for the child had worsened. In a phone call later that day, Rene' reported to her mother that the doctor had sent the pair home with a prescription for the malaise of the baby. The young mother was worried and concerned because Grace did not seem to respond to the medicine or rest.

Tuesday afternoon at school, I was called out of class to take an emergency phone call. Dottie had packed clothes for me and herself and we were needed in Rochester. Grace had been admitted to Strong Memorial Hospital. Prayers filled the chaos of the rush to my home, to the airport, and through the lines of travelers waiting to obtain tickets and boarding passes. People left us through the queue of a hundred travelers as they heard our pleas to catch an already departing flight for an emergency medical reason.

At Strong Memorial, the vigil was underway. Rene' and Phil related the various tests and procedures that their infant had been put through. Rene' cried at the mention of spinal meningitis and the spinal tap. "She's almost in a coma, Mom," sobbed the frantic young mother. "She doesn't respond to either of us."

Heartsick, we tried to console and encourage the young couple, but the medical news seemed to be preparing us for the worst possible outcome. The medical staff dropped in and detailed the medications and tests results. They had no indication of any illness that, at this point, might be causing Grace to drift farther from us. "I hope we can turn this around, Rene' and Phil," the head physician comforted, "but I must tell you that it has to be soon because her vital signs are growing weaker." We prayed that we would not lose our grandchild. We prayed for Rene' and Phil. We prayed for the medical staff to solve this mystery.

An hour later, the family was summoned to the waiting room. A team of four doctors followed the head pediatrician as he entered the room. The last intern carried a clip board heavy with sheets of fingered papers. The doctor requested any information on Grace that occurred prior to this illness. Rene' recounted the trip to Pennsylvania, and Dottie and I remember the evening babysitting the cranky Grace and our giving solid food to the child.

"No, I don't see any reason for these symptoms," volunteered the doctor. "Any of you pick up anything?" he directed at his staff. Heads shook negative responses. "Rene', did you and the child encounter any sick children or adults?"

"No, and I was careful about checking for any kind of cold or flu," she confessed.

"This is not easy for me, Rene' and Phil," he paused searching for the correct phrase or words, "we have to prepare ourselves… because we may lose Grace. There's not much more we can do."

Muffled sobs and gasps of breath filled the static air. The room was warm, and the discomfort of the people within rose on many levels.

"Have any of you thought about infantile botulism?" rang clearly into the somber atmosphere of the quarters. All eyes darted toward the speaker. Dottie had calmly directed her question to the staff. Stunned by her clarity and the medical term that she introduced to the topic, the head pediatrician scanned his bewildered staff. At the end of the line, the intern flipped through the documents on his clip board. "It's here, Doctor, on the last page here. Yeah, the symptoms match somewhat," he delivered with a satisfied air.

"Why do you ask this?" he queried. "We've never had a case of this in Rochester."

Dottie narrated a tale that had begun to rummage through her thoughts and prayers. The grandmother had the full attention of the entire room. She recounted how her cousin had a son who came down with similar symptoms. She remembered that the child lapsed into a coma for a month or so because of the poison in his system.

The doctors began reading the description of the pathology of infantile botulism: "Occurs after ingesting first solid food, listlessness, high fever, medication should be not administered as this releases more toxins as the spores carrying the botulism are killed."

"If this is the culprit, we must discontinue the doses of antibiotics," he hurried the words.

From the depths of despair a message of hope sprang into being. As it would be, Grace did have infantile botulism. She did slip into a coma in her grandmother's arms that lasted almost four weeks. The child recovered completely without knowing the celebrity status she had gained. Pediatricians from all the northern states came to Strong Memorial to learn and observe Grace's progress. This illness occurs in only four areas of the world; Doylestown, Pennsylvania, reports eighty percent of the one-hundred or so cases each year. The ground born spores leave the soil and reside in the child's digestive tract. The toxins are released when the infants digests its first solid food.

Grace is a gift of God, but her survival depended on the teamwork of professionals, a grandmother, and the Providence of Heaven. Anyone of the earthly team could have ignored the message, the prophecy. What prodded Dorothy to discern the story and bring it to life? At that moment, all others were in the throes of ignorance, sorrow, fear and torment. She, too, could have submitted to the course of the disease and the eventual outcome, but she spoke, "In Tongues!" For her, the medical jargon was surely a foreign language. God speaks in a myriad of ways, and someone amongst us has to be listening. Hope is always present: in quiet or confusion, in roars or whispers, and in heaven and on earth.

I would like to thank the Ronald McDonald House in Rochester, New York, and other locations for their wonderful charity and care of people in need of support. It is truly an exceptional organization!

***

"Dear St. Anthony, please come around. Something is lost and can not be found." The item is occasionally precious, but frequently it is a mundane, cherished trinket for which the owner has special emotional significance. I have had reason to bother this patient and kindly saint with my petition to assist with the retrieval of some part of my world.

I frequently drove my little Honda Cosmopolitan, fifty cc, scooter to work at the golf course where I worked on a part time basis. My day started with setting up golf carts for members and getting their bags on the carts. As they completed their round, my job shifted to cleaning the carts and bags and, then, finally storing clubs in the bag room or putting the carts in the storage barn. At times, the day ended with one cart and its passengers still on the darkening course.

One particular night, I chose to take the scooter onto the course to check on the missing vehicle and its riders. The possibility that the cart had broken down, prompted me to begin my search. The scooter had a two beam headlight, and that facilitated my scouring the now dark golf course for the golfers.

At the first check point, I dismounted my motor bike to walk on foot near the practice area and the pool. No one was milling about, so I remounted the scooter and headed toward the front nine. Proceeding down the third fairway cart path, I stopped and set the motor scooter on its kickstand. As I scoured the visible fairways on foot, I spotted the wayward cart and its passengers heading towards me. Remounting my two wheeler, I returned to the clubhouse. All ended normally, and I ventured home in the dark, enjoying the warm summer evening on the Cosmopolitan.

Once home, I realized that the two bladed, wooden handled pocket knife that I carried with me had fallen from my pocket.

My twin brother Frank had given it to me many years before for a birthday present. I never went anywhere without it. My first thoughts went to the foraging on the golf course for the missing golfers. Perhaps I had dropped it at one of the stoppages that I had made? After checking the house thoroughly and all my clothing, I was determined to hunt for my pocket knife early the next morning.

At the course, I retraced my path but had no luck locating the missing item. I left word at the golf shop that I had lost it and waited hopefully that someone would retrieve it for me. Two weeks later, I received a call that the knife was returned to the shop. When I reached the course, I was filled with hope and goodwill. Inspecting the penknife at the shop, I sadly had to announce that it was not mine. It was a single bladed, wooden handled knife.

A month passed and I sadly decided to purchase a replacement. At a local Dick's Sporting Goods store, I bought a single bladed knife similar to the one that remained unclaimed in the golf shop. The warmth and feel of the original pocket knife was no longer with me.

At the end of the season over Labor Day weekend, my son Jeremy and his family came for a short visit. We spent countless hours on that screened-in porch enjoying food, fellowship, and good stories. I remembered that I had the newly purchased knife in my pocket. Jeremy had heard my tale of woe over the phone shortly after I had lost the original.

"Hey! Jeremy," I spouted from my seat next to him. "I bought a new knife."

"Oh, yes, I remember. You lost the one Frank gave to you," he posed.

"Here!" I exclaimed as I thrust my hand into my pocket and passed the knife to him to appraise my newly purchased replacement.

"Hey, Dad?" he questioned. "This isn't a new knife, this is your old one," he declared.

"What're you talking about," I retorted, a little set back and angry with his attempt to tease me. "That's the one I bought at Dick's," I affirmed.

"No, it isn't, Dad!" he added. "Look! Check it out yourself, Dad!" He pushed the small knife toward me.

"No, way! No, way, Jeremy! That can't be possible." Stunned, I managed to lean forward and view the item he held. There, in his hand, rested Frank's gift to me. I could not take it from him at first. I thought somehow he had pulled some hoax on me. Had he found it? Did he buy me an exact replica? Had I, somehow, found it in the pants that I wore that day?

Taking it into my hand, I immediately sensed its warmth and comfort in my palm. Confused, I hurried off to my room to bring the new knife out for comparison. Searching every nook and cranny of my life in that bedroom, I could not locate the Dick's Sporting Goods knife. Befuddled, I returned to the porch and questioned everyone present about their possible part in this turn of events. No one had any idea of what had transpired. To this day, the one bladed penknife has never turned up. The two bladed, woodened handled pocket knife remains with me.

St. Anthony, you have proven to me the value of trust and faith. It is my unflinching belief that the good saint traded knives that day. Somewhere on that golf course is the Dick's Sporting Goods knife. He left it right where I had lost Frank's gift. I am forever grateful for his intercession then and always.

Miracles are not always great, wondrous healings. They may be only the whisper of daily events and not the traumatic thunder that changes lives. I am content to have them occur on a regular basis; we have to become accustomed to perceiving them in their infinitesimal effect and also in their grandeur. Keep watch and dream.

Postscript: Frank B. Blanche, born on January 30, 1944, died suddenly on April 30, 2014. He rests in peace with Francis, Camille, Dennis, and his grandparents, Martin and Mary Bernot and Timothy and Mary Blanche.

Review Requested:

If you loved this book, would you please provide
a review at Amazon.com?

CPSIA information can be obtained at www.ICGtesting.com
Printed in the USA
BVOW08s0336090216

436040BV00001B/2/P

9 781681 814339